THE SIMULTANEOUS TREATMENT OF PARENT AND CHILD

THE SIMULTANEOUS TREATMENT OF PARENT AND CHILD

SARALEA E. CHAZAN

BasicBooks
A Division of HarperCollins*Publishers*

Designed by Ellen Levine

Library of Congress Cataloging-in-Publication Data
Chazan, Saralea E.
    The simultaneous treatment of parent and child / Saralea E. Chazan.
        p.   cm.
    Includes bibliographical references and index.
    ISBN 0–465–04552–9
    1. Problem families.   2. Child psychotherapy.   3. Family psychotherapy.
4. Parental influences.   5. Child psychotherapy—Case studies.   6. Family
psychotherapy—Case studies.
RJ507.P35C49   1995
616.89'156—dc20   95–15309
                                                                     CIP

95 96 97 98 ❖/HC 9 8 7 6 5 4 3 2 1

To Bob

Contents

Acknowledgments

Many people have supported my clinical interest in parent-child treatment. Charles Wenar, Solveig Wenar, Malcom Helper, and Herbert Rie encouraged me to pursue professional studies in clinical child psychology. Robert C. Lane mentored me over many years in the practice of psychotherapy, always supportive of my autonomy and curiosity. Kenneth Zucker, Thomas Lopez, and David Shapiro contributed to the clinical approaches taken in several of the case studies in this book.

The idea for this project took form within the context of my supervisory work on the volunteer faculty at New York Hospital–Cornell Medical Center/Westchester Division. In this setting, colleagues and friends were willing to listen to and debate the issues involved in simultaneous treatment. I shall always be appreciative of their receptivity and encouragement. Specifically, Paulina F. Kernberg and Paul V. Trad gave me their active and sustained support. Amy Bloch, Joseph DeMore, Richard Hill, Mary Raine, and Elizabeth Senekjian participated by including this approach when working with their own clients. I am most grateful for their willingness to try a new perspective; I gained considerably from their experience.

Additional support for this work came from a variety of sources. The Department of Health of Westchester County, Department of Children with Disabilities, contributed toward the cost of one treatment case. In addition, at different times during the work I had recourse to my colleagues in Division 39, Section II, and the Committee on Infant Mental Health, led by Ed Corrigan, for discussion and constructive suggestions. Risa Ryger contributed valuable clinical observations. Stephen Francoeur of Basic Books made this book a reality. Nina Gunzenhauser was a perceptive, discriminating, and sensitive manuscript editor. Marcia Miller and Pamela Quinn assisted in locating references in the literature. Louise Taitt helped to organize the final bibliography with efficiency.

It would have been impossible to write this book without the collaboration and cooperation of my patients. The persons who agreed to participate in this project understood the value and importance of the clinical work. They were willing to share their personal experience so that others might benefit; this is how scientific work proceeds. Although many of the transcripts are of necessity verbatim, every precaution has been taken to protect the participants' identity and confidentiality. I am most grateful to all of these people for their openness and contribution.

It is my good fortune to be part of a family group to whom I can always return as a secure base. The generations include my parents, Ethel and David Engel and Ida and Abe Chazan, as well as my children, Daniel, Michael, and Rachel. My abundant gratitude is extended to Bob, husband and friend, to whom this book is dedicated. It is a small way of indicating my appreciation for his good-natured understanding and sustained confidence in my endeavors.

Introduction

SOMETIMES CHILD THERAPY is doomed to failure from the outset. All child therapists have had the experience of engaging children in treatment, only to have the parents prevent the process from going forward, although on a manifest level the parents are bringing the child in the hope that troubling symptomatic behaviors will be ameliorated. If something within the parent-child relationship does not permit the child to change, the outcome is compromised, no matter how well accomplished the treatment. In such a case, the only effective treatment involves changing both members of the dyad. If the therapist engages both parent and child, there can be hope for progress and ultimate resolution.

Simultaneous treatment is defined as the treatment of both members of a dyadic relationship, parent and child, separately by the same therapist. What characterizes this treatment method is not just external arrangements but also the complex nature of the developing transference-countertransference relationship. The therapist is the nodal point of treatment, integrating levels of reality by sharing in new understandings with each member of the dyad. Simultaneous treatment focuses on the points of contact between parent and child that are keeping the two individuals dependent on each other in a struggle to survive. These points of contact constitute the core of the child's problem.

In simultaneous treatment, the therapist is concerned not only with the interactions between parent and child but also with the individual representational worlds of both. Simultaneous treatment is a natural extension of the process of individual ego psychoanalytic supportive-expressive psychotherapy, integrated with concepts of learning theory, developmental psychology, and attachment theory.

1

This approach accepts the concept of treatment as individually based, with the traditional analysis of transference, resistance, and defense, but adds to it the dimension of examination of the parallel events that occur when parent and child are treated concurrently by the same therapist.

In simultaneous treatment, the therapist works to reconstruct the subjective experience of each of the patients. The issues of relationship within the dyad are both fundamental and complex. They deal with the basic differentiation between self and other, the creation of adaptable boundaries between self and other, and the capacity to differentiate between what is imagined and what is real.

Child psychotherapy begins at the initiative of a parent or both parents, who also control its ending, in consultation with the therapist. In all child psychotherapy, therefore, the therapist relates at some level to both parent and child. In simultaneous treatment, the relationship with the therapist is pushed to a therapeutic level for both the parent and the child. The parent not only is involved at the beginning and end of treatment but also is an intimate partner throughout the process and the resolution of the treatment problem.

In nonsimultaneous treatment, the end result is that the parent's life is improved because a difficulty in the ecological context of the family is diminished or resolved. In successful simultaneous treatment, not just one element but a whole constellation of family features is transformed because two members of the family have changed simultaneously. A critical relationship has been transformed by changing both partners. That change radiates outward to other groupings within the family, including siblings and adults. Simultaneous treatment deals with the ubiquitous reality that a child never comes to treatment alone. It does not isolate the child from his parent but rather focuses on the conflicts within the dependent dyadic relationship that are hindering growth and development.

This book provides a rationale and framework for conducting simultaneous treatment. Although simultaneous treatment has been practiced widely for pragmatic reasons, it has never been explicated fully as a valuable and sometimes preferred method of treatment. Contamination of feelings within the transference and the use of the parental role as a defense have been cited as reasons for avoiding treatment of the parent and child by the same therapist. I argue the opposite case. Beginning with the adult as parent is often the only avenue toward negotiating the complex issues of parent-child relationship. The parental role does not close off infantile feelings but provides a safe passage to the probing of deeper issues.

Often the choreography between the members of the dyad reflects an intricate dance of attitudes and feelings. Nothing is lost in working with this complexity, and potentially there is much therapeutic gain. By focusing on the context within which the child lives and not on symptomatic behaviors alone, therapy can be incisive and perhaps shortened. Even when treatment is not shortened, the results are likely to be sustaining and to represent a conservation of effort over time.

This book describes both the theory and practice of simultaneous treatment. Chapter 1 is an overview of simultaneous treatment and includes some theoretical background as well as a review of the literature. The ideas of John Bowlby, Robert Emde, Irene Fast, Otto Kernberg, Paulina Kernberg, Arnold Modell, Paul Trad, Anne-Marie Sandler, and Joseph Sandler are considered in relation to their implications for simultaneous treatment. Chapter 2 describes the psychological processes underlying simultaneous treatment. The dyadic processes of parallel events and shared fantasies are defined. The concept of representational worlds is central to the understanding of how these dyadic processes become enmeshed. Empathy, intersubjective validation, and identification are other processes observed in simultaneous treatment. These psychological processes are implicated in the differentiation of roles within the dyad and the intergenerational transmission of trauma. Chapter 3 is a description of the pragmatics of the course of treatment, including beginning, middle, and ending phases.

Chapter 4 begins the clinical section of the book; it describes the case of a 7-year-old boy with a gender identity disorder. Chapters 5 and 6 describe the simultaneous treatment of a mother and her 8-year-old son who had a narcissistic disorder. Chapters 7 and 8 describe the case of a 2-year-old child with pervasive developmental delay. These cases were chosen to represent an array of diagnoses to demonstrate the flexibility of this approach. Cases 1 and 3 concentrate on a 9-month period of treatment. Case 2 is more extensive, covering a period of almost 3 years. Other vignettes in the text present examples from briefer treatments of approximately 6 months in duration.

The intent of this book is to present a guide to treatment that provides hope for troubled children who are enmeshed in conflict with a significant adult and unable to proceed with their development.

CHAPTER 1

An Overview of
Simultaneous Treatment

ERIC, AGE 7 YEARS, originally was referred for psychotherapy because of a recurrent eye tic, which sometimes generalized to a facial grimace or a neck spasm. He has kept appointments regularly for 2 years, but the symptom persists, with only minor diminution. His parent's concern remains high, and this recurrent, visible irritant often precipitates arguments at home.

The therapist reviews the course of treatment for clues to how intervention strategies might be altered. Should Eric's once-a-week appointments be more frequent? Should a trial of medication, originally rejected by the family, be reconsidered? How could management sessions with the parents be more helpful? Are there some behavioral measures that are not being applied consistently? Are the parents somehow acting covertly in a way that is sabotaging the treatment? Are there family roles that require more clarification?

The therapist's relationship with Eric seems to be going along well enough. He appears to like coming to treatment, although he was initially shy. He enjoys drawing fantasy creatures, and these imaginative creations are an open avenue to feelings of alienation from family and peers. Despite this strong connection to the therapist, however, Eric continues to experience his world frequently as frightening and overwhelming.

Eric's mother regards his drawings with dismay and worries that he might be headed for "serious" emotional difficulty such as her younger brother experienced. Eric's problems trigger increasing anxiety, and his mother begins to despair and lose hope. The therapist shares the parent's concern for Eric and wonders what to do. How can she be more effective in reaching this troubled child?*

At this point in treatment, it becomes clear that both Eric and his mother require intensive and focused intervention. Some clues to the appropriateness of simultaneous treatment include the mother's high level of enmeshment with her child, the parent's degree of sensitivity and reactivity to her child's symptoms, and the recurrent need of the parent to cast her child in the role of a character from her own childhood. Anxiety and fear seem to emanate from the relationship between parent and child. The stress of these emotions exceeds the stress imposed by the presenting symptoms. This therapeutic dilemma is encountered commonly by child therapists, who must master a variety of techniques and yet continue to search for and create new avenues for rapprochement with their child patients and their families. The child therapist needs to be flexible and versed in many different methods to be able to shift approaches when appropriate to fit a particular patient or phase in the treatment process.

Lauren, age 13 years, comes to therapy at a time of crisis. Her parents have separated recently, and divorce proceedings are pending. Lauren is an only child; her closest attachments outside the nuclear family group include her maternal grandmother and aunt. The maternal grandfather is deceased. Although Lauren suspected her parents were unhappy together, she was unprepared for the immediacy of the separation and her father's disclosure of an extramarital affair.

Abruptly surrounded by family chaos, Lauren faces new, disturbing issues regarding her identity shortly after she begins treatment. She is beset by fears of being a lesbian. She has strong desires for sexual relationships with women, desires that threaten to overwhelm her. In addition, she has nightmares in which a male intruder is going to do her harm. A memory of an incident of sexual exploration with a female friend as a younger child upsets her. Lauren feels perplexed by these alien and frightening sexual feelings.

*Feminine pronouns are used throughout the book to refer to the caregiver, reflecting the prevalence in our culture of women as principal caregivers for children. Although in some instances of simultaneous treatment, the adult patient has been the father, and in others, both parents have been seen individually, in most cases the parent is female. Masculine pronouns are used to refer to the child patients, reflecting the high incidence of male children among clinic referrals.

Lauren's mother is similarly perplexed and overwhelmed by her life situation. In addition to seeking help for her daughter, she seems to be seeking clarification from the therapist regarding her own experience. She is beset by guilt regarding Lauren's circumstances; angry toward her estranged husband, who is negative toward treatment for their daughter; and frightened about what the future might hold. The therapist is confronted with two individuals seeking treatment and wonders if it would be appropriate for her to treat both mother and child concurrently.

Clearly, in each of these presenting situations, the underlying problem resides not within the individual child but within a complex set of connections between parent and child. Separating the patients by assigning different therapists would remove the areas of enmeshment from direct scrutiny. For example, what aspects of Lauren's fears link with her mother's fears? How do Lauren and her mother relate to each other regarding concerns about gender identity? What rigid attitudes are holding in place frightening and distorted perceptions? What are the risks imposed on one member of the dyad as the partner begins to change? What are the shared barriers to forming secure and trusting bonds that encourage individuation? Broadening the therapeutic sphere to focus on the contextual framework within which parent and child reside, with each member of the pair treated separately by the same therapist, marks the therapeutic intervention as simultaneous treatment.

Child therapists never lose sight of the contextual relationship within which children and caregivers live. This is a context that grows, changes, and develops over time and defines the actual, as well as the potential, identities of each of its members. In some cases, to treat the child without treating the adult family member closest to him is to eliminate the most important component of the treatment.

RELATED APPROACHES

Other approaches to treatment stress dyadic relationship factors as important in determining the cause and course of childhood disorders. Group therapists (for example, Gottsegin & Grasso, 1973; Holman, 1985; Weil & Boxer, 1990) structure therapeutic groups containing parent-child dyads. Family therapists, emphasizing the importance of the family group, stress the necessity of treating the child within the context of the entire family unit (Combrenick-Graham, 1989; Feldman, 1988; Sholevar & Schwoeri, 1994; Zilbach,

1986). In conjoint treatment, the larger family unit is broken down into smaller units (Davies, 1991; Satir, 1967).

Simultaneous treatment differs from conjoint therapy in that it does not focus on the understanding of family systems but is a natural extension of the process of individual ego psychoanalytic supportive-expressive psychotherapy, integrated with concepts formulated by learning theory, developmental psychology, and attachment theory. This approach accepts the concept of treatment as individually based, with the traditional analysis of transference, resistance, and defense. However, it adds the additional dimension of examination of the parallel events that occur when parent and child are treated concurrently by the same therapist.

Two other treatment approaches also conceptualize parent-child interaction as the focus for the treatment of pathology in children. The first, behavioral therapy, examines autism, attention deficit disorder, and conduct disorder within the context of the dyadic relationship. Parent-training paradigms are constructed on the basis of working with parent and child together (for example, Dumas, 1984; Eisenstadt, Eyberg, McNeil, Newcomb, & Funderburk, 1993; Maddux, Eyberg, & Funderburk, 1989; Robinson & Eyberg, 1981; Short, 1984).

Simultaneous treatment does not disregard the critical treatment components that provide adequate structure for optimum parent-child interaction; direct work on management issues always must be a facet of treatment. In the simultaneous treatment model, however, the problem of maladaptation exists not only in the child's behavior or the parent-child interaction but also within the child's internalized representational world.

The second treatment approach, parent-infant psychotherapy, most closely addresses the concerns of the simultaneous treatment model. Parent and child are seen together by the same therapist with the purpose of intervening within the matrix of earliest relationships (for example, Dodge, 1990; Hopkins, 1992; Kalmanson & Pekarsky, 1987; Lieberman, 1992; Lieberman, Westin, & Paul, 1991; Trad, 1993b; Williams, Nover, Castellan, Greenspan, & Lieberman, 1987; Zeanah & Klitzke, 1991). Attachment theorists, continuing the pioneering work of Selma Fraiberg (1980), study the development of pathological internal working models within the parent-child dyad that lead to maladaptation (for example, Bretherton, 1990; Erickson, Korfmacher, & Egeland, 1992; Main & Goldwyn, 1984; Main & Hesse, 1990; Main, Kaplan, & Cassidy, 1985; Sroufe, 1983; Zeanah & Anders, 1987). Paul Trad (1991a, 1991b, 1993a) introduced the concept of "previewing" as a metaphor to understand the parent-infant couple. Daniel Stern (1985) traced the earliest steps in the formation of the child's representational world to the matrix of the parent-child dyad.

These approaches to infant treatment, however, by definition are limited in chronological scope. Also, both members of the dyad are present continuously. In the simultaneous model of treatment, the emphasis is on the internal representational world of each of the partners. From this perspective, transactions between partners are not necessarily immediately observable but emerge over time in individual sessions with the therapist. The therapist, in maintaining her therapeutic stance at a midpoint between parent and child, is in an optimum position to observe and participate in the parent-child relationship, never losing contact with either member of the dyad. In her reverie, the therapist is a partner for each of them and can empathically relate to their individual issues. Reciprocally, each partner engages in treatment with the same therapist. The therapist thus provides both continuity and integration for the many qualitatively diverse experiences that make up the shared reality of the parent-child dyad.

All these treatment models—conjoint therapy, behavioral therapy, and parent-infant psychotherapy—converge at many points and are important areas of study in their own right (Stern-Bruschweiler & Stern, 1989). They also may be combined by the individual therapist in a flexible approach to meet the needs of her patients, so that simultaneous treatment may not be the exclusive method used. Group sessions, conjoint sessions, and parent-training sessions all may intersect with simultaneous treatment in a treatment plan. Although in the simultaneous treatment of very young children, child sessions usually are conducted in the presence of one or both parents, the focus is on the intersection of individual representational worlds.

THE BACKGROUND OF SIMULTANEOUS TREATMENT

Treating both parent and child in simultaneous individual therapy was a natural outgrowth of my clinical work with patients. In many cases, a parent saw the need to pursue her own treatment when her child's problems occasioned a referral. In other cases, the parent requested treatment after the child had a positive experience in therapy. In still other instances, the parent began her own treatment and subsequently referred her child. In all these instances, the parent asked that the same therapist work with both parent and child, citing several reasons: the therapist's familiarity with the family unit, the security and attachment already experienced with the therapist, and anticipated difficulty in maintaining multiple therapeutic contacts with different therapists. In the most poignant requests for treatment, the parent observed that she now felt the confidence to approach issues she had been unable to confront in a situation independent of her child.

It was this comment more than any other that stimulated me to think further about these issues. Was it possible that children afforded their parents an opportunity not otherwise available to them to confront fundamental feelings and conflicts? Could the key to continuity in treatment and resolution of children's difficulties lie in full recognition and acceptance of their dependence on their parents? Were traditional approaches to child treatment closing possible avenues to therapeutic effectiveness? The classical psychoanalytic approach rejects the simultaneous treatment of parent and child. From my discussions with colleagues and scattered references in the literature, however, I was presented with the possibility that simultaneous treatment has been practiced widely by many therapists although not extensively reported. This unspoken tradition among therapists indicated to me a need both to understand and to conceptualize publicly what had become common practice.

I found direction in and drew confidence from the wisdom of Melitta Sperling (1950, 1951, 1954, 1970), whose voice broke the collusion of silence surrounding this commonly used method of intervention. According to Sperling, simultaneous treatment of mother and child permits a new approach to the observation of the development of the ego and the superego within the context of object relationships. The mother plays a central role in her child's life, often functioning as an auxiliary ego. Simultaneous treatment facilitates the detection of parental attitudes toward instinctual control, separation with the child, and changes in dependency. Therefore, Sperling writes, "an approach based on psychoanalytic insight, confronting the mother with her unconscious conflicts concerning her child, is not only the most effective therapy for both the mother and her child but is also the best prophylaxis for the child's future development" (1982, p. xiv).

Of interest is Sperling's argument that simultaneous treatment often shortens the course of therapy. Goals can be accomplished more readily because the therapist understands the parent-child dilemma from different perspectives, has the ability to establish rapport with the mother, and can relate to the child with appropriate tact and empathy. Simultaneous treatment of mother and child allows this sensitive synchronization between parent and child to be understood and resolved. "Treatment of the child alone in [certain] cases does not reveal those forces to which the child is reacting nor does it make growth possible unless the mother can give up her own infantile strivings, which are reflected in the child's illness" (1982, p. 41).

Sperling's emphasis on the importance of simultaneous treatment has been matched by the views of Dorothy Burlingham (1951; also,

Burlingham, Goldberger, & Lussier, 1955); Anna Freud (1950); and others (Chethik, 1976; Kolansky & Moore, 1966; Levy, 1960; Shapiro, Fraiberg, & Adelson, 1980; Sholevar, Burland, Frank, Etezady, & Goldstein, 1989). All these authors have agreed on the need for alteration of treatment parameters as a means to an end, that is, a way to deal with the unconscious resistance of the symbiotically enmeshed dyad.

Margaret Mahler (1949), however, expressed concern that if the same therapist saw both parent and child, a double transference-countertransference problem might arise. In her tripartite model, the parents and child were seen together, and the parents were seen separately by a different therapist for their individual treatment. This treatment model was extended by Eleanor Galenson in her work with young children (for example, Galenson, 1993; Galenson & Fields, 1989). Conversely, Peter Buirski and Cathy Buirski (1980) wrote about the risks of a split transference that might occur when two therapists treated members of the same family.

A useful summary of the early literature on this topic appears in an article by Ben Kohn (1976), in which the author reflects on the technical problems arising when both parent and child are seen by the same therapist. Kohn concluded that the double countertransference creates more distractions than a less contaminated analytic effort. Specifically, this approach permits the mother to focus on the role of mother as a defense and tends to shift the focus from her transference reactions to a consideration of her reality. On the positive side, Kohn noted that seeing both mother and child permits the therapist to observe the effects of the parent on her child and to be in the middle of the child's defense and character formation. He was able to observe how a child identified with maternal attitudes and reacted defensively against his mother's intrusions, her withholding, and her sadistic attacks on him. In a tone of conciliation, Kohn commented that possibly just as much can be learned from a purposeful, controlled contamination as can be gleaned when the field is kept uncontaminated.

James Anthony (1970) suggested a position affording therapeutic consensus. He noted an array of points for therapeutic observation of the reciprocal interchange between mother and child. As I noted previously, data usually are derived from separate analyses of mother and child or from direct observation of family interaction, as in conjoint treatment, parent training, infant psychotherapy, or tripartite treatment. Simultaneous treatment of parent and child offers an additional vantage point. It affords the therapist the opportunity to experience the dynamics between parent and child in all of their complexity. Conversely, it affords the patients a common therapeutic focus.

THE FOCUS OF SIMULTANEOUS TREATMENT

Simultaneous treatment focuses on parent and child both as separate individuals and as a dyad. It is concerned not only with the interaction between parent and child but also with the representational worlds of both patients.

The concept of the representational world of the child was first introduced to refer to the subjective world of the child, which is differentiated gradually in the course of development owing to processes of biological and psychological adaptation (Sandler & Rosenblatt, 1962). This notion of a child's subjective world has become a central one for researchers and clinicians. Particularly in the field of infant observation, the concept of developing representations has helped the therapist to capture the immensely complicated early transactions occurring between parent and child.

Systematic infant observation has provided clinicians with a wealth of information. Most striking is the irrefutable evidence that babies are born with many inborn propensities for forming early relationships with their caregivers. Followers of Melanie Klein (Segal, 1974) assume that the infant's inborn capacities for subjective differentiation are evidence for the existence of innate memories and fantasies.

Joseph Sandler (1993), agreeing that the baby "is born with highly complex inherited dispositions and capacities . . . from a subjective, experiential view," added that "the infant is, in a sense, the active experiencer and observer of his own complex behavior and has to make sense of it" (p. 340). In other words, although the infant is capable of interacting with the external world in a variety of complex ways, he still must build up his internal world on the basis of his subjective experience. Sandler listed the tasks the baby needs to accomplish: to learn to differentiate between self and other; to create boundaries between self and other that he can impose when appropriate; and to build up a capacity to differentiate between what is imagined and what is real. As the young child continues to develop, he acquires not only recognition memory but also the capacity to associate sensory and perceptual images to evoke memories of absent people and objects. The child also learns to construct coherent narratives about his experience (fantasies), which may be shared or private and conscious or outside the realm of awareness.

In simultaneous treatment, the therapist works to reconstruct the subjective experience of each of the patients and can observe, as well as participate in, the kinds of experience that have contributed to maladaptation. Because the dyadic relationship is a two-person system, issues of boundary formation and interpersonal regulation (merger and separation) are central concerns.

Two types of conflict arise and are commonplace within the dyadic relationship. One is the quantitative dilemma of "too much" (the fear of incorporation or enmeshment) versus "too little" (the fear of impoverishment or abandonment). What is "just right" is always relative to the transactional relationship created between two individuals.

A second dilemma arises because transactions always involve a dynamic state. The relationship created is a balance that can vary from an extreme of fixed rigidity to an extreme of indeterminate chaos. Although these polarities threaten the existence of a sense of balance between the two individuals, they nonetheless define end points of theoretical possibility. Most experience within the dyad falls somewhere between these two extremes.

Emotional regulation is a focus of the therapist in simultaneous treatment. The therapist does not view conflict as the outcome of libidinal and aggressive needs alone but also considers the role of affects. Both conscious and unconscious feeling states are central to the regulation of subjective experience and are motivating forces in behavior and development. Attachment theory broadened the therapist's concern to include the needs for security, admiration, and safety. It drew the therapist's attention to the need for relationships with others that are gratifying and pleasurable and the need to reduce anxiety, guilt, shame, and other unpleasurable aspects of relationship to others. Toward meeting these needs, parents and children construct complex representations of themselves and others that act to create, restore, and maintain a sense of well-being. Simultaneous treatment strives to discern and understand these representations along with their associated constellations of feelings indigenous to the emotional life of parent and child.

SOME RELEVANT THEORETICAL CONCEPTS

Otto Kernberg (1966) introduced the notion that a dyad represents a self-image and an image of the other, joined by an affect. In agreement with Edith Jacobson (1964), Kernberg viewed these early units of relationship between people as the consequence of a previously existing set of introjective ego processes. Joseph Sandler and Anne-Marie Sandler (1978) extended this viewpoint further to suggest that constellations of "subjective experience in which self and nonself have not yet been differentiated" (p. 292) are, in fact, the earliest units of experience. In this formulation, human existence originates within the undifferentiated dyadic relationship. Joseph Sandler described the notion of primary identification, or primary confusion, between self and object as "in representational terms . . . the state which exists before a firm boundary between self and object (or self and object representations) has been established . . . a state in which the infant cannot differentiate the representational aspects of his own self from those of the object . . . a 'fleeting primary identification' or 'fleeting confusion' between self and object [that] has been described as a ubiquitous normal phenomenon . . . which can be regarded as a basis for empathy" (1987, p. 345).

Irene Fast (1985), in a modification of psychoanalytic theory based on Piagetian concepts, proposed that the earliest experience and cognitive registration of events is of actions, not of self as actor in relation to an object of action. Self and other are initially undifferentiated aspects of actions. Mental representation occurs in action schemas energized by affects. From the beginning, therefore, affects are basic to the child's active and adaptive engagements with the environment. The emphasis in this approach is on activity, including both psychic and mental activity, as the functioning from which the construction of psychic structure can be inferred.

According to Fast's event theory, self and other are originally undifferentiated aspects of affective events. Affective events are organized psychically into discrete schemas representing similar actions. Affect is one dimension of similarity. The pleasure-pain dimension of affect is one principle governing the organization of events into discrete schemas. Event theory makes explicit the fact that many discrete schemas are possible, among which the pleasure-pain dimension of dissimilarity is only one determining factor, although probably one of particular importance.

Generally, in patient dyads entering simultaneous treatment, early affective experience has been organized rigidly, primarily along the pleasure-pain dimension. In this polarized organization of their experiential worlds, these dyads approximate the model proposed by Otto Kernberg (1975), which suggests two discrete affective organizations, one of pleasure and one of pain. As parent and child improve in treatment, they more closely approximate the event theory formulation, with many intermediary types or categories of affective organization. At the same time, parent and child begin to become aware of the nonhuman environment as another important source of experience, in which actions and affective states are less saturated by, and at times independent of, interpersonal relationship.

Event theory proposes further that "objectification is one process by which self and nonself are articulated out of undifferentiated event experience. Objectification occurs when two discrete [affect] schemas are activated simultaneously" (Fast, 1985, p. 74). In this manner, self and other are differentiated from each other.

This principle of differentiation is particularly relevant to simultaneous treatment, because the experience of each member of the dyad is reciprocal to the experience of the other. For example, Fast suggests that no objectification of the nonself (such as of mother as both gratifying or withholding) can occur without a concurrent objectification of the self (as one who may be satisfied or frustrated). Thus both the Sandlers and Fast link self and object into reciprocal units. Fast, however, emphasizes quality of affect as the organizer of differentiated schemas.

The affective compatibility or incompatibility of schemas is a significant factor in determining the possibility of their objectification. For example, Fast states that schemas with dissimilar but compatible affects (such as disappointment and anger, or pity and affection) are probably more readily integrated than ones with incompatible affects (such as to welcome home a returning parent and reject him, or to take in food and spit it out).

Event theory argues that primitive thought (primary process) occurs as a function of the nondifferentiation of self and nonself in the early experience of events. Symbolic thought (emerging at approximately 2 years of age) results in a revolution whereby it becomes possible for the child to think about something in the absence of what is thought about (evocative memory). At this point, the child is able to construct a world of actualities independent from the self (the objective world) and to test his own ideas against this new reality. Events excluded from the objectification process because of anxiety or other intense affects retain to varying extents the characteristics of primitive experience.

Because of its focus on the dyadic relationship, simultaneous treatment deals primarily with preoedipal issues, including narcissistic injury, impulse control, emotional regulation, and negotiation of boundaries, in the domains of both actuality and fantasy. Oedipal concerns, including rivalry and competition, are always present, if not yet succeeding earlier dyadic concerns. Event theory is helpful in assessing the interaction of these developmentally earlier and later modes of functioning.

The perceptions of parent and child are organized into schemas that enable the two to relate to each other and to themselves in a meaningful way. The relative use of more primitive coping-defensive strategies, such as splitting, or of the developmentally more advanced coping-defensive strategy of repression depends on the extent to which objectification has been accomplished. According to Fast (1985), "when the processes of objectification have resulted in a largely coherent and integrated self-structure and construct of nonself and reality, repression predominates . . . [but] when, due to the pervasiveness of affectively incompatible schemas, the psychic structure remains one of relatively discrete schemas representing disparate patterns of affectively motivated interactions, splitting—the anxiety-based substitution of one schema for another—is likely to prevail" (p. 76). When this definition is used, the demarcation between oedipal and preoedipal experience becomes permeable, and the two types of experience are distinguished by the degree of specific modes of defensive response present.

Peter Fonagy (1993) emphasizes the strategic role of the caregiver's sensitivity to both the child's inner (mental) world and his physical world in determining the formation of coping-defensive strategies. The parent helps to contain the child's overwhelming affects and binds the child's anxiety so that the child can use fantasy to play out conflicts and express fears symbolically. However, if the parent's capacity to understand the child is interfered with by incoherent mental representations arising out of the parent's own life experience, the child's affective experience will be chaotic and dysregulated. The parent's capacity to reflect on the mental states of her child is described by Fonagy as an active creative process giving coherence to the child's affective experience. It implies the parent can identify with her child without becoming the child.

The parental capacity for reflection parallels Joseph Sandler's (1987) description of emergent self-awareness in the infant, who must gradually make sense out of his ongoing activities. Hobson (1993) comments further on the dyadic process of infant self-awareness and parental reflection. He describes how the infant comes to relate not only to the world around him as he perceives it but also to the parent's psychological relation to the same world. Because he is aware of his caregiver's reaction to events, the infant learns that objects and events can have multiple person-related meanings. Thus the child's first experience is of being understood. Subsequently, the child can progress to reflecting on his own diverse states and the diversity of experience in others without resorting to maladaptive coping-defensive strategies. Understanding the developmental course and outcome of these early dyadic parent-child issues is a primary concern of simultaneous treatment.

LEVELS OF EXPERIENCE WITHIN SIMULTANEOUS TREATMENT

Dyadic experience in simultaneous treatment occurs on different levels. The first level is the level of observable actions. On an intermediate level are shared and unshared subjective states, both articulated and unarticulated. A third level consists of experiences occurring outside conscious awareness, usually referred to in the analytic literature as unconscious, including wishes, fantasies, and memories.

The boundaries between these levels of experience fluctuate, reflecting variable levels of emotional regulation between parent and child.

Although dyadic relationships include both shared and unshared elements, even the unshared elements are experienced by each partner, although in different ways. Moments of private meaning that exclude the other contain the potential to lead to the experience of rejection and alienation if there is no reference point, or background, against which the experience can find form and meaning. The receptivity of parent to child and child to parent provides such a background, enabling the integration of the personal moment to occur within a milieu of acceptance. If the context, or receptivity, is deficient or lacking, the private experience of each partner is isolated from that of the other, incapable of being validated or objectified.

There are many instances in which a private moment can be read and understood by the other without destructive consequences. Such moments are described by Donald Winnicott's (1971) concept of the child's capacity to play alone in the presence of the adult. The child is safely contained within the benign acceptance by the adult of the child's need for space and independent exploration.

The concept of background of safety (Sandler, 1960a) is encountered here, wherein the child feels comfortable to play alone, given unintrusive acceptance by the adult. As the adult allows the child to "go on being" and the child suspends the need for validation, possibilities for individual exploration and creativity are opened. Essential for these conditions to exist is a climate of understanding within the dyad that supports individuation.

SIMULTANEOUS TREATMENT AND THE
DIFFERENTIATION OF GENERATIONS

Two important components of simultaneous treatment are the definition of roles and the articulation of generational differences. Sigmund Freud (1913) described the risk of oedipal desires that thrust the child into rivalry with the parent of the same sex. These oedipal dangers were previewed by the biblical patriarch Jacob, who punishes his first-born son, Reuven, for "alighting onto the sleeping place of his father."

As noteworthy as these admonitions are, they focus on genital desires and overlook earlier, more crucial articulations of generational differences. Mahler's (1968) stages of separation-individuation delineate these earlier developments, in which awareness of generational differences and the capacity for self-reflection permit the adult to parent the child and to acknowledge his individuality while emphasizing his continuity with other human beings.

This view of the parent-child relationship is consistent with the viewpoint of the concept of the self as paradoxical. According to Stephen Mitchell (1991), the self functions to maintain unity and coherence, while at the same time it contains variety and change. This paradoxical definition of self is compatible with the principles of differentiation and objectification enunciated by event theory.

It is this perspective, acknowledging the need for sameness yet recognizing the existence of difference, that defines the transactional relationship studied by simultaneous treatment. Parent and child in simultaneous treatment present to the therapist a portrait of role reversal and confusion in the formation of boundaries between self and other. The concept of the self to be used in this book is that of a person embodying a variety of perspectives, who is able to reflect, with some sense of separateness, continuity, and integrity, on his or her own identity.

In the patients who are appropriate candidates for simultaneous treatment, perceptions of self and other have become polarized, rigid, and confused. The attacker becomes the attacked; the child becomes the parent. When this kind of communication occurs between parent and child, the separateness of levels of intergenerational reality is lost, with subsequent loss of effectiveness in parenting and trauma for both members of the dyad. When it occurs in treatment, the therapist experiences an intrusion into her relationship with parent and child by perceptions that are disorienting and confusing. Progress in treatment depends on the ability of the therapist and patients to sort out these perceptions and understand them within the context of past and current relationships.

Countertransference, the feelings evoked within the therapist by the patient, can be valued as important communication informing the therapist about ongoing dynamics within the dyad, rather than as error factors to be eliminated. The therapist's awareness of her own feelings brings an added dimension to the unfolding scenario. These feelings provide clues to the underlying difficulties or unresolved issues that need to be addressed. The more aware the therapist is of her patient, the more aware she can be of her own feelings. This attunement does not imply enmeshment as the goal of treatment. It does imply, however, that enmeshment in some cases may be the means to finding the shared experience leading to the language necessary for treatment to proceed.

Simultaneous treatment implies therapeutic relationship and understanding arising from within the relationship. These understandings are ultimately personal and intense. The therapist recognizes the theme and terrain as familiar. She is able to respond in a manner that is both resonant and unique. Part of the therapist's artistry is the careful balancing of realities and the capacity to meet and communicate with her patients wherever they are at any moment in treatment.

THE INTERGENERATIONAL TRANSMISSION OF TRAUMA

John Bowlby's (1969, 1973, 1980) theory of attachment postulates the construct of internal working models to account for the organization of an individual's subjective experience in relationships. Internal working models are mental representations, maintained largely out of awareness, that guide an individual's appraisal of and response to others. According to Bowlby, working models determine how incoming personal information is perceived, determine what affects are experienced, select the memories that are evoked, and mediate behavior with others in important relationships. Bowlby's concept of internal working models shares many of the attributes of Joseph Sandler and Bernard Rosenblatt's (1962) concept of the representational world of the child. Both constructs suggest that the crucial factor in the transmission of experience is the individual's subjective experience of others in relationships, rather than isolated objective events, discernible behaviors, or personality characteristics.

Attachment theory researchers redefine the categories used in examining the intergenerational transmission of maltreatment. In their work, they have shifted the focus from observable behaviors in the maltreated-maltreating cycle to the underlying themes organizing a parent-child relationship and their associated internal working models. This perspective is especially relevant to simultaneous treatment, which proposes to work within the reality of everyday life and the subjective experience of both parent and child, with the goal of changing repetitive maladaptive patterns of relationship. It is not my intention to review the literature on the maltreated-maltreating cycle (for example, Cicchetti & Aber, 1980; Kaufman & Zigler, 1987; Steele, 1983) but to point out several aspects of the general problem of intergenerational transmission of trauma that are particularly relevant to simultaneous treatment.

Charles Zeanah and Thomas Anders (1987) point out the motivational qualities of working models. These constructs act to compel an individual to recreate experiences congruent with his relationship history. For example, in addition to presenting distorted social signals to adults with whom they are interacting, abused children often behave in ways that invite punitive responses from others (Gaensbauer, 1982; George & Main, 1979; Wasserman, Gardier, Allen, & Shilansky, 1987). Susan Crockenberg (1987) demonstrated that mothers who are angry and punitive have toddlers who are angry and noncompliant.

Apparently these toddlers internalize their mother's aggression and learn both the provocative and the punitive aspects of the relationship (Sroufe & Fleeson, 1986).

Attachment theorists argue that child maltreatment is a kind of relationship disorder in which intergenerational transmission is mediated by the internal working models of both parent and child in the manner of the aggressive toddler just described. Patterns of relating are considered to have farther-reaching consequences than specific traumatic events. Simultaneous treatment is focused on the subjective experience of parent and child and their mutual linkages. It appears to offer an excellent approach to changing the ongoing cycling and recycling of parent and child pathology.

Parents' retrospective reports of childhood maltreatment on the Adult Attachment Interview point to three patterns of maltreatment. Each pattern of maltreatment is characterized by a different organizing theme of the relationship and associated with a different type of internal working model. This evidence suggests that rejection, role reversal, and fear are organizing themes of maltreating relationships transmitted across generations. What is transmitted across generations is not necessarily a behavior but an organizing theme of the relationship and a way of experiencing that theme, or internal working model (Zeanah & Zeanah, 1989). These organizing themes (of rejection, role reversal, and fear) are common to the simultaneous treatment cases included in the clinical section of this book, although none of the clinical cases described include physical maltreatment.

In the pattern of rejection, the child is turned prematurely away from the parent toward independence. The affects toward the child range from coldness and sternness to wishing the child away or dead. Essentially, the parent communicates to the child that he is disliked or unwanted. The parent in addition may neglect the child by being physically or psychologically unavailable. The child learns at an early age to turn his attention away from the parent when needing comfort and that independence and individual strength are highly valued (Main & Goldwyn, 1984).

Role reversal is a major theme of maltreatment relationships in which the parent's psychological well-being becomes the burden of the child. Although there is no direct rejection of the child in the sense of turning the child away, the child's needs are subservient to those of the parent. Guilt-inducing criticism results in conformity to please the parent. Despite feeling that no accomplishment or behavior is ever good enough, the child persists in his efforts to please the parent. If the child is physically abused, it is not a rejection but an angry retaliation against not pleasing the parent. The child's inability to obtain responsive care from the parent leads to a working model of relationship characterized by confusion. Adults who experienced role reversal as children are inconsistent as parents. Their children construct models of relationship reflecting confusion and struggle.

Fear of the parents or of frightening parental behavior is the sequela in relationships reflecting severe unresolved trauma or parental mental illness. Fear of the parent is the major theme of these relationships. For example, Radke-Yarrow, Cummings, Kuczynski, and Chapman (1985) found that parents of disorganized infants tended to suffer from bipolar affective disorder. Children whose mothers have an anxiety disorder tended to show increased levels of inhibition (Biederman, Rosenbaum, Hirshfeld, Faraone, Bolduc, Gersten, Meminger, Kagan, Snidman, & Resnick, 1990; Hirshfeld, Rosenbaum, Biederman, Bolduc, Faraone, Snidman, Reznick, & Kagan, 1992) as do children of depressed mothers (Kochanska, 1991). Parental behaviors derived from fear are especially frightening to children, who cannot comprehend their cause. In these cases, the child is presented with an unresolvable paradox inherent in the parent-child relationship: The safe haven is also a source of alarm. Moreover, the conflict between opposing tendencies to approach and to flee from the attachment figure stems from a single external signal (threatening or fearful parental behavior). This approach-avoidance conflict is internalized by the child (Main & Hesse, 1990; Sroufe, 1988; Zeanah & Anders, 1987; Zeanah & Klitzke, 1991).

Mary Main (1993) described the child's response to frightening parental behavior as a collapse of behavioral and attentional strategies. Dissociation on the parent's part—trancelike behavior induced by her own history of maltreatment—induces a state of disorganization in the child. These shifts in the parent's mental state frighten her child and link the child to unresolved states of mind in the parent. When parents were interviewed about their children's behavior, gaps occurred in their reporting, reflecting profound parental insecurity and disorganization. Parents were unable to perceive or accurately interpret their child's signals that threatened to alter their defensive affective state. Main (1991) suggested that alteration in attentional patterning (in the service of control or manipulation of behavior) is an important feature of caregiver and child development. Rigid organization of these processes in the caregiver compromises her capacity for self-reflection, which is so essential to her child's development (Fonagy, 1993).

It is the human context of subjective experience that contains the imprint of trauma. Situations in which the parent is unable to receive the child's communications in an empathic manner, perhaps because of her own psychopathology or traumatic experience, tend to exacerbate the child's difficulty and perpetuate the internal conflict. For the child, the result is confusing, frightening perceptions of external reality. Burdened by these intense experiences, the child resorts to maladaptive defenses of denial, avoidance, and splitting. These defenses curtail differentiation and integration of feelings and result in enmeshed pathological representations of self and other, which transcend time through intergenerational transmission.

THE ORIGIN OF PATHOLOGICAL REPRESENTATIONS

Pathological representations are based on distorted perceptions reflecting failures of differentiation within the parent-child relationship. In the usual course of events, subjective experience within the dyadic context results in boundary formation between the real and the imagined. Parent and child share a world that gradually becomes organized into patterns of affective expression, symbols, and perspectives on the self and others. Will these events coordinate smoothly, resulting in pleasurable and playful illusions about the reality of the self and other? Or, alternatively, will the parent-child experience be disrupted in a way that produces conflict and dissonance?

Martin Hoffman (1978) suggested that a capacity for empathy predates a capacity for symbolic thought and is fundamental to the infant's earliest experience. In the instance of positive empathic experience, the infant is in harmony with the other person and introjects his experience into an early sense of personal good feeling. Intense negative affective arousal has disorganizing effects as the infant attempts to avoid or flee from the source of disturbance (Fraiberg, 1987).

The parent responds to her child by attuning to the expressive signals of comfort and discomfort. For example, when the infant whimpers, cries, or smiles, the parent turns to focus on her child and fully respond to the message communicated. The parent may respond by amplifying, or elaborating on, the child's signal, sending back a message that the child has been understood. This kind of empathic attunement to the child's need states is essential for survival (Ainsworth, Blehar, Waters, & Wall, 1978; Bowlby, 1969, 1973, 1980). Both Robert Emde (1980) and Stern (1985) argue that a parent's attunement to her child is an essential ingredient in the formation of human bonds. Furthermore, attunement is a reciprocal process; each member of the dyad attunes to the other. Failure of attunement is a failure of relationship.

In its most advanced developmental form, empathy is an affective and cognitive process that includes attunement. Mature empathy, predicated on autonomy from the other person, is the capacity to recognize and be aroused by the familiar in the other person's experience and yet remain separate from it.

Furthermore, mature empathy assumes a capacity for differentiation and forming part-whole relationships. One person resonates to the other without being overwhelmed by wishes to be the same and to merge. In other words, similarity with another person is not experienced as confusing, frightening, or overwhelming. Rather, the person is capable of reflection and perspective. The bond to the other is flexible yet bounded by limitations imposed by the person's own sense of who he is—his personal identity.

This mature form of empathy, therefore, begins with attunement. It also includes, to a greater or lesser extent, several other faculties. One constellation of abilities is involved in socialization, namely, the capacity to decenter from one's egocentric concerns and the capacity for perspective in understanding roles. A second constellation of abilities is involved in individuation, namely, the capacity for conservation of a sense of self and the capacity for self-reflection. A third constellation of abilities is involved in the development of conscience, namely, the capacity for inhibition and control of wishes, the capacity for postponement of actions, and the capacity to integrate one's own aggression. It is this set of three constellations of abilities that I call *complex empathy*. It is essential to adequate parenting and is acquired gradually by the child as he proceeds in his development. (Chapter 2 includes a description of the child's acquisition of empathy.)

When a parent is deficient in her capacity for mature empathy, her relationship to her child is also impaired. The synchrony within the duet is not harmonious, and the relationship becomes symptomatic. The symptoms may vary from avoidance and rejection, to role reversal, to aggression and fighting, to immoral acts such as lying and stealing. Regardless of the manifest symptom, underlying the difficulty is a fundamental failure of empathy within the dyad, resulting in a failure of regulation of perceptions, feelings, and behavior. Maladaptive coping-defensive mechanisms are efforts to reinstate regulation and prevent disorganization. However, these maladaptive solutions always exact a cost and run the risk of blocking further opportunities for development.

Simultaneous treatment is geared toward helping parent and child to restructure the subjective experience of their relationship. It depends on the capacity of restored empathy to nurture and heal impaired pathological representations. Within the safety of treatment, parent and child can explore new avenues of experience to create new models of relationship.

THREE LEVELS OF REALITY IN
SIMULTANEOUS TREATMENT

Simultaneous treatment is defined as the treatment of a dyadic relationship in which both parent and child are seen separately by the
same therapist. What characterizes this treatment method is not only
external arrangements but also the complex nature of the developing
transference-countertransference relationship. The therapist is the
nodal point integrating levels of reality by communicating new
understandings to each member of the dyad. This schema of therapeutic realities was formulated by Arnold Modell (1990). Each of the
levels of reality may be conceptualized as a different aspect of the parent-therapist or child-therapist relationship. They emerge sequentially with the unfolding of treatment. The levels of reality are not
necessarily mutually exclusive and intertwine in various patterns
within the dyadic parent-child relationship. Each of these aspects of
reality is examined individually in the following paragraphs.

In the everyday reality, the parent in her adult role perceives the
child and his behavior as the presenting problem. The child may be
more or less aware of his difficulties. The therapist helps the child to
focus on the behaviors and attitudes his parents experience as problematic. The child perceives the therapist as an adult trained to provide guidance to himself and his parents.

In the dependent/containing reality (the safe haven), the parent
and child gradually come to perceive the therapist as supportive and
benign. This function of the therapist has been described in the
metaphor of the therapeutic relationship as a container within which
the patient is contained (Bion, 1962) and in the metaphor of the therapist as providing the holding function of the "good enough" mother
(Winnicott, 1958). The concept of the self-object (Kohut, 1972) relates
to the mirroring aspects of the dependent/containing reality; it does
not address the issue of regulation and limit setting.

In the dependent/containing reality, the parent in the role of parent
receives from the therapist support and assistance, advice, and prob-
lem-solving techniques. The child as child likewise receives educational and supportive suggestions and guidance. The parent in the
role of child has the opportunity to experience safety and caring. By
contrast, the child is curtailed in his role as parent. His identity is
established as separate, and he is freed from the bonds of precocious
tending to the needs of others. He can feel reassurance in the recognition that someone else can provide for the parent and limit inappropriate parental intrusions.

The projective reality for parent and child develops in relation to the therapist when she is perceived as repeating some aspect of a past relationship and its concomitant affects. In projective reality, the parent in the role of parent confronts her disturbing perceptions of her child. The parent in the role of child reexperiences with the therapist specific trauma of her childhood. The child in the role of child perceives the therapist as embodying the threatening aspects of the parent that he was unable to confront in everyday reality. The child is limited in the role of parent and no longer needs to perceive himself as omnipotent and responsible. As this projective aspect of the relationship diminishes, the therapist functions increasingly as an everyday rather than fantasized person. For both parent and child, the therapist in her capacity for reverie transforms unpleasant sensations into acceptable ones. Clarification and confrontation are used by the therapist to point out crucial differences between past and present realities. Parent and child then reintegrate modified emotional experiences into the context of a transformed parent-child relationship.

DESCRIPTIVE SUMMARY OF SIMULTANEOUS TREATMENT

Simultaneous treatment focuses on the points of contact between parent and child that are keeping the two individuals wrapped in dependency with each other in a struggle to survive. These points of contact constitute the core of the child's problem. Often it is the birth of this child that unexpectedly confronts the adult partner with unresolved past issues of child-parent relationship. At times it is a particular child who seems to be targeted because of specific characteristics such as gender, appearance, birth order, or some other trait that is more obscure. Characteristics triggering unconscious parental issues allow the child to become a focus for unresolved feelings. For example, the child's physical characteristics may remind the parent of an envied sibling. Unaware of these feelings, the parent might convey a disdainful, resentful attitude toward the child. To the extent that the child is compliant with parental wishes and feelings, he becomes a container for them and surrenders part of his autonomy and sense of identity to the parental prerogative. Realistic issues of childhood dependency act to reinforce the child's vulnerability and his submission to parental needs.

For the parent who brings her child to treatment, at first the therapist is a "real" person who will help the child while assisting the mother to cope with her parental role. When the therapist forms an association with the child patient, this connection in turn links the therapist to the parent's representation of herself as a child. In this way, the therapist becomes linked to the child within the inner life of the parent, an aspect of the adult that previously may have been hidden.

It seems as though the only way the parent can bring her "split-off" child to treatment is by allowing it to come alive within the transference relationship with her child's therapist. First the parent brings her child; then she presents her "split-off" internalized child. The therapist becomes the caregiver, securely "holding" the child in both individuals.

At this juncture, the child gradually experiences freedom from being the container for the projected identity of the "parent's child." He is able to experience himself and be experienced by others as the separate person he really is.

The therapist becomes increasingly a fantasized parent for the parent, relieving the child of functioning in this role. With increased separation, the dyad becomes capable of tolerating a triad, in which one can be left out without being annihilated, and one can experience envy without the threat of destructiveness or retaliation. Progress is enhanced when positive feelings between parent and child lead to experiences of reciprocity and the growth of confidence and caring. These experiences take the place of the pathology of extreme ambivalence, merged boundaries, role reversals, lack of autonomy, terror of mutual destructiveness, and lack of confidence in the survival of the child, the parent, or both.

The pathology in simultaneous treatment resides within the dyadic relationship. The treatment required is for each partner, separately, to experience the same therapeutic context. A change in the original dyadic relationship occurs when each member of the dyad relates to the same third partner, separately. The new partner is the shared component in the therapeutic experience, which combines both real and illusory components.

This introductory chapter has given an overview of simultaneous treatment and outlined three aspects of reality that occur in this method of treatment. The next chapter describes in detail the psychological processes underlying simultaneous treatment. These are the concepts that help therapists to understand how pathology develops within the context of the parent-child relationship.

CHAPTER 2

Psychological Processes Underlying Simultaneous Treatment

THIS CHAPTER DESCRIBES the psychological processes a clinician uses as guidelines and measures of progress in conducting simultaneous treatment. Although every case is unique, several general concepts are common to dyadic intervention with parents and children.

Parallel events are events that signal shared therapeutic experience. These events are of major importance to both the therapist and her patients. They form the basis for communication that can lead to the development of empathy and intersubjective validation. The chapter summarizes the reasons that this optimal growth fails to occur and how distortions of empathy and emotional trauma result instead in pathology. Finally, this chapter describes how new dyadic narratives can be composed and can bring about positive therapeutic outcomes in new identifications.

PARALLEL EVENTS

Parallel events occur within the framework imposed by simultaneous treatment because both members of a dyad interact with and are observed by the same therapist. The therapist is able to share in the parent's subjective experience of being a caregiver as well as being a recipient of care. In simultaneous treatment, the caregiver replicates emotions to both therapist and child, which results in the caregiver behaving in similar ways toward both therapist and child, allowing the therapist to perceive similarities between the caregiver's mode of functioning with her child and within the therapeutic relationship. Similarly, with the child in treatment, the therapist is able to observe the child's responses that reflect his subjective experience with his caregiver and responses that reflect his experience of the more neutral role of the therapist within the context of the therapeutic relationship.

Parallel events that occur in simultaneous treatment may be affective interchanges, behaviors, or defensive or receptive attitudes (Trad, 1992). Parallel events are not always easy to delineate; however, they are always in operation either impeding or facilitating treatment. What is unique to simultaneous treatment is that these events occur in the presence of a new, shared partner. An event that occurs with one patient in the therapeutic context is paralleled by an event the original partner experiences in therapy. For instance, a parent mentions that her child seems to be less anxious about coming to therapy sessions and that somehow she also is finding it easier to come to her sessions. In another instance, the child berates the therapist for having no interesting toys, and his parent complains that "time-out" procedures are not helping and that there must be other techniques the therapist can suggest.

In simultaneous treatment, there are instances when events experienced within one dyad are not duplicated in the other dyad but are experienced as inverse patterns of subjective experience. Role reversals often become evident as inverse parallel events. For instance, the therapist experiences precocious caregiving qualities of the youngster in treatment. These characteristics may not be reported by the parent, who takes these mature qualities of her child for granted. Parental reports may focus on the child's infantile behaviors rather than the child's mature caregiving capabilities. In a set of parallel events within the therapeutic relationship, the parent reveals infantile attitudes, demanding behaviors, and expectations for gratification that are unrealistic. These inverse parallel experiences afford the therapist an opportunity to observe reversed parent-child roles.

An important subcategory of parallel events is that of *shared fantasies*, in which two individuals have the same fantasy and the fantasy serves as a common bond. Harold Blum (1988) described specific features of these fantasies. Communicating a fantasy to a person is part of an invitation to identification, shared living out of a fantasy, or a shared defense intrinsic to the fantasy. When a parent shares a fantasy with his child, it becomes part of the parent-child reality, with implications for the child's development. The child also influences the caregiver with his fantasies, but in most cases not to the same extent, because the child is dependent on the caregiver's more advanced development.

Blum argues that the shared fantasy of a child is always anchored in some measure of reality. Thus a childhood seduction fantasy usually contains some kernel of truth, although the truth may be elaborated on and distorted by the child's wishes. Shared fantasies influence a child's sense of morality, defining boundaries between right and wrong and between acceptable and unacceptable behaviors. Shared fantasies also influence parent-child attitudes toward the future, personal ideals, and strivings.

Shared fantasies tend to shape personal and familial history subjectively. Intrafamilial fantasies may shape a child's identity according to the role ascribed to him by others. For example, he may be the child destined for great deeds to fulfill parental ambition, the child chosen to serve a scapegoat function, or the child needed to replace a loss.

An extreme form of shared fantasy that depends on pervasive symbiotic attachment and identification is *folie à deux* (Anthony, 1970). In this instance, parent and child believe a fantasy that binds them together to be real. For example, a father might perceive his daughter as a son, and the little girl might believe she has a penis. This mistaken identity connects the two closely as a pair, wherein the father validates his daughter's delusions, and the daughter confirms her father's wishes. The disturbance may be less extreme, however. Phyllis Greenacre (1959) described focal symbiosis, a circumscribed area of the child's development in which the child's and parent's needs are interwoven with incomplete separation. More recently, attachment theorists have attributed these difficulties to insecure attachment.

A case of focal symbiosis can present as separation anxiety. Four-year-old Annie, a bright, vivacious, coy, verbal child, could not leave her mother. In sessions, she was very quiet and spent most of her time tracing female heroines from the Walt Disney books of fairy tales she found in my office. She insisted that every feature be duplicated exactly or else she would cry uncontrollably. Over time, we became more expert at our pictorial renditions. Our work together soothed her; if her mother left her pocketbook with us, she was free to wait in the waiting room. Annie's favorite character was Sleeping Beauty, who was awakened from her deathlike trance by a handsome prince. Annie "read" this story countless times, always focusing on the beautiful young princess and her consort.

Annie's mother revealed to me that she herself was a twin. Her twin sister was chronically depressed and lived in their parents' home. The grandparents were dependent on Annie's mother to help them to organize their lives. When Annie was anxious and clingy, she reminded her mother of her sister; in fact, at times they seemed identical—demanding and helpless. Although Annie's mother knew her attitude toward her daughter was distorted, she felt compelled to view her in this troubling way. As we continued to meet, Annie's play became more joyful and less grim. She allowed mistakes and began to draw free-form pictures of her fantasy characters, always reminding me, "not to worry, the prince will come." Before too long, original creatures were appearing, and the drawings became totally Annie's creations. Concurrently, ambivalent ties binding mother and daughter loosened, as the symptoms of separation anxiety diminished.

In many cases treated by simultaneous treatment, failure to negotiate separation-individuation had resulted in impairments in self and object constancy without implying a complete symbiotic state (Mahler, Pine, & Bergman, 1975). Telepathy, magical thought transference, or empathy without communication is not the source for these shared experiences. Rather, there are always cues for and clues to the transfer of unconscious communication. The work of Rene Spitz (1965) on archaic parent-infant reciprocal identification and the establishment of dialogue; Margaret Mahler's (1968) delineation of mutual cueing; Robert Emde's (1983) work on social referencing and procedural knowledge; Daniel Stern's (1985) description of an infant's experience of self; and Judy Dunn and Robert Plomin's (1990) naturalistic studies of young children and their parents all focus on points of origin for shared fantasy.

In simultaneous treatment, the fantasy shared between parent and child is acknowledged in the presence of the therapist. This opens the secretive aspects of the relationship to exploration and participation by a third party. Acknowledgment of the shared fantasy is a prologue to recognition of the separate existence of parent and child. A crucial clinical judgment is whether the child contends with communicated fantasies or with manifested fantasy enactments, such as physical or sexual abuse, bizarre rituals, or masquerades.

INTERSUBJECTIVE VALIDATION

Intersubjectivity refers to an awareness of shared meaning with another person (Bretherton, McNew, & Beeghly-Smith, 1981; Stern, 1985; Trevarthen & Hubley, 1979). In intersubjective validation, two people agree on the occurrence of an event and by doing so establish it as an actuality. Such an event has a meaning shared by two individuals, who together have a sense of past and expectations about the future, with shared intentions and emotions. Because intersubjectivity is the means of processing shared fantasy, it is basic to the understanding of simultaneous treatment.

Research with infants indicates that shared meaning begins between 2 and 7 months of age, prior to language. Stern (1985) believes that mother-infant interactions are averaged and represented mentally as representations of interactions that have been generalized (RIGs). Beatrice Beebe and Frank Lachmann (1988) argued that mutually regulated bidirectional interactions between infant and caretaker provide the basis for an infant's presymbolic representations of self, other, and self-with-other. They term these patterns *interaction structures:* characteristic patterns of mutual influence that the infant comes to recognize and expect in his interaction with others. Alan Sroufe and Everett Waters (1977) suggested that at approximately 9 to 12 months, the infant is capable of constructing an internal working model of the dyadic relationship. Later on, at approximately 12 to 18 months of age, the infant forms a working model of the self.

Intersubjectivity can be observed in infancy in the form of emotional signaling (Emde, 1988) and social referencing (Campos & Stenberg, 1981; Feinman & Lewis, 1983; Klinnert, Emde, Butterfield, & Campos, 1986; Sorce & Emde, 1981). In a typical social referencing situation, the child is presented with a novel toy or unexpected event and looks toward the caregiver for a signal on how to proceed. Shared meanings form a basis not only for exploration of the world and acquisition of language, but also for rules and a sense of "we" in addition to self and other.

Private events contribute to the establishment of personal realities, which then must be tested against consensually based actuality. Harry Stack Sullivan (1953) termed this process *consensual validation,* emphasizing the need for agreement between individuals. The concept of intersubjectivity brings out the subjective nature of these agreements and their pervasiveness in the interpersonal realm. In this context, pathology can be understood as a disorder of regulatory mechanisms occurring within the dyadic relationship, or interaction structure, rather than solely within the individual.

One can speak also of *intrasubjective* validation, the internal agreement within the individual concerning behaviors, feelings, attitudes, and beliefs—his own and others. Simultaneous treatment uses both the therapist's and the patients' intrasubjective perceptions that influence the intersubjective process among therapist and patients. Consensus between participants in the treatment process facilitates differentiation and integration both for the individual patient and within the dyadic relationship. By treating both child and parent, the therapist has the potential to enhance the development of each, with benefits resulting for both. Sharing the same therapist provides gains to the dyad in terms of providing a sense of continuity and coherence.

EMPATHY AND IDENTIFICATION

Empathy is a major means by which a child gains understanding of the feelings of others and therefore is a prerequisite for intersubjective validation. Moreover, empathy has a central role in the child's development of prosocial interactions (Radke-Yarrow, Zahn-Waxler, & Chapman, 1983; Zahn-Waxler, Cummings, McKneur, & Radke-Yarrow, 1984). In simultaneous treatment, empathy is important because of its function in the transfer of feelings from parent to child and child to parent.

THE DEVELOPMENT OF EMPATHY

The development of empathy is crucial to the development of mutual understanding. When this process is interfered with or is deficient, a major obstacle to positive parent-child relationship is created. Therefore, it is important to understand the usual course for the development of empathy.

Martin Hoffman (1982a, 1982b) described four stages in empathic development. During the first year of life, infants act as if what happens to others happens to themselves. In a distressing situation, they interpret the distress of others as their own. Because cognitive immaturity prevents infants from identifying the source of distress correctly, during this stage they may be more vulnerable to other people's distress than at subsequent stages. If the distress is too great, infants use pathological defenses to keep from being overwhelmed. These defenses protect them from the empathic onslaught, but they are costly in terms of individuation and further development.

Hoffman described a second stage in empathic development, which he termed *egocentric empathy*, which lasts through the third year of life. The child at this stage is able to share another person's emotional distress yet is aware that it is occurring to another person. Reciprocally, the child is aware that others share his feelings but realizes the feelings are his own.

Dunn (1988) also described the child's self-interest between 2 and 3 years of age as a strong incentive to the development of an understanding of others. Whether arising from situations of conflict and threatened self-interest or a desire to cooperate and comply, the emotions aroused motivate the child to understand others. This description of the child between 2 and 3 years of age corresponds with Hoffman's concept of *egocentric empathy*. Dunn argued that both cognitive advances and affective responses contribute to the child's growing social understanding and awareness of himself within the family context.

Hoffman warns, however, that errors in the reading of empathic cues at this stage may lead to the child's misperceiving the extent of his personal influence and control. In a similar analysis, Paul Trad (1986) described how, in the natural progression of causal understanding, children may come to accept unrealistic responsibility with accompanying feelings of guilt and self-reproach. The illusion of control is a misperception of both the contingency of events and the level of personal competence involved in affecting the outcome of an event. The child mistakes an externally caused event for one within his own or another person's control. A variety of distortions can arise from the young child's egocentric perspective.

The third stage in the development of empathy occurs, according to Hoffman, when the child is able to assume another person's perspective. Moreover, he can empathize through symbolic expression as well as through facial and somatic distress. Symbolic play flourishes, and the child is able to characterize roles with distinctive personalities, behaviors, and feelings. The child creates scenarios depicting his understanding of these fantasy personae and how they interact. As these empathic understandings are consolidated into personages, they can be openly communicated and verified. The possibilities for intersubjective and intrasubjective validation at this point proliferate and take on abstract permutations, forming a complex repertoire of meaning available to the child for self-regulation in his relating to others.

Hoffman's fourth stage in empathic development occurs in later childhood, when children can experience empathic distress for someone's general life condition rather than just for specific events. They can understand that immediate behavior may be at variance with another person's general condition and make sympathetic allowances for outside factors contributing to a person's behavior. These capabilities introduce a relativistic perspective that renders the older child less personally vulnerable to the impact of empathic understandings but not less receptive. This advanced level of empathic development facilitates parental self-reflection. Self-reflection is the caregiver capacity described by Fonagy (1991; 1993, chap. 1) as promoting self-awareness and well-being in the child.

EMPATHIC DISTORTIONS: COPING AND DEFENSIVE STRATEGIES

A smooth coordination between caregiver and child resulting in a progressive development of intersubjective states and their validation is possible. It is also possible for several less than ideal scenarios to ensue involving the misreading of cues and the resulting chaos, confusion, disappointment, pain of miscommunication, and failure of relationship. Something pervasive impairs the reciprocal functioning of the pair, and instead of a meeting of minds, there occurs a forced sharing (Bretherton & Waters, 1985). This sense of coerciveness is experienced as painful by the child because it results in lack of synchronous regulation within the dyad.

Selma Fraiberg (1987) described the pathological defenses the very young child erects against the painful experience of lack of regulation: freezing, withdrawal, avoidance, hyperactivity, aggression, and sadness. In each case, these defensive strategies, employed by the child for survival, further sabotage his efforts at adaptation, his understanding of himself and others, his comprehension of causation, and his possibilities for further growth.

Distortions in empathic understanding may occur at many different levels within the parent-child relationship. The parent or child may be overwhelmed by or totally immersed in the experience of the other. In psychoanalysis, this type of incorporation of experience is termed *introjection*. The word refers to the taking in of partial or complete characteristics of another person. These attributes can be attitudes, fantasies, gestures, language, or behavior. Imitation and accommodation are similar processes in which the individual incorporates or introjects aspects of another.

Projection is the opposite process, the expulsion onto or into another person of one's own attitudes, behaviors, or feelings. Boundaries disappear, and the other is perceived as possessing a quality that belongs to the self. Fantasy and assimilation are characteristic of projection. In projection, the feeling projected is repressed; there is no longer an experienced empathy with the feeling projected. There is a distancing, or estrangement, from the other person as a completion of the defensive effort.

Another, more primitive type of empathic distortion occurs because of a failure of differentiation akin to stage 2 *egocentric empathy* (Hoffman, 1982a, 1982b), when the child misreads the cues of another person, attributing to him or her characteristics that pertain to himself. In this type of projection, the child's feelings are split, or polarized, with pleasurable attributes ascribed to the self and aversive attributes ascribed to others. Although these intolerable aspects of experience are projected into another, empathy is maintained with these feelings.

The child attempts to control the other person and in interaction with the other person induce in that person what is projected. In psycho-analytic literature, these processes are termed *projective identification* (for example, Bion, 1967; Kernberg, 1975; Klein, 1946; Ogden, 1979).

When projective identification as a defense affects the relationship between parent and child, it can eventuate in maladaptation and destructive distortion. Parental expectations are potent contributing factors to a child's general development, particularly on the child's emerging sense of self. This defensive intrusion on the autonomy of the developing child by parental expectations can be experienced by the child as overwhelming trauma.

In fact, in daily living an array of varied interactions occur between parent and child, serving the functions of both adaptation and defense. Projective identification as a defense occurs only at points of intense vulnerability within the dyadic relationship. The parent-child pair at these moments are sharing less differentiated, or less objectified, rigidly organized, intersubjective experience. Even if these moments occur only occasionally, as infrequent regressions within the dyadic experience, their impact is intense, immediate, and widespread.

Joseph Sandler (1993) suggested that projective identification is also a normal process, an integral part of all emotional relationships, and an especially vital aspect of love relationships. It is observable when a parent lives vicariously through his child or when a partner in a love relationship lives to "too great" a degree through the other. These excesses seem necessary at points of intense sharing of feelings, when the imagined figment becomes embodied in the identity of the other. These moments, like shared memories, link the partners in a unique bond of attachment (Blum, 1988).

Sandler argued that *primary identification,* or *primary confusion,* in which the boundary between self and other is lost, occurs for a fleet-ing moment whenever we relate to another person. Fleeting confusion between self and other allows for an extremely rapid and "continual to-and-fro: an unconscious alternation between the momentary state of 'oneness' and a process of boundary setting, of sorting out of dif-ferences between self and other. What was one's own a short moment before is now located in the object. What is projected is fleetingly 'mine,' but then a microsecond later, reassuringly 'not mine'" (p. 346).

The therapist uses her own primary identifications as a source of data to speak vicariously in the other's voice and playfully feel the other's feelings. How the infant uses projective identification is less clear. Certainly some perceptions of the self may be perceived initially primarily as aspects of the other. For example, where can we locate the source for that special gleam in the baby's eye or his curious, intent gaze at the world around him? Does the event reside within the infant himself, or is it the expression of dyadic interaction? Any projection, Sandler pointed out, requires a representational boundary across which the child can displace unwanted aspects of himself within his representational world.

Sandler is in agreement with Beebe, Jaffe, and Lachmann (1994), Irene Fast (1985), and attachment theorists in arguing that it is not simply a perception of the self or a perception of the other but rather the dyadic perception of the self in relation to the other that is represented in the experience of both child and adult. What vacillates and is flexible is the boundary between the partners.

Important issues for simultaneous treatment are how and when boundaries are triggered and their degree of permeability and flexibility. At what levels of relationship do the boundaries function adaptively and when are they dysfunctional? Are there different parameters functioning in boundary formation in the reality of everyday life, in the dependent/containing reality, and in the projective reality?

Sandler and Kernberg are in agreement that the characterizations that dominate the intrasubjective world of the parent and are duplicated within the psyche of the child can have pervasive and enduring implications. Inge Bretherton and Waters (1985) described the enduring effects of these representations. If an attachment figure frequently rejects or ridicules the child's bids for comfort in stressful situations, they note, the child may develop not only an internal working model of the parent as rejecting but also one of himself as not worthy of help or comfort. Conversely, if the attachment figure gives help and comfort when needed, the child will tend to develop a working model of the parent as loving and of himself as a person worthy of such support.

Concerning the maladaptive extreme of parent-child experience, Donald Meltzer (1975) described the catastrophic anxiety that pervades the state of autism. In the autistic state, dyadic emotions are stressed to the utmost extent. Autistic children have an exquisite sensitivity that renders them, according to Meltzer, "naked to the wind." They show a subtlety of emotive response to the mental and physical state of the therapist that far exceeds that found in other child patients. The autistic child has a primitive permeability to the emotions of others and experiences other people as similarly permeable. Because of their sensitivity, they are likely to be bombarded with the awareness of pain in others and expect others to be sensitive to them as well. They insist on uncompromising possessiveness of the caregiver.

Meltzer described the defense of *dismantling*. By the process of dismantling, ongoing transactions between individuals relating to each other are not linked and therefore are unavailable for memory. Dismantling is different from splitting, a strategy used in connection with projective identification. *Splitting* is an active division of subjective experience by the child in an attempt to avoid aversive feelings about the self. Dismantling occurs in a passive way, which permits the various senses to attach themselves to the most stimulating object of the moment. This scattering of attention brings about the dismantling of the self. The autistic child, by suspending his attention, cannot sustain his experience of himself and others.

This primitive state, lacking in differentiation, is the failure of relationship in its most extreme form. Other people are reduced to the sensual qualities that can be apprehended from their surfaces. For example, an autistic child manipulates objects for their sensory qualities in a perseverative way. Similarly, he engages in perseverative autoerotic activity, such as bubbling saliva, for the sensation in the mouth. There is no penetration into a firm object; there is no concept of orifices that can open or shut. According to Meltzer, it is only once the struggle commences between the child and parent over the opening and closing of orifices that potential space can develop. With this separation, there is space for omnipotence to emerge and create the fantasy of projective identification.

This chapter so far has described several qualitatively different possible outcomes of child-caregiver relationship within dyadic experience, ranging from the most benign to the most pathological. Following is a discussion of how trauma impacts on the process of identification, with adverse effects on the emotional development of the dyad.

IDENTIFICATION AND TRAUMA

Given the operation of parallel events, the therapist is in a unique position to observe how parental expectations operate. When and how are parental expectations expressed? How are these expectations of parent and child evidenced in interaction during daily routine? What expectations does the child have of himself and others? How do the child's expectations impact on parental predictions? Often the therapeutic course is a torturous one, leading to unanticipated encounters with shadows of past generations that continue to exert their influence in the form of unacknowledged expectations from the past (Fraiberg, Adelson, & Shapiro, 1975; Zeanah & Klitzke, 1991). Future time and anticipations of the future exert their influence as well. Forecasting and parental previewing are powerful influences on the child's continuing development and on events yet to unfold (Trad, 1991a, 1991b, 1993a).

In undergoing traumatic experience, the individual has been overwhelmed by stimulation and experienced a loss of boundaries or sense of individuation. The trauma interrupts the safe, secure background of life, what Winnicott (1958) referred to as "going on being." In the face of this loss of security, any person—child or adult—is vulnerable and impressionable.

If a child experiences loss of connection with an important person in his life, for example, his perceptions of the experience may cling to one frightening characteristic of the person. For example, children characterize "Bigfoot" as a large monster who looms over them and threatens to crush them. A benign parent may be perceived as Bigfoot by the child, who must comply with parental demands. The memory of Bigfoot may linger to frighten the child long after the disciplinary event has passed. Alternatively, under catastrophic conditions, the child is unable to conceptualize in a coherent way any aspect of the dyadic experience. His fear is of something vague like the howling wind or the scary ghost who returns to frighten him. In these instances of trauma, the intensity of the exposure as well as the attendant feelings of helplessness cause the child to become traumatized. He experiences a loss of secure context and also a loss of synthesis— how the parts of the experience hold together and who he is in relationship to the important person in his life.

To be sure, there is usually an external triggering traumatic event that therapist and patient can point to and make reference to in treatment. It is the internal event, however, occurring intrasubjectively, that is difficult to fathom at the moment of traumatic experience and is therefore unavailable for intersubjective validation. Because of unexpected disappointment or frustration, the child is overwhelmed and at the same time encapsulated within his experience. His perception of the other person may be diffused, as in the autistic state of dismantling; thus the autistic child is unable to attune to other people, insensitive to their presence, and seemingly unaware of their intentions. Alternatively, the perception of the other may be polarized, for example, as an aggressor, a victim, a rescuer, or a comforter. Because of the use of splitting as a coping-defensive strategy, these perceptions are potent, disparate qualities.

When the child's perception of the other is sufficiently differentiated, the child may respond to trauma by needing to make restitution, to repair damage to himself or others, or to take revenge. In pursuit of mastery and to counteract castration anxiety, the child may identify with the aggressor and continue to perpetuate a sadomasochistic relationship. The compulsion to repeat the trauma can be viewed as another effort to attain mastery; however, these perseverative efforts to attain resolution usually result in maladaptive outcomes.

Parent-child interaction may mirror maladaptive efforts at resolution, reflecting a compulsion to repeat. Intergenerational cycles of trauma have been documented by survivors of physical and sexual family abuse as well as by survivors of the holocaust in Europe. Identification with the aggressor and identification with the martyr are two defenses against intense suffering used by survivors. The internal world of the child of survivors is inhabited by personages of epic stature, larger than life in their idealization or demonization. In contrast to these heroic images, the child feels helpless and inadequate. Failure to pattern themselves after their parents leaves a void. Defensive adaptations arise to deal with the anxiety aroused by this alienation and lack of connectedness. The comfort of belonging is denied to these survivors of trauma and their children; thus the dyad perpetuates and relives the experience of the previous generation.

As discussed previously, simultaneous treatment reveals parallel events that are clues to the shared fantasies underlying the distress of parent and child. Blum (1988) argued that shared fantasies also result in positive identifications. These constructive identifications are characterized by the comfort of sharing, not overburdened but open to the subtleties and the fluid reciprocity of intimate relationships. The role of the therapist is to facilitate the definition of the contours of a relationship, promoting optimum coexistence for both members of the parent-child dyad.

Clues to understanding parent-child relationships can be detected in the signaling smile or cry of the child, the attitude of the parent, and the harmonious or disharmonious interaction of the dyad. The therapist, through her patience, containment, concern, and capacities for empathy and communication, furthers not only the enhancement of the relationship but also the autonomy of each of the partners. The partners' individual autonomy emerges out of shared understandings, which remain as a source of security and delineate their sense of the actual as differentiated from the imaginary, the permissible as opposed to the forbidden, and the competence and individuality of each partner.

NARRATIVE: THE TELLING OF LIFE EXPERIENCE

Clinicians are accustomed to hearing stories that recount life experiences. As listeners, they witness and participate in significant events that have shaped the life of the storyteller. Roy Schafer (1992) and Jerome Bruner (1986, 1990) have studied the narrative form because of its richness for clinical work and human development. The events of the distant past are combined with imaginary events and events experienced in the present. All these components merge in a single moment of lived experience when retold in a story.

Stern (1990) composed a diary of infant experience based on a parent's need to imagine an inner life for her baby. It is through these imaginings that the parent comes to know what to do next, how to feel, and what to think. Stern commented that when parents cannot identify their baby's experience, they simply make their best guess. This approximation inevitably is biased by the way in which the parents view the world. Moreover, a parent's interpretation of her baby's experience determines her choice of response to the baby. For instance, if the parent reads anger in the baby's cry, she is likely to respond with guilt or anger, but if the parent hears only distress, she is more likely to be able to feel and express empathy easily and directly.

The parent's response is intuitive and depends in large part on how she was treated as a child. In simple, direct language, Stern (1990) reconstructed the story of how the experience of self emerges in these first dyadic interactions. Indeed, how parents imagine their child is feeling and responding serves as a framework for how the baby will view himself for life. Similarly, it affects how the parents will perceive themselves in the future. The name given to this shared reciprocal process is *identification*. The need to ascribe meaning to behavior, therefore, to assign roles within a structure of social understanding, is a human need common to parents, families, and societies. The stories begun in infancy last a lifetime and form the basis for understanding oneself and others.

As the young child grows, he becomes able to narrate his own subjective experience. What began as vicarious efforts to understand another become the events of an individual life, which then can be told as a story. Clinicians listen to these stories of their patients and try to comprehend the similarities and differences in the representational worlds of child and adult. When does an event seem distorted as described? When does there seem to be discordance between the content of a narrative and the manner of telling, or between narrative content and the attitudes expressed toward self and others? When does there seem to be a distortion favoring overcontinuity, a theme resonating from the past?

As discussed in chapter 1, the clinician listens within the context of three intersecting realities. The everyday reality describes daily events, similar to that of a logbook. The dependent/containing reality describes a secure context enabling the patient to feel comfortable and express his inner thoughts and feelings. The projective reality describes the reality of imaginings and vicarious meanings, in which the patient elaborates his tale with creative experience, often of a private nature and difficult to discern. These three levels of reality intersect and often occur simultaneously in the telling of a narrative. Parallel events—the subjectively shared dyadic experiences discussed earlier in this chapter—can serve as a key to unraveling the many levels of meaning concealed within patient-therapist and parent-child interactions.

THE THERAPIST'S INTERVENTIONS AND THE FRAMING OF A THERAPEUTIC NARRATIVE

The therapist's goal is to enhance understanding between herself and her patients by assisting the patients in organizing their themes into a coherent narrative. This sense of coherence and continuity acts as a regulator of relationships and events occurring in the past, present, and future. The themes that emerge are expressions of affective states, such as happy or sad, frustration or gratification, curiosity or disgust, and surprise or fear. Some experience can be reorganized or told differently as a result of experience within simultaneous treatment.

The therapist needs to bear in mind that all verbal and nonverbal interventions occur within the context of a relationship. It is the quality of this relationship that determines the efficacy of treatment. A careful balance must establish the safe boundaries of treatment. This balance within the therapeutic relationship recognizes the pain experienced by the patient and the differences existing between therapist and patient. The awareness of these differences must not be too great nor too little. The differences in age, life experience, and knowledge are counterbalanced by the feelings of empathy for the patient and his need to be fully understood. Threatening, disapproving images are balanced by approving and guiding images. It is the complex, varied, shared experience that leads the patient to accept possible change in nuance or character of the personal narrative.

Ann-Marie Sandler (1994) emphasized the role of a therapist's interpretations in helping the patient to get on good terms with fantasies and wishes previously considered unacceptable. She stressed that the therapist must monitor her patient's conscious and unconscious receptivity to communication by carefully following what is happening in the "here and now." The therapist must deal with the patient's concerns and maintain contact with the patient by dealing with immediate issues.

Thus "holding," according to Sandler, is a metaphor for conveying in words that the therapist knows and understands the patient's inner experience. The therapist interprets the source of the child's anxiety, such as being with a new person or in a new situation. Instead of focusing on the child's outbursts, the therapist focuses on aroused feelings of shame, guilt, and humiliation. Because these feelings have been subject to defensive maneuvers, they may be difficult to decipher. The therapist addresses directly the child's feelings that have been hidden and now are being expressed within the context of treatment. For example, the therapist might say, on noticing her patient's irritability: "How awful you felt after last session when you became so angry, and how upset and afraid you still feel."

The essence of this approach is in the therapist's attitude toward unacceptable feelings and thoughts. Using a calm, containing, enduring attitude of recognition and acceptance, the therapist conveys to the patient her capacity to maintain relations in the face of the primitive feelings aroused in the transference. The patient experiences safety within the firm frame of the therapeutic relationship.

In addition to verbal interventions, the very presence of the therapist represents a nonverbal intervention. This presence of the therapeutic other is taken as a given of treatment, yet it represents a powerful statement in and of itself: "I am here, and I am able and willing to participate with you in this process." It is often left unverbalized, yet the nonjudgmental availability is communicated in gesture and attitude. It may be that this openness to engagement is the therapist's most powerful tool.

Paulina Kernberg, I, and some colleagues (Kernberg, Chazan, Frankel, Rosenberg-Hariton, Kruger, Saunders, & Scholl, 1991) compiled a hierarchy of verbal interventions used by therapists. The schema identifies seven levels of verbal intervention, each level subsuming and incorporating those below it. In simultaneous treatment, the therapist may choose from any of these levels of verbal intervention with either parent or child.

1. Ordinary social behaviors. Through appropriate conversational dialogue, the therapist establishes herself as available to engage in mutual interaction and as someone not to be feared. For example: "Good morning, come right in." "Hello, you must be Johnny!"

2. Statements related to the treatment. The therapist allays the anxiety of patients by making the unknown known and explaining the procedural aspects of treatment, including the boundaries, rules, and work of therapy. The structure of the session, behavioral limits within the session, responsibilities of the patient for fees and attendance, and roles of each of the participants are communicated. For example: "We will be meeting twice a week for 50-minute sessions." "In this room, you may play with any of the toys you see."

3. Requests for factual information. The therapist elicits information she needs to know to understand her patients, including family history, information about activities, and other objective information. For example: "And where did you live before you came to New York?" "How many sisters and brothers do you have?"

4. Supportive interventions. The therapist increases her patient's sense of self-esteem and mastery through the use of education, suggestion, encouragement, and empathy. The therapist labels perceived affects, provides factual information, teaches new skills, and suggests new ideas or courses of action. For example: "The way we tell time is by looking at the big and little hands of the clock." "You seem angry when you talk about your brother."

5. Facilitative interventions. The therapist initiates, enhances, and maintains an exchange with her patient through the use of invitations to continue and review statements. These comments convey the therapist's ongoing attention to, interest in, and comprehension of what the patient is experiencing. Statements by the therapist may mirror what the patient has said, pick up a theme the patient has begun, or summarize what the patient has said or done, currently or in the past. For example: "Tell me more about the game." "The alarm went off again and you still didn't hear it."

6. Directing attention. The therapist focuses the patient's attention on events, affects, behaviors, and ideas to imply the possibility of new meanings or connections through preparatory statements; "look at" statements about the past, present, and future; and "see the pattern" statements. For example: "Whenever you mention your mother, you look very sad." "You are smiling when you tell me how you were late for school."

7. Interpretations. The therapist helps her patient to see links between behavior, feelings, and ideas of which he is aware and attitudes, assumptions, and beliefs of which he is unaware. The links between states of awareness and unawareness include defenses, wishes, and past experiences. Using these defensive strategies, the patient has kept himself protected from unacceptable feelings. For example: "The smile tells us you like being late. Maybe you enjoy having Mommy all to yourself when she drives you to school." [Within the metaphor of play] "The big bunny can never be little again. He seems to like being big; he brags to all the little bunnies about how big he is. But maybe he also misses being little."

The goal of simultaneous treatment is to assist in the development of parent and child by contributing to the revision of narrative. What was formerly an apparent jumble or, alternatively, a rigid catechism becomes reorganized into a flowing experience of dyadic interaction. This shared therapeutic experience is constantly being enlarged, to include new individuals and encourage creativity, and then receding again. Always in the background is the early source, or lexicon, of dyadic interaction.

The experience contained in the narrative has a theme. Several emotional themes may be aroused by one interactive event. For example, Stern (1990) described how themes of aggression-anger, loneliness-sadness, and reconciliation are all aroused by the dramatic events of one child behaving aggressively with another and having "time out" in his room. These themes help to organize the child's story. If the child remains angry, he returns to the adult, recounts the story, and disclaims indignantly, "It isn't fair." If the child remains sad, he may be withdrawn, reclusive, and unavailable, expressing silent reproach. If he has had time to contain his emotional reaction, he will emerge from time out in a conciliatory manner and ready to get on with the day. Thus emotional themes act to organize the story. The narrative retells the events in accordance with the child's subjective experience.

Reunion and reconciliation occur in the process of the telling of any therapeutic narrative or in its attempted deciphering and telling. In simultaneous treatment, the parent and child strive to put their personal and shared experience at the behest of the therapist's understanding. For it is only by being understood by another that they can become truly themselves. The clinician helps both parent and child to reconnect with their own personal experience, the experience of their cultural heritage, and the experience of the interactive moment in the telling of their stories.

The concepts discussed in this brief review of psychological processes are basic to the next chapter, which deals with the practical aspects of practice in simultaneous treatment. This framework of ideas is the foundation for forming the therapeutic perspective necessary to conduct simultaneous treatment in a reliable and accountable manner.

CHAPTER 3

The Course of
Simultaneous Treatment

S IMULTANEOUS TREATMENT INVOLVES both parent and child in all phases of treatment. The focus of simultaneous treatment is on the interaction between two partners in a dyadic relationship and the actions, ideas, symbols, and themes that characterize that relationship. Initially the partners are the parent and child; during treatment, the parent and child are paired separately with the therapist, forming two new dyadic relationships. This change in partners results in changes within the dyad, which in turn impact indirectly on the larger family group. As rigid patterns change, the treatment dyads become more flexible and resilient, and parent and child are able to respond more adaptively in family interaction. This chapter traces parent and child through beginning, middle, and ending phases of treatment. The process of simultaneous treatment in each phase is described.

SCHEMATIC REPRESENTATION OF THERAPEUTIC
RELATIONSHIPS IN SIMULTANEOUS TREATMENT

Simultaneous treatment can be represented schematically as two intersecting triangles set in a horizontal axis. This therapeutic model incorporates the concept of *interaction structures* defined by Beatrice Beebe and Frank Lachmann (1988) as mutually regulated, bidirectional interactions between therapist and patient. One triangle represents the interactions of parent, child, and therapist in everyday reality. The second triangle represents the interactions of parent, child, and therapist in projective reality. The midpoint is the position of the therapist, representing the dependent/containing reality. Through her understanding, the therapist is able to help the dyad to construct a new sense of shared understanding, incorporating these three levels of reality.

In simultaneous treatment, one therapist shares in the conflictual and nonconflictual feelings previously confined to the parent and child. When aspects of the projective reality become linked in new patterns with everyday events, therapeutic change occurs. Irene Fast (1985) described objectification as the step forward in development that follows the simultaneous activation of two discrete affect schemas. In simultaneous treatment, aversive experience of the past finds expression and new meaning within the safe context of the dependent/containing therapeutic relationship. Disorganization, avoidance, resistance, and rejection are replaced by more adaptive coping-defensive strategies. Because of this unique treatment design, the linkage between parent and child can be worked on directly, and parent and child are treated within the same period of time and by the same person. These shared aspects of simultaneous treatment enhance the occurrence of objectification and the developmental progress of parent and child.

In simultaneous treatment, the issues arousing intense ambivalence usually revolve around boundary formation and role clarification. The therapist participates with each member of the dyad separately and becomes a partner in the activities of each, in the absence of the other. This therapeutic support for separation enhances each partner's sense of individuation and leads to reregulation of aggressive and libidinal impulses, objectification, and improved capacity for adaptation.

THE BEGINNING PHASE OF TREATMENT

It was mentioned in chapter 1 that simultaneous treatment may be instituted at any of several points. It may be clear at the onset that simultaneous treatment is necessary and that the parents are receptive to it. This situation usually occurs when the problem involves a conflict in which one parent is enmeshed with and overwhelmed by the child. It also may occur in a single-parent situation, in which the parent realizes that the child's problems require more than behavior management. The parent may have been in treatment previously and may suggest spontaneously that she too see the therapist on a regular basis, recognizing the reemergence of unresolved issues.

In other instances, recognition of the need for simultaneous treatment is a therapeutic development that emerges gradually in the course of the child's treatment and the family's involvement. Although a new therapeutic framework needs to be established, the transition is relatively smooth, because the plan makes sense to all the participants in the natural course of events. Changes in scheduling as well as billing may be necessary, and these changes need to be understood by all those involved: the child and both parents.

Another possibility is that the parent or child may seek individual treatment with the same therapist following the conclusion of the partner's therapy. This more widely accepted practice shares some of the aspects of a simultaneous treatment intervention. Often simultaneous treatment emerges in combination with family therapy. In these instances, treatment of the family group may precede or follow simultaneous treatment.

CRITERIA FOR SELECTION AND EXCLUSION OF PATIENTS FOR SIMULTANEOUS TREATMENT

Patients who are potential candidates for simultaneous treatment present with problems within the dyadic relationship between parent and child. Parents need to possess a strong desire for change despite tensions and hardships that might be encountered. They must be willing to explore the self in the present as well as the self of the past. They need to have sufficient strength to sustain the relationship despite the intense envy, rage, or guilt that may be evoked. Finally, they must have the capacity for introspection and must be able to resist fleeing from conflict.

It is important to exclude from consideration parents who lack sufficient impulse control and therefore cannot enable their child to experience safety with the therapist. Included in this category are parents who intrude on the privacy of their child and, because of their own needs, fail to support the therapeutic contract. For example, parents may be noncompliant by not paying bills on time or not keeping scheduled appointments or by acting out on a behavioral level in any of a variety of ways to undermine treatment. These impulsive parents usually fall within the spectrum of severe borderline personality disorders and would benefit from a different therapeutic approach, such as family treatment or parent training.

Children who are candidates for simultaneous treatment present with deficits in autonomous functioning. They must possess the potential to contain conflict and grow toward constructive interaction, however. Although the capacity to introspect may be blocked or inhibited initially, the children must have the potential to evoke it in treatment. One way of assessing these capacities for growth is to observe the child's use of symbols in play and verbal expression as well as his ability to delay gratification and tolerate frustration.

Clearly, simultaneous treatment is not a technique of choice for all patients or all therapists. Because of the complexity and intensity of feelings aroused, the parents need to have the capacity for self-control and the ability to introspect, or to observe and reflect on their own behaviors. They must be capable of understanding the need for boundaries and be able to use the support of the therapist to respect their child's autonomy.

Children with a variety of presenting problems may be appropriate patients for simultaneous treatment. Younger children may present with psychosis, failure to thrive, communication problems, or more specific developmental deficits such as language delay. Behavioral outbursts, delayed toilet learning, and sleep problems are all difficulties that respond well to simultaneous treatment. Older children may have diagnoses ranging from internalizing problems, such as thought disorders, anxiety disorders, depression, and somatizing disorders, to externalizing problems, such as conduct disorders. Generally, adolescents require their own therapists and benefit from other approaches, although in crisis situations and when earlier traumas prevent entry into adolescence, simultaneous treatment can be beneficial.

CRITERIA FOR THERAPISTS

Therapists working in simultaneous treatment need to be versed in both child and adult therapy. In addition, they must have the capacity to tolerate ambiguity and must have a welcoming attitude toward points of view other than their own. Working with the parent-child dyad is to come to grips with understanding experience as complex and multidetermined. If the therapist is overinvested for personal reasons in any one perspective, she will be unable to appreciate the complexity of her position as participant-observer and will be ineffective in her therapeutic interventions. The therapist's own therapy is a valuable source of insight, which cannot be achieved through a didactic approach, even an intensive one. The integration of personal and professional knowledge is essential for maintaining both therapeutic understanding and endurance.

FORMATION OF THE THERAPEUTIC ALLIANCE WITH PARENT AND CHILD

The therapist's alliance, or collaborative relationship, with the parent is based on the parent's recognition of a need to receive help for her child and her unconscious wish to repair the damage done to herself and her child. This self-awareness on the part of the parent permits access to the adult parent's infantile needs, wishes, and insecurities. Access to these parental feelings otherwise would not be possible because of entrenched defensive barriers. Because the parent sees the therapist accepting the unlovable parts of her child, she can bring her own hidden pain, disappointment, and sadness to the therapist.

A collaborative relationship between the therapist and the child depends also on a mutually accepted set of understandings. The manner in which these first meetings are conducted has been described at length (Kernberg, Chazan, Frankel, Rosenberg-Hariton, Kruger, Saunders, & Scholl, 1991). The child needs to know explicitly why he is being seen in therapy, what the goals of treatment are, and the meaning and limits of confidentiality. Specifically, the child needs to know what types of information will be shared with his parents as well as what types of information will remain private between therapist and patient. He also needs to comprehend the rules of treatment sessions. This consensus is reached during feedback sessions following the assessment interviews.

Although the child may or may not be happy at the prospect of treatment, he needs to understand why it has been recommended. If the child is unable to recognize any existing problem because of his age or resistance, he still should be offered a clear explanation of his parents' and the therapist's understanding of the problem. In addition, he needs to know that his parents have decided in favor of the course of treatment and have accepted responsibility for his regular attendance.

If the child's attitude is positive, an initial honeymoon period is made possible in which to lay the groundwork for a secure beginning. If the child is unable to comprehend the therapeutic goals, however, or despairs of finding a solution, this lack of conscious cooperation need not deter the treatment. In these cases, a firm therapeutic alliance with the parents, independent of conflictual feelings, is especially important.

Whether or not the child is aware that one of his parents is in treatment depends on the individual situation. In some instances, although the child is aware that his parents confer with the therapist, it may not be appropriate for the child to be privy to the knowledge that his parent is in treatment. This decision must be considered carefully in each case. Because of the child's need for protection from the parent, it may be hurtful for him to share the therapist at first. On the other hand, there are child patients who feel safe when they know that their troubled parent is receiving help from the same doctor. If sharing the same therapist is likely to recreate the child's illusion of an ever-present, hovering parent, the information that the parent is in treatment may not be helpful. In some instances, the child may be aware of parental meetings but unaware of their personal nature. Over time, he gradually may become aware of the therapeutic relationship with the parent, or it may be decided not to reveal to the child the personal therapeutic aspect of the parent-therapist relationship.

The frequency of visits also needs to be determined on an individual basis. In most cases, once a week for the parent and once a week for the child seems to work well, but this pattern can vary. In some instances, occasional meetings with both parents present are conducted to discuss issues of child management.

CONTINUED ASSESSMENT IN THE
BEGINNING PHASE OF TREATMENT

Early work in simultaneous treatment is characterized by a continuing assessment of problems in the dyadic relationship. In each case accepted for simultaneous treatment, a preliminary assessment procedure determines that simultaneous treatment is the method of choice for intervention. Data are collected from the parents, including detailed family and developmental history and behavior checklists such as the Achenbach Behavior Check List (Achenbach, 1978; Achenbach & Edelbrock, 1981) and the Conners Scales (Conners, 1985a, 1985b). The child is interviewed and observed and, possibly, given psychometric tests including projective tests. Information from a family interview might be included as well as a diagnostic impression of the child, the parent, or both. The therapist reviews all these materials before proceeding with her own contacts with parents and child.

The first interviews are conducted, if possible, with both parents present. The therapist reviews the findings of the referral source and asks parent and child for their reactions to the recommendation for simultaneous treatment. At this point, a family meeting might be helpful to give the therapist an opportunity to observe the entire family unit. When the idea of simultaneous treatment emerges in the natural course of a deepening individual treatment of a child, it is advisable to conduct a transition interview with both parents. At this joint meeting, the meaning of the decision to pursue simultaneous treatment can be reviewed. Is guilt or shame ascribed to the parent now declaring herself a patient, or is the new path willingly taken toward enhancement of relationships within the family?

It is important at this juncture for the therapist not only to comprehend the details of the referring problem but also to observe carefully the parental attitudes toward these problems. Are the child's problems viewed as syntonic with or alien to the parents' views of themselves and other family members? Is there a split between the parents in the way they describe and appraise the child's difficulties? What is the nature of the relationship between the parents? Is the marital atmosphere one of calm, anger, competition, or sadness? Are the parents overwhelmed by the child's difficulties; is the child diminished because of his problems; or are both of these attitudes present? The therapist needs to preview with the parents their expectations for their child's future (Trad, 1991b).

Reviewing the family history with the parents, the therapist needs to glean an understanding of the social hierarchy in the family group. What impact do extended family members have on the nuclear family? Are there family myths that influence how the parents perceive their child? Does their child remind the parents of anyone from their own families of origin or extended families? Do any intergenerational issues emerge?

Unresolved relationships, particularly concerning separations, both temporary and permanent, need to be identified. The impact of deaths, births, illnesses, and anniversaries should be explored. The dynamics of rivalry within the nuclear family unit—in particular, subordinate, loser roles versus successful, winner roles—are useful indicators of possible treatment issues. The therapist needs to listen keenly and be alert to the manner in which the family story is told. Do both parents participate in the telling? Is the story organized into a beginning, a middle, and an end? Do the parents agree on a common, shared narrative, or is there disagreement?

From these data, the therapist can begin to construct for herself an understanding of the representational world of the family unit as perceived by each of the parents. Communicating this understanding to the parents helps to clarify their perceptions of themselves and deepen their sense of involvement in the therapeutic process. Although only one parent will be continuing treatment in an intensive manner, this initial work affords both parents an opportunity to know the therapist and contribute to a firm therapeutic alliance.

The next line of extended assessment focuses on observations of the relationship between the two identified patients. These observations may be conducted formally in scheduled interviews, or the information may be obtained over time in an informal manner. In the case of an interview, the therapist should be prepared not only to review the reasons the parent and child are coming to the clinic, but also to present the parent and child with the opportunity to play together or solve a common problem. These shared situations usually arise spontaneously in the course of a session with parent and child in the playroom.

Observation of the interaction of the dyad focuses on several issues. Are the parent's responses to her child directly responsive and appropriate to the cues her child gives her? Does the interaction between mother and child include reciprocal sequences of interchange between them, that is, back and forth, active-passive alternations of give and take or turn-taking? Does the child initiate reciprocal interchange with the mother? Does the child succeed in his demands that the parent fulfill his needs? Is the child successful in his efforts to assert himself with the parent? Does the parent initiate reciprocal interchange with the child? Is the parent successful in his efforts to assert himself with the child, for example, in limit setting? Do the parent and child experience pleasure in being together? Do the parent and child allow themselves space for their independent activities?

These issues are parameters that provide markers for early assessment as well as a framework against which to chart the progress of treatment (Emde, 1983; Sander, 1964). The questions rarely are answered in all-or-nothing terms, because these observations are either more or less present in each parent-child dyad. In research using simultaneous treatment, observational measures can be taken at the beginning of treatment and repeated at the midway point and at the end of treatment.

In addition to the measures already cited, scales of emotional availability (Biringen, Robinson, & Emde 1988; Clark, 1985; Rothbaum & Schneider-Rosen, 1988), attachment behavior of parent and child (Ainsworth & Wittig, 1969; Main, Kaplan, & Cassidy, 1985; Bretherton, Biringen, Ridgeway, Maslin, & Sherman, 1989), and peer relationship (Kernberg, Clarkin, Greenblatt, & Cohen, unpublished manuscript) might be considered. Some of these measures are rating scales for direct observation; others are based on information gathered from interviews. Most of the scales of direct observation were written for infants and young children and require adaptation.

Finally, the beginning of treatment continues the process of gathering first impressions of each of the partners in the dyad. Does the parent present with a consistent parental style? Does she seem characteristically submissive, authoritarian, abusive, permissive, threatening, seductive, overwhelmed, intrusive, suspicious, or fearful? Does she have a combination of these attributes? Perhaps instead of a consistent picture, the parent presents with a fluctuating set of attitudes and behaviors. The manner in which these behaviors occur and whether they tend to seem organized or disorganized in any comprehensible way should be noted.

Similarly, increased contacts with the child patient enable the therapist to gauge the type of attachment bond (Ainsworth, Blehar, Waters, & Wall, 1978) between parent and child. Are the child's insecurities demonstrated by clinging behavior, negative behaviors, avoidant behaviors, or disorganized behaviors? These behaviors can be understood as maladaptive efforts to deal with failures of secure relationship between parent and child.

In addition, the therapist gains impressions of the child's preferred means of self-expression and level of cognitive development. Is he primarily nonverbal, expressing himself through actions, gestures, or sensorimotor play? Alternatively, does he rely almost exclusively on words to tell his story and describe fantasy events? Or does his repertoire include both abilities and, if so, in what permutations? Is the child's development commensurate with his chronological age? What are the child's temperamental characteristics? Is he easy to care for, irritable, or slow to warm up? Are there unexpected gaps or is there unevenness in his development? What are the neurological or cognitive deficits or precocities that might impinge on the receptive and expressive capacities of the child? The therapist needs to understand the child's means of communication to collaborate with him as a partner in treatment.

The therapist also observes the child's level of development in separation-individuation. Is the child concerned with being physically held by the parent? Is the child primarily focused on continuous physical contact with the parent? Alternatively, can he use her as a base for refueling while he begins to walk away from her and exercise independent capacities? How dependent is the child on keeping the parent in his perceptual field? Is he able to extend his orbit from the mother and, if so, to what extent? Is the mother available to her child when he needs her? Is she also unobtrusively available when he does not seem to need her? Does the child demonstrate elements of the rapprochement crisis with oscillation between "shadowing" and "darting away"? Does the parent respond with annoyance, or is she able to survive her child's fluctuating demands without retaliating? Can the parent demonstrate interest in her child's activities and adventures? Can she gently yet firmly push him away when encouragement toward independence is necessary?

All these observations are possible within the microcosm of beginning simultaneous treatment. The sphere of shared experience of separation-individuation development is widened to include the therapist.

At times, simultaneous treatment begins as a tripartite model (Galenson, 1991), gradually fostering separation of the partners.

CHALLENGES TO THE THERAPEUTIC ALLIANCE

A strong collaborative alliance is necessary to provide a background of safety and a secure feeling of well-being for all participants. If the parent is unable to form a strong bond with the therapist and with her child, simultaneous treatment is not possible. In other words, for simultaneous treatment to proceed beyond these initial observations, the parent must be capable on one level of accepting the separateness of her child and the child's need for privacy with his therapist. Thus the strong urge to protect and nurture her child provides the parent with what may be the first opportunity in her life to tolerate a triangular experience. The tolerance for this type of work may need to build gradually and emerge over time as the parent begins to view her child's progress.

Single-parent families present special challenges and opportunities for simultaneous treatment. The therapist becomes intimately connected to each member of the dyad. In comparison to treatment of two-parent families, the involvement of the therapist with both parent and child may become more intense. Whether the family is in transition or the parent has been a single parent since the child's birth, simultaneous treatment leads to intensified treatment bonds and helps to allay the loneliness of each partner. The adult shares some of her burdens as a parent and is listened to attentively, and the child feels there is another adult who shares in caring for him and is concerned with his welfare.

In the single-parent family, in which there is heightened dependence of the children on one parent, particular anxieties are naturally more pronounced. Confidentiality is an important issue, and the willingness to have separate sessions may require tact and patience. It is not at all unusual for an otherwise independent, older child to manifest separation anxiety in the treatment situation. It may take several meetings before the child is able to meet with the therapist alone. The therapist should not force the issue, because there is much to be learned in the process. Sometimes it is possible much later in treatment to explore the fantasies underlying these anxieties. In many instances, the underlying fear is of being abandoned by the parent and is accompanied by the wish to be adopted or kidnapped by the therapist. In some instances, the anxieties are never made explicit but lessen as the members of the dyad come to feel secure enough to explore other issues. In many ways, simultaneous treatment may be the natural choice for single-parent families, because it can effectively diminish loneliness for both parent and child.

Another special circumstance arises when there are reasonable concerns that either the child or the parent is being abused. In the rare instance in which the abusive parent is the one involved in the treatment dyad, the therapist is in an excellent position to intervene. Usually the abusive parent is not the parent in simultaneous treatment, however, and in that case it is mandatory that every effort be made to involve the abusive parent in treatment. In either case, it is crucial that the therapist avoid the position of investigator or judge. If abuse is evident, the authorities must be notified as designated by law. This exception to confidentiality is always described to the family as part of the rules of treatment; when someone is being hurt or is hurting others, confidentiality is breached. The therapist's role is to remain equidistant from all persons involved and to contain the different perspectives and reactions experienced in response to the violent acts. In the case of an abusive parent, simultaneous treatment affords a direct window to view the pathological parent-child relationship.

ISSUES OF THE BEGINNING PHASE OF TREATMENT

Issues dealing with everyday reality usually dominate the beginning phase of treatment. In a few cases, the child and parent are so enmeshed in fantasy that everyday reality issues do not become the focus until well into the middle phase of treatment. In most cases, however, after the therapist explains the rules of treatment, the patients begin to ask for information and direct advice. Giving assistance in these matters is appropriate as a supportive intervention, but the therapist is cautioned to avoid the role of expert or authority. Rather, the more productive stance is as an ally in problem solving. For example, the parent inquires concerning how she can help her son with his homework. The therapist might proceed to describe a daily routine and approach to the management of homework. Alternatively, the therapist might reflect that the parent seems to feel she is not doing enough, that perhaps she feels there is some magical way to handle homework. The therapist might go on to inquire about the routine the two of them currently are following and how they think it could be improved. Various possibilities for change might be explored together.

Suggestions given to parent or child are part of the larger category of supportive interventions. Empathy and encouragement are other responses at this level of intervention. The therapist may feel that it is appropriate to help the child patient with social skill learning. The therapist commonly finds it necessary to educate parents in ways to provide structure for children in the home. Specifically, keeping a log and observing special times, quiet times, and "time out" are all techniques that can be implemented. These techniques have been described in detail elsewhere (Kernberg et al., 1991).

When educative efforts are unsuccessful or when efforts that were successful at first begin to diminish in effectiveness, it is clear that other factors are implicated. Rather than perceiving these events as a source of disappointment or frustration, the therapist considers that they may signal the operation of new projective realities and a deepening of the therapeutic relationship.

The therapeutic problem consists of the negative, oppositional, and angry or helpless and depressed attitudes that surface in response to unfulfilled expectations. These are the fundamental issues that have brought the dyad to treatment, and they finally are being brought into sharper focus. A note of caution, however: As the relationship becomes more complex, the necessity for tact and sensitivity on the part of the therapist increases. As Anne-Marie Sandler suggests, the therapist must stay attuned with her patients and follow their lead. Supportive interventions of encouragement and empathic responses can yield only gradually to more facilitative interventions as the dependent/containing reality is put firmly in place. Indeed, too much understanding too soon can seem like no understanding at all.

THE MIDDLE PHASE OF TREATMENT

The middle phase of simultaneous treatment is marked by a flourishing of independent activities in separate domains. The child is able to construct with the therapist a relationship based on his needs and interests. The content of therapeutic activity varies with the age and inclinations of the child. Infants and young preschoolers engage with the parent and therapist in interactive games. School-age children typically engage the therapist in play. Make-believe, games with rules, and artistic projects are all avenues for self-expression. In addition, the therapist becomes familiar with friendships, conflicts with authority, and other details of daily routine, viewed from the child's perspective.

As the parent pursues her therapeutic path, issues of child management and coping with household demands continue in tandem with a developing narrative concerning her life's story. Varied periods of the parent's life are reviewed: childhood, adolescence, young adulthood, marriage, career pursuits, goals attained and unattained. From each of these perspectives, different attitudes arise concerning the self and others, some of which were not previously available to the parent's conscious awareness.

ISSUES OF THE MIDDLE PHASE OF TREATMENT

The elaboration of themes, symbols, and fantasies is the hallmark of the middle phase of treatment. Traumatic experiences often are condensed by one or both partners into symbolic characters. At times the child and parent present, simultaneously or sequentially, with corresponding characterizations. Robert Lane and I (1989) described three symbols commonly encountered in treatment: the witch, the spider, and the shark. These symbols form a sequence reflecting decreasing differentiation and increasing anxiety along a continuum of terror. These three symbols are condensations of the self and other, expressing in symbolic form conscious and unconscious attitudes arising from past experience and occurring in the present between therapist and patient.

The witch is part human and part magical; with her powers, she can be both good and bad. She can be frightening, but she can also make wishes come true. The spider spins a diabolical web to ensnare her victims and then consume them. However, even the spider can be portrayed, as in the book *Charlotte's Web*, as a benevolent creature. The shark arouses terror from the depths of the sea. He never sleeps but is always on the move, jaws ready to devour his prey with certain swiftness.

In symbolic play, dreams, and stories, these three characterizations depict the quality of past relationships and present tensions within the transference relationship. The meaning of a symbol can be interpreted not only on the basis of its content but also on the basis of the affective response it evokes. Clearly, patients who use the same symbol are not equally terrified. In fact, a wide range of pathology might be expressed through the same symbol. Also, one person might use different symbols at different times in his life to represent the same underlying wishes and conflicts.

Cognitive development is an important factor in determining symbol choice. Between 18 and 26 months of age, the child becomes capable of using a single symbol to stand for a variety of objects. For instance, the child begins to use the word *ball*, a verbal symbol, to describe a class of round objects of various sizes and shapes that can be used for rolling. Similarly, the child learns that frustration leads to angry feelings and can anticipate anger when he spills milk, even though anger is expressed by different members of the family in different ways. He can translate diverse cues as signaling one affective state.

As the child grows older, he learns that even though perceptual attributes change, a substance may remain the same in size, weight, or volume. Jean Piaget (1954) observed the child's capacity for object permanence that enables the child to recognize this quality of sameness and to form abstract concepts. In the interpersonal realm, secure in his attachment to his parent, the child comes to be familiar with various parental moods and behaviors and is able to conserve a feeling of being loved despite variation in parental attitude. Another example of interpersonal conservation is when a child learns that although people grow older and change, bonds of affection although altered can still be maintained.

The symbol acquires personal as well as shared meaning. In fact, all symbols in varying degrees have shared and private aspects. Charles Sarnoff (1987) described an aspect of symbolic development he called *masked symbols*. By school age, the child is able to disguise the true meaning of events represented by a symbol. He does this by choosing a symbol that has no direct linkage with the object or feeling it represents. With this disguise, the child is able to deal with primitive wishes and feelings that otherwise would be unacceptable. The child becomes acculturated by using these masked symbols instead of direct representation. For instance, although murderous rage toward a sibling at home is unacceptable, it is acceptable to play competitively in sports. Through the mechanisms of displacement, projection, and repression, these symbols mask latent content, which is no longer available to conscious awareness. Masked symbols enable the school-age child to sublimate aggressive and libidinal impulses and use acceptable channels for self-expression. In simultaneous treatment, the deciphering of masked symbols often leads to greater self-understanding.

Patients who enter simultaneous treatment often do not present with an organized representational world. The prerequisites for consistency and coherence—namely, object constancy for persons and things and, later, conservation of classes of objects and persons—are not consolidated achievements. Rather, the therapist is presented with a chaotic world, evocative of overwhelming and disorganizing anxiety. As the representational world takes form in the course of treatment, it often is filled with powerful, polarized images, such as the three symbols described previously. The origin of these creatures can be understood in part as the failure of the transitional object to bridge internal feeling states and external experience.

In these early representations, instead of two separate and autonomous individuals, the experiential world consists of four percepts: the good me, the bad me, the good you, the bad you. In each pair, one percept is unavailable to conscious awareness and is externalized into a symbolic other. Differentiation of self from other occurs by splitting of experience and disavowal. This polarization creates serious difficulties in the process of separation and individuation.

As patients feel comfortable and safe enough to share their subjective experience, the therapist is better able to discern their projective reality. Salman Akhtar (1991) described three fantasies related to unresolved separation-individuation, all of which are common in simultaneous treatment.

The "someday" fantasy implies unrealistic expectations that someday all hopes will be realized and the patient will not have to deal with disappointments in his unrelenting optimistic pursuit. This fantasy takes the form of the perfect child or the perfect parent. The therapist is seen as embodying these virtues, until the idealization somehow is diminished and ends in disappointment. These magical wishes may lead to an impossible life goal that keeps the patient ever hoping for a time that is forever peaceful and conflict-free.

A variant of the someday fantasy is the "if only" fantasy, common in cases of divorce: If only an event had not taken place, everything would have turned out alright. Life before that event is glossed over or retrospectively idealized. Akhtar traces both of these fantasies to incomplete mourning over the premature and painful loss of adequate maternal attention. A clear connection can be seen between these fantasies and the wish-granting witch characterization described previously.

The second fantasy is that of a tether, a long rope or cord that connects the therapist and the patient. A young child may enact this fantasy with a ball of string, connecting all the furniture in the playroom in one large web. In another instance, a child plays a game with checkers with his own rules, instructing the therapist to follow his lead and his moves. The child sings, "Follow me up and down, here and there and all around." One adult patient enacted this fantasy by phoning the therapist from each stop in his travels so that he could maintain his sense of being with her all the time.

The main issue is of distance versus safety. The purpose of a tether is to maintain a connection between the therapist and patient that is experienced as a comfortable sense of distance. The tether is an aspect of the spider characterization described previously, in which the web can be portrayed as either frightening or comforting, or both.

The third fantasy discussed by Akhtar is the fantasy of the "long embrace," which will satisfy forever the longing for contact with another person. The child wants the therapy hour not to end and wishes he could live with the therapist forever. Other children fear that the therapist wants to kidnap them and hold them prisoner forever and ever. Indeed, these fantasies often emerge after the therapist has been of some assistance in helping the child to play creatively, and the wish is that the source of support not be withdrawn until the child's needs are fully met.

The therapist may experience these demands (for personal information, a hug, more sessions, or extraanalytic contact) as burdensome and coercive. The patient, however, feels only a desperate need for the other's presence, to which he feels entitled. The therapist may experience these demands by the patient as intrusive and threatening, like a shark from the deepest waters. The demands may arise unexpectedly and, if they are gratified, may arouse destructive anxiety rather than reassurance.

The therapist must do everything possible to maintain therapeutic limits tactfully to retain an arena of safe relationship. As with all wishes, acknowledging them openly often satisfies the need. The bond between therapist and patient is strengthened as they share in the magic of the moment, in mutual understanding and trust.

Lane and I (1990) described a fourth fantasy that is common to simultaneous treatment. It is the fantasy of "fixing and being fixed," terms that have both positive and negative connotations. The need to fix implies that a former state of wholeness somehow has been shattered or damaged; pieces are missing, and the whole is no longer perfect. Within this context, an addiction to the prior state of intactness may occur, and efforts may be made to restore or recreate the original state of unity, as implied by Freud in the concept of repetition compulsion (1914, 1920, 1926).

Fixing can be both reparative and creative in two contexts: making something new that feels like the old and making something work that never has worked previously. In the latter case, the focus is on something in the future that will be better; in the former instance, the focus is on recreating the past. In either case, the outcome is never identical with the original intention. A new entity emerges that is never totally identical to or free from the past.

In its positive connotations, "to fix" means to bring together, to fasten, or to attach; in therapeutic terms, it implies an interaction between the healer and the one who presents himself to be healed. But to fix has negative implications when it connotes one person imposing his will on another. Another negative implication of to fix is to avenge oneself, or to get even with, punish, or chastise. These negative connotations of the term may be experienced in treatment as the negative transference, when the therapist is perceived as threatening rather than helpful. Depending on the context, therefore, to fix means to help and to hurt, to benefit and to hinder.

Parents bring their child for treatment because they feel that something is in need of repair, and their own feelings of competence are in question. These issues reflect concerns about personal integrity and fears of damage and castration (Lane & Chazan, 1990). The attitudes often barely disguise fantasies of being rescued by the therapist, the omnipotent parent of childhood, and the desire for a "quick fix." The therapist also must attend to the anxieties accompanying these wishes, however, and provide disillusionment in manageable doses.

These four fantasies, which refer to underlying deficits in parental caregiving and availability, occur frequently in simultaneous treatment. It must be stressed that identification of a deficit is always relative to a specific dyad, and inherent in this subjective judgment is the problem of "the fit," or dyadic regulation. Temperamental characteristics determine the extent of lack of attunement that forecloses the possibility of development of rapport. For example, an irritable child might fare well with a relaxed, slow-to-react parent, whereas an active parent would be uneasy with a child who is slow to warm up (Thomas, Chess, & Birch, 1968). It is in the match between members of a dyad that understanding is fostered within a context of harmony. The therapist needs to be attuned to individual constitutional factors complicating the development of relationship.

THE THERAPIST'S INTERVENTIONS IN THE MIDDLE PHASE OF TREATMENT

The verbal interventions described earlier in this chapter—ordinary social behaviors, statements related to the treatment, requests for factual information, and supportive interventions—continue into the middle phase of treatment. In addition, the therapist begins to use the verbal interventions that are higher in the hierarchy (described with more detail in Kernberg et al., 1991).

Facilitative Interventions

One way that the therapist facilitates the therapy is by mirroring, or sharing the patient's experiences and perceptions. Pairing with the patient in this fashion, the therapist articulates and focuses on experiences that heretofore may have been unarticulated. For instance, with a child referred because of distractibility in the classroom, the therapist might note how sad the child looks when telling about being unrecognized by the teacher and how much he seems to want the teacher's attention all the time. The therapist orients to the experience and deepens the actuality of its occurrence through sharing.

Similarly, the therapist might reflect to the parent that she sounds tense, even though the parent is reporting saying reassuring things to her child. The therapist can feel the tension in the moment. Thus the therapist not only orients to the experience—what is verbalized and what is communicated nonverbally—but also sanctions the experience by becoming a part of it. This empathic sharing is an additional component unique to mirroring statements and is not included in the more general category of facilitative statements (see Kernberg et al., 1991).

As the therapist participates in mirroring, some confusion might arise, especially in connection with ambivalent attitudes. It is important to remember that the source of the confusion is the patient's set of contradictory attitudes and does not reside within the therapist. However, using projective identification, the patient may seek clarification of his conflicted feelings by perceiving the therapist as his adversary. For instance, in the following vignette a parent describes how he spoke to his teenage son regarding his future plans. He is speaking in irreverent tones, as though hardly convinced of the worthiness of this undertaking.

THERAPIST: You seem be trying to convince yourself of the necessity to speak to Ricky in this way.

MR. R [in earnest]: Well, this is how a parent should speak to his child. It is his responsibility. No one ever spoke to me that way [with a smile], and I wish they had.

THERAPIST: You are smiling, as if you are amused by what you are saying to me.

By continuing to mirror her patient's demeanor as well as the content of his statement, the therapist removes herself from an adversarial position and facilitates Mr. R's understanding of his own conflictual attitudes. Rather than establishing who is right and who is wrong, the focus of treatment is on the need for therapist and patient to understand each other so that a broader, more adaptable context for communication may be constructed.

Invitations to continue are another form of facilitative intervention. The therapist elicits further comments or feelings by asking the patient to say more about a particular subjective experience. The therapist queries, "Isn't there more we might know about this?" and thereby broadens the patient's sphere of conscious experience.

Directing Attention

The therapist uses "look at" and "see the pattern" statements to encourage the patient to view the connections between feelings, ideas, actions, and ensuing events. The therapist is an auxiliary observer encouraging the patient to attend to the linkage between thoughts and feelings and what happens next. The patient may be surprised or unwilling to see what is being pointed out. A strong element of tact is necessary to locate a good time for such a comment. Indeed, the first notice of such connection might simply occasion the query "what happened there?" eliciting the participation of the patient. The next occurrence might be followed by the comment "it seems to be happening again." To a child in play, the therapist might say, "Whenever the policeman sees the car go by fast, he looks the other way. Did you notice?" To an adult, discussing limit setting, the therapist might say, "Whenever you want to say no, he smiles, and it slips by, just that fast, did you notice?"

Interpretation

Interpretive statements by the therapist point to underlying complexes of attitudes, feelings, or behaviors the patient otherwise might not be capable of accessing or integrating. The emphasis here is on synthetic understandings, the integration of parts of experience of which the patient may not be aware into comprehensive understanding. The interpretation itself may take the form of a complex statement or merely a recognition by the therapist communicated as "oh!" There may be various ways of communicating an interpretation, but the desired result is an integration of understanding. Sometimes interpretation results in verbalized insight; at other times, it causes a heightened sense of shared understanding.

Insights gained in simultaneous treatment deepen both parent and child's sense of their own separate identity, confront paradoxical roles, and unravel irrational patterns of relationship. For example, in the next anecdote the therapist listens attentively as the parent becomes aware of her irrational attitudes.

PARENT: But I always look to Billy to see if what I am saying is okay. [Parent makes eye contact with therapist, looks surprised, and says, as if in self-recognition, "Oh!"]
THERAPIST: You seemed to have surprised yourself.
PARENT: I suddenly realized, I look to Billy for approval, as if he is the parent and I am the child.

In another example, the therapist intervenes with an interpretation to an aggressive child: "Your mom comes in unexpectedly and you are playing; you run over with the bat raised in your hand. It seems like you want to reach out to her. Could it be you want to hug her?"

In simultaneous treatment, it is especially important that the opportune moment for understanding be presented by the patient. A didactic approach on the therapist's part arouses perceptions of her in the role of authority or judge. The patient, whether parent or child, will experience intensified feelings of inadequacy. Because of the enmeshed pathology presented by the parent-child pair, the risk of polarization within relationship is enhanced whenever support is withdrawn. In simultaneous treatment with these vulnerable parent-child dyads, the therapist uses tact to maintain close contact with her patients. Sensitivity of the therapist minimizes the possibility that her perspective will be experienced as an imposition. Integration occurs not because of didactics, but because of a spontaneous shared experience.

When the patient and therapist are able to share different perspectives and agree or disagree, the process of differentiation is enhanced (Fast, 1985). An interpretive moment occurs on two levels. On the interpersonal level, there is mutual recognition of differing perspectives. On an intrapsychic level, the patient comes to identify the difference in perspective as another aspect of his internal experience. In this acceptance by the patient of a broadened perspective, the projective aspect of reality is altered within the safe haven of a dependent/containing therapeutic relationship. The therapist strives to keep the therapeutic frame of observation sufficiently secure to facilitate the emergent understanding of the patient.

To endure this convoluted path takes courage and commitment on the part of all persons involved. During the middle phase of treatment, therapeutic encounters still reverberate with trauma and test the confidence and resilience of all participants, who no longer can take solace in the repetitive past and must strive toward new and different patterns of integration.

THE ENDING PHASE OF TREATMENT

The issues of the ending phase of treatment are the same as those of the middle phase, but the emphasis is different. Simultaneous treatment often induces conflict where it was not apparent before. For instance, for the adult, the therapist unexpectedly becomes threatening in a way the parent previously had experienced only with her child. Alternatively, the child's attitude toward the therapist changes, and he acts toward the therapist in a manner formerly reserved only for his parent. These exchanges of intimacy are frightening only when they are experienced as something familiar suddenly undergoing involuntary transformation.

One of the signals that therapy may be reaching the ending phase is not a change in issues or focus but rather a change in affective reaction and sense of competence. Specifically, the patients may refer to the narrative scripts of their lives (expressed in words or through play) with an increasing sense of familiarity and mastery. Some themes remain merged, and others become autonomous. The outcome of their narratives may have changed because the underlying images and feelings are less overwhelming and more manageable. In a sense, the world becomes a better place for both participants.

This sense of well-being is accompanied by greater flexibility and variability in response pattern. The patients feel greater mastery in the selection of modes of response and greater readiness to invest effort in exploring possibilities for relationship. Defensiveness gives way to coping and managing, which is increasingly autonomous of therapeutic intervention.

The types of intervention used by the therapist range from facilitation to interpretation. The patient usually welcomes interventions, often anticipating the response of the therapist. However, some patients remain negative toward the therapist and indicate that they believe their progress occurred in spite of the continuing presence of the therapist. As the end of treatment approaches, it becomes clear that the issues struggled with can now be pursued outside the therapeutic context without incurring further debilitating trauma.

For some patients, the cast of characters within their narrative changes to become more benign. In other cases, the cast of characters remains constant, but the characters undergo transformation. For instance, a malevolent character may take on an impish or playful tone.

The Urist Scale of Object Relations (Urist, 1977) has been adapted for the purpose of measuring changes in play therapy (Kernberg et al., unpublished manuscript). The adaptation delineates a series of points in the management of aggression and the development of autonomy. This scale also can be used to trace changes in the quality of relationship in the separate narratives and within the dyad in simultaneous treatment. The scale is included here as another instrument (in addition to those mentioned in chapter 1) that can be adapted to measure change over time and treatment outcome:

• Autonomous relationship. Characters in the narrative (or members of the dyad) interact and are involved with each other, reflecting a sense of mutuality within the relationship.

• Parallel relationship. Characters in the narrative (or members of the dyad) engage in parallel activity. There is no overt mutuality, nor is there any indication of a negative relationship.

• Dependent relationship. Characters in the narrative (or members of the dyad) lean or hang on each other. Some of the characters may not be standing on their own two feet but instead require some external source of direction or support for the narrative to unfold.

- Twinning relationship. One of the characters (or member of the dyad) in the narrative is the reflection or imprint of another. The relationship between the characters (or members of the dyad) conveys a sense that the definition or stability of one character (or member of the dyad) exists only insofar as it is an extension, reflection, or duplication of the other.

- Malevolent controlling relationship. One character in the narrative (or member of the dyad) is in the clutches of another. Themes of influencing, controlling, and casting spells are present. Some characters are powerless or helpless, whereas the others are omnipotent and controlling.

- Destructive relationship. The imbalance between narrative characters (or members of the dyad) is definitely destructive. An attack on the psychological integrity of one character by another may occur through torture or strangling. Alternatively, a parasitic relationship culminates in the diminution or destruction of the other.

- Annihilating relationship. The narrative (or dyadic relationship) is characterized by an overpowering, enveloping force. Characters are swallowed up, devoured, or overwhelmed by forces completely out of their control, ending in total annihilation and physical destruction.

As treatment ends, the quality of the relationship in the themes of the separate narratives should become more benign and correspond more closely to the quality of relationship observed within the dyad.

As in all therapies, when gains become consolidated during the ending phase of simultaneous treatment, old issues paradoxically may become vivid once again. It is important to discern the difference between this inevitable malaise of ending and a genuine setback.

In assessing whether or not patients are ready to end, it is necessary for the therapist to conduct a private inventory of the various constellations of attitudes presented by the patients. Particularly important to assess is the capacity of each patient for self-soothing, which provides a cushion during moments of upset and enables the patient to retain or regain connectedness in times of stress.

A sense of shared reality and limits as well as role clarification are other important indicators of goals achieved. The therapist may wish to review the series of questions posed as observations relevant to the initial assessment. What is the quality of the observed and reported interaction between parent and child?

It is particularly important in simultaneous treatment to end slowly, if possible, because of the complexity of issues involved. Many times, one of the members of the dyad wants to continue in some other mode of treatment, such as individual, group, or family therapy. The remaining issues to be explored need consideration before a new direction is pursued, with an awareness of both patients that the therapeutic relationship will be ending.

Sometimes an ending presents itself more precipitously than is desired. What is important in all instances, whether treatment is brief or extended, is that the therapist remain accessible for further contact if necessary. Because of the intensive nature of simultaneous treatment, it is not unusual to be consulted at other points of family transition.

To illustrate both the underlying concepts and the practical aspects of simultaneous treatment, the remainder of the book is devoted to three clinical case descriptions. The first child described presents with a gender identity disorder, a manifestation of overincorporation in identification with his mother. The second child presents with aspects of a narcissistic disorder, including omnipotence, splitting, and projective identification, in which a primary issue is identification with a devalued self. The third child presents with pervasive developmental delay and aspects of experience within the autistic state.

CHAPTER 4

Adam: A Case of Gender Identity Disorder

*I*DENTITY REFERS TO an awareness of the self's continuity and individuation, a sense of "who I am" related to one's body, one's significant others, and one's inner life over time. Many aspects of the
self are transformed with age or with changes in locality or social status. Gender identity is unique in that it generally is established early
and permanently. At a young age, a child comes to classify him- or
herself as a boy or a girl, and any challenge to this assignment usually
brings a strong response, such as "Of course I'm not a boy—I'm a
girl."

Gender identity seems to emerge between 2 and 3 years of age.
During the preschool and school-age years, gender role preferences
are consolidated. These preferences are demonstrated by choices concerning sex-typed toys, dress-up and role play, same- versus opposite-
sex peers, and outlets for aggression. Sexual orientation (eroticism)
develops later, at about the time of puberty.

Children with gender identity disorder demonstrate a marked
identification with the opposite sex. They also tend to misclassify
their own gender, out of some discontent with their own sex.
Although the confusion diminishes with time, these children continue
to voice the desire to belong to the other sex and find little that is positive about their own sex.

DSM III-R describes two diagnostic criteria for gender identity disorder of childhood. The first indexes the child's sense of discomfort with the assigned sex and the desire to change sex. Descriptively, this is the criterion most directly tied to the concept of gender identity. The second criterion emphasizes the child's preference for cross-gender roles and activities and aversion to roles and clothing more typically associated with the child's own sex, as well as an aversion to the child's own sexual anatomy. The DSM-IV subcommittee has recommended that the expressed desire to be of the opposite sex no longer be considered as a distinct criterion but rather be listed among a number of behavioral criteria required for diagnosis. Research in the area of gender identity disorders among children has been summarized extensively by Kenneth Zucker (1982, 1985; Zucker & Green, 1992) and others (Fischoff, 1964; Loeb & Shane, 1982).

Adam and Andrew, 7-year-old identical twins, afforded me an unusual opportunity to study the emergence of gender identity in the struggle of a child to free himself not only from the symbiotic matrix with his mother but from the polar pairing with his brother as well. These two focal relationships strongly impinged on this child's developing sense of self. At the time I met him, Adam's self was imprisoned by the limitations imposed on him and in search of new definition. Clearly, a case of discordance for gender identity between monozygotic twins presents evidence that psychosocial influences can override genetic similarity. Interestingly, Richard Green and Robert Stoller (1971) reported on the assessment of two monozygotic twin pairs discordant for gender identity, one pair involving boys close in age to the case to be described. Such a case also sheds light on the controversy between viewing the disorder as an outcome of conflict and seeing it as the result of nonconflicted development.

THEORETICAL BACKGROUND

Stoller (1966), studying adult male transsexuals, concluded that male transsexualism begins in infancy as a primitive and pervasive identification with the mother's femaleness. The basis for this pronounced identification is the intense, blissful symbiotic relationship the mother establishes with her son—a relationship characterized by endless hours of physical and emotional closeness, continuous preoccupation with the child, and instant gratification of all his needs. At the core of the disturbance is the mother's unconscious need to share in her son's being and the strong wish to remain mutually tied with him. Prolonged physical contact, unusual nudity, and a desire never to be parted are the features of this paired relationship. In these behaviors and feelings, according to Stoller, the mother is expressing her own unresolved conflicts over gender identity (generally seen earlier in a history of tomboy behaviors and interests), her own mother's critical attitude, and her subsequent identification with her father. The tie with the father is a defense against the destructive rage in the relationship with the mother. In relating to her son, she does not perceive him as a separate being but as an extension of herself, part of her own body. The child fills the role of transitional object (Winnicott, 1960b), bridging the incomplete separation between herself and her mother.

As a result of longitudinal observations of fifteen feminine boys in the oedipal period, Lawrence Newman and Robert Stoller (1974) concluded that the significance of this later developmental period is in the failure to modify or in any way alter the already existing feminine orientation of the male child. It is the absence of the significant oedipal conflict that permits the feminine identity of the child to develop undisturbed. The father is usually a distant figure emotionally and physically; he does not present himself as a rival for the mother's affection or as a model for masculine attachment. The son remains enmeshed in the symbiotic web of earlier infancy, gratified by his mother, who makes no effort to introduce masculinity into his life. The child usually is not viewed as problematic by either parent but is brought for professional assistance at the insistence of others, such as teachers or friends. This hypothesis suggests that transsexualism is the outcome of unconflicted identity formation.

An alternative hypothesis suggested by Ethel Person and Lionel Ovesey (1974) states that, in primary male transsexualism, the child resorts to a reparative fantasy of symbiotic fusion with the mother to counter separation anxiety. To avoid the conflict presented by the necessities of individuation, child and mother become one, and the anxiety is allayed. The cost to the child, however, is an ambiguity of core gender identity that interferes with the normal development of gender role identification. Unlike Stoller, who suggests that male transsexuals have a coherent female core gender identity, Person and Ovesey suggest that the "true" identity is confused and ambiguous. This underlying ambiguity derives from the unconscious fantasy of symbiotic fusion with the mother. As young children, these males possessed no other major defense than this fantasy, which markedly inhibited masculine behavior. In Person and Ovesey's sample of ten primary male transsexuals, the common shared characteristic of early mother-child relationship was the mother's insensitivity and lack of attunement to her child's needs. Mothers and sons were not excessively close but rather excessively distant, as retrospectively described by these subjects. Person and Ovesey concurred with Newman and Stoller, however, with regard to the father's distance and noninvolvement. They found that the critical etiologic factor was not physical separation from mother during the first 4 years of life but a deficit in the quality of empathic mothering. The extent of conviction with regard to gender identity varied with the degree to which the fantasy defense prevailed. As the underlying separation issues were resolved, the rigid defensive posture relented, and progress was made toward individuation consonant with sex.

Zucker (1985) focused on the child's own contributions toward socialization in the adoption of internal rules that guide gender behavior. In contrast to a critical-period model, which suggests a poor prognosis following an irreversible pattern formation during the first 2 or 3 years of life, Zucker's model suggests a possibility for change as late as 11 or 12 years of age. The reorientation occurs within a familial context. To the extent to which others, particularly the father, value the change and support the child's efforts, change is possible.

Several other important clinical reports have involved treatment of male transsexual children (Gilpin, Roaza, & Gilpin, 1979; Loeb & Shane, 1982; Fischoff, 1964). In two cases, the primary therapist was female, and positive outcomes were achieved. Aaron Esman (1970) gave a brief description of transsexual identification in a 3-year-old female fraternal twin. In this instance, the pathological twin used identification to deal with the trauma of repeated seduction by the father. Her "choice" of this solution seemed to be the consequence of two factors: unconscious pathological patterns of parental response specific to each twin and her own slow speech development. This maladaptive, defensive identification with the father later threatened an appropriate resolution of individuation. Esman's analysis followed a model outlined by Mahler, which includes consideration of both the psychodynamic context of the family and the individual coping capacities of the child in accounting for etiologic factors. This model is used to analyze the psychodynamic factors that contributed to the case under consideration.

ADAM'S PRESENTING PROBLEMS

Adam was referred by his mother at the suggestion of his classroom teacher. The mother described him in an initial phone conversation as wanting to be a girl, sometimes appearing to think that he was a girl, and exhibiting several characteristics of cross-gender identity difficulty:

feminine walk, occasional cross-dressing, feminine voice inflection and gestures, choice of female friends and toys, and avoidance of rough and tumble activities. These characteristics, confirmed in interview, meet the criteria for gender identity disorder of childhood as described in DSM III-R. In addition, Adam demonstrated avoidance of any overt expression of aggression and manifested multiple fears, including fear of the dark and of strangers, which resulted in continued seeking out of protection. He was described as the opposite of his twin brother, Andrew, who was both outgoing and friendly.

The boys were identical twins, 7 years old, in separate second-grade classes at school, and both were reportedly excellent students. They were monozygotic twins, had shared the same placenta, and showed several mirror characteristics at birth; for example, they had cowlicks going in opposite directions; they had birthmarks on opposite legs; and whereas Andrew was right-handed, Adam was left-handed. From an early age, Adam shied away from the activities of his brother and seemed to have a low opinion of himself. Feminine behavior, such as primping his hair, enraged his mother (she reported saying to him, "God damn it, you are a boy!") and made her feel ashamed. She felt that their father was not sufficiently sensitive to the differences between the two brothers.

Following these initial interviews, the parents and I agreed to the need for therapeutic intervention. The basic framework set was six meetings a month: weekly sessions for Adam (initially the brothers alternated, until Andrew voluntarily deferred the session to his brother) and two meetings a month for the parents, which became primarily individual sessions for the mother. It was predetermined that treatment would continue for 9 months, after which I was going to be leaving the clinic.

Immediate interventions included placing the twins in separate rooms with responsibility for upkeep in their own areas, emphasizing the need for privacy for individual family members, and insisting nudity in front of the children be stopped. The boys were not to shower with their mother, sleep with her, or come into the parents' room unannounced, nor was their mother to bathe with them. The parents were to respond to all of Adam's feminine activities and gestures by distracting or, more directly, by enjoining him.

During the 9 months of treatment, three distinct phases emerged, each typified by a dominant theme and accompanied by changes at home and in school. Diagnosis was a continuing aspect of the initial weeks of treatment, providing hypotheses to be supported or disproved by further work. Along the way, Adam's teacher and the parents were strong allies.

BEGINNING PHASE OF TREATMENT: IDENTITY CONFUSION AND ANXIETY

ADAM

In his first session, Adam came reluctantly; he was extremely verbal and abusive. Physically, he was of average height for his age, with a slender build, fair coloring, a generous smattering of freckles, and thick glasses that made his wide-eyed inquisitive glance seem a bit blurred and gave him a definite bookish appearance. As I engaged him in conversation, he immediately took a girl doll and began running his fingers through its hair.

He attributed his problem to his teacher, who "acts crazy sometimes, and I get angry with her." He reported that he kept slipping and falling from things; he was angry because his teacher would not call on him first; he was angry with his mother for not letting him pet his hamster; he was angry with his brother for not leaving him alone. There was no mention of his father. He freely explored the room, continually returning to stroke the doll's hair. Feminine gestures and voice inflections were obvious and frequent. I explained to him that we would be meeting to explore his problems further and that I was a doctor who dealt with children's feelings. He seemed to accept this plan, especially if I would give heed to his complaints.

During the first weeks of treatment, strong paranoid feelings were aroused as well as a desire for protection against what others and I would think of him. Adam would enter the room, slam the door, look for his mother's shoes under the crack of the door, and insist she was listening. Themes of oral deprivation were dominant; he appeared extremely hungry, demanding, and needy. Complaints continued against his teacher, with considerable whining and demanding behavior.

Adam enjoyed drawing, and as he spoke he worked with pencil and paper, accompanying his dialogue with drawings. His first picture was of a water spigot with a small boat by it, as if in a bathtub. This was followed by two pictures of tornadoes, which led us to talk about stormy feelings. Comments like "sometimes I don't like my pictures" led to other statements of low self-esteem. I asked him to draw a picture of a person, and he copied the picture of a little girl in a batik on my wall. He claimed that the little girl was himself. When I inquired about this statement, he wrote, "I am a g," erased it, turned the paper over, and wrote "man." He then took a second sheet of paper and wrote, "No, I am a grown-up boy." It was difficult for him to share these confused ideas, which were accompanied by feelings of anger and impatience. The drawing permitted him freedom of expression that otherwise would not have been possible. When I inquired concerning the difference between boys and girls, he responded, "They have a different kind of wiener . . . ; girls have my vagina" [touching his crotch]. Material from this initial period was voluminous and contained many loose associations as well as magical thinking (such as referring to me as a "miracle worker").

Fears at night emerged following separation from his brother. He drew pictures of Dracula and expressed fear of a boy in his brother's classroom whom he liked but who frightened him, because he might "come over and bite me, get me, and take me to his castle." His reality testing was poor at times, and the fantasies that emerged from his reading seemed to dominate his thoughts. He claimed that Dracula would force him to be a little girl and bite him "like you do to pretty girls." These thoughts caused him considerable suffering, which could be relieved by sweets—candies available in the room. In play he wanted to take the part of "people who do things to Dracula . . . we kill him. I only played that part once . . . other times I'm the little infant . . . I bet Dracula is afraid of you." Thus I became enmeshed in his fantasies in the role of aggressor and protector.

During sessions, he often braided the doll's hair while he verbalized his troubled thoughts. "Mom says I wish we had two girls, especially when we are messy . . . at times I wish I was a girl. [Defensively] Has my mom been talking to you?" At these moments, he seemed to merge with his mother's thoughts and would rid himself of these intrusions by projecting the ideas onto me, along with accompanying paranoid fears that I was collaborating with his mother. We worked again and again on the meaning of confidentiality, and gradually I began to see the beginnings of trust in our relationship. But then he would turn on me destructively—"Oh, you just have to love children"—and complain that I did not provide enough sweets (there was always a limited supply of candy available). This resentment of me seemed related to his fears of being rejected and deprived of love.

Specifically, although he possessed a phallic identification, as expressed in his first picture of a spigot, he felt threatened by a male emasculating figure who forced boys to become girls by biting off their wieners and then took them to his castle. This sadistic castrating image was a clear one, but the confusion in thinking stemmed from a conflicting identification arising from his mother's expressed wish that he had been a girl. His own wish paralleled that of his mother: "At times I wish I were a girl." Castration fears and mother's wishes were linked and assimilated by Adam as components of his personal identity.

MOTHER

Mrs. A was a tall, strong woman. She related in an aggressive manner, with many open expressions of feeling that ranged from delight to anger and disappointment. At first, she was quite ill at ease with me and seemed to be containing tremendous rage at having to seek help. This tension expressed itself in overt mocking of me as a doctor with all the answers. In subsequent weeks, as her dependency on me grew, there was some mellowing and softening. She seemed to seek approval and reassurance from me, to want me to mother her as well as to function as a mother-surrogate for Adam. Mrs. A was attending graduate school, and there was a considerable role reversal in the family, with Mr. A assuming household duties because of his wife's demanding schedule.

Mrs. A's father was in the health field, someone she trusted and admired. She chose him as a role model. Her mother, also a professional, was critical of her daughter and overbearing to the point of creating extreme tension between them. Mrs. A felt that she had never been able to please her mother and yet had never stopped trying. These strong feelings manifested themselves as painful stomach spasms in her mother's presence. Until the family moved 5 years previously, when Adam and Andrew were 2 years old, contact with the grandparents had occurred with regularity; Mrs. A's mother had assumed most of the responsibility for child care, especially of the identified patient, who reciprocated by becoming especially devoted to her.

Mr. A was a natural scientist. He had made prolonged trips away from home in the past but none within the previous year. He was a large man, sturdily built, and easygoing in relating to people and the world about him. He completely enjoyed the children. Nothing about their development caused him serious concern (although Mrs. A had considerable anxiety), and he was somewhat defensive of Adam's interests. He valued creativity and did not want to squelch his children's natural tendencies. Mr. A seemed a bright and warm individual, with an air of softness and gentleness, who enjoyed receiving the affection of others. He had been an only child, adopted by his parents when they were well along in years. As an adult, Mr. A became closely attached to his in-laws, who were in turn quite fond of him. The couple often sought advice from Mrs. A's parents in making a decision.

The pregnancy had been planned. Mr. and Mrs. A had been married for 5 years, a first marriage for both, and both were in their late 20s. Mrs. A was ill throughout the pregnancy with complaints of vomiting, dizziness, and loss of appetite. She gained only 20 pounds. According to Mrs. A, the couple did not find out that "Adam was in there" until 4 or 5 weeks before delivery, and their reaction was of mixed pleasure and concern, because they did not feel ready for so much responsibility. Delivery, at full term, was described as quick; Andrew was born, and Adam "slipped out" 3 minutes later. Mrs. A was awake throughout the delivery, and the children went home with her from the hospital.

From the beginning, the ambivalent feelings about being the parents of twins focused on Adam. It was he who was greeted as the unexpected arrival. At birth Adam was found to have undescended testicles. In addition, he had bilateral hernias. One hernia repair was performed at 8 weeks of age, and the second side was repaired 1 month later. In addition, Adam had eye muscle surgery at 3 years and, since then, wore thick glasses to correct for depth perception.

As Mrs. A grew more comfortable with me, she was able to describe her need for close physical contact with Adam, her feelings of helplessness and inadequacy with infants, and her horror of any "birth defect." She felt that babies had to be born perfect; she was especially revolted by abnormal genitalia. These reactions need to be understood in relation to her earlier fear of rejection by her mother. Mrs. A's need for closeness with Adam was connected in turn with Adam's attachment to his maternal grandmother. Thus he seemed to represent both his mother's feelings of being damaged and her need for close support and nurturance, providing an essential link between generations.

The maternal grandfather assisted at both hernia operations. Mrs. A felt that she needed to rely on him completely, as "he knew what he was doing," and she clearly derived comfort from his presence. The impression gained was of an extended family, with Mr. and Mrs. A functioning, during these early years, more like siblings than as parents. Andrew became close to his grandfather; Adam was attached, as previously noted, to his maternal grandmother. The twins slept well as infants and woke only to be fed. They were both breast-fed for 3 months; solid food was given as a supplement at 3 weeks of age. There was no undue crying, except surrounding trauma associated with hospital procedures. Milestones were within normal limits. Adam sat up at 5 months, stood alone at 9 months, took his first steps at 11½ months, and was walking freely by 14 months. Andrew did everything about 1 month later. Subsequently, after age 3 years, Adam became clumsy in gross motor movements, disliked running, and experienced difficulty throwing a ball. Rather than helping him overcome his dislike of activity, the family avoided dealing with the concern.

The boys were still in diapers at age 3 years, as a convenience. They were weaned from the bottle at 3 years, 6 months, while simultaneously using a cup. Weaning and toilet training occurred together, when the couple moved and the twins were put on a schedule for the first time. The boys continued to be good sleepers. For the most part, they shared a room and liked to sleep together in the same bed. When they were sick, they slept in bed with their mother, who felt a need to be constantly vigilant.

Although Adam was always perceived by his mother as different, the first feminine characteristics did not appear until age 2 years, 6 months. Artistic interests and sensitivity appeared earlier. Adam was drawn to colors and touching objects. After age 2 years, 6 months, feminine gestures and a special attraction to female-typed toys developed. He identified with Laura Ingalls in "Little House on the Prairie," mimicked her, acted out the "old days," and wanted to wear a bonnet. Andrew was described as the easier of the two twins to control. He responded to parental threats and peer pressure. Adam was a loner; he did not do well in groups and did not interact with other children. According to his teacher in first and second grades, when he did play with another child it was usually a girl. He needed to be forced verbally into physical activity at recess time and in class demanded the teacher's undivided attention.

It is interesting to note that Adam presented with characteristics that combine observations made by both Stoller and Person and Ovesey. He was described by his parents and teacher as sensitive, creative, and artistic but also as a loner who did not relate well to his peers. Perhaps because of the complexity and intensity of his problem, the primary transsexual gender identity disorder was reflected clearly in his behavior at an early age and was not deferred until adolescence.

As Mrs. A told me the story of her family in her sessions, Adam's behavior in sessions became less confused and his play activity became less chaotic. Mother and child settled into the therapeutic relationship; each formed an alliance with me, and a transition occurred into the middle phase of treatment. The middle phase was marked by coherence of play themes and the mother's continued sharing of her experiences. Adam became less clingy, letting go of his mother, and the relationship within the dyad became less tense.

MIDDLE PHASE OF TREATMENT: EMERGENCE OF BEGINNING IDENTIFICATION WITH FATHER

ADAM

At about this time, Adam began writing stories for his father. He described "a land where there are no grown-ups, just a king, a queen, and kids." He began building crowns, and in reference books he located a crown with gems to replicate. That year for Halloween he wanted to be a ghost because he felt scared; the following year he planned to be a king. Adam created a nature center in his home, similar to the one at the museum; it contained a hornet, a bee, and some wasp nests. He would show his treasures to anyone who would pay attention. Whenever there was company in the house, Adam would dominate by lecturing; Andrew would retaliate by taunting him and calling him a girl.

Adam saw a man lecturing and inquired, "Can a boy be a teacher?" At the historical society, he saw an exhibit of dolls, returned home, and put his dolls away for storage in the "museum." The symbols of king, queen, jewels, and nests were significant recurrent themes, reflecting a need to rework relationships with his parents and search for a secure home. A nest would provide the containment within which even the tiniest bird could grow and flourish.

In therapy, artwork continued to be a primary medium of expression. Adam was drawn to water paints and used primarily soft pastel colors (with several exceptions, such as black for Dracula). He drew in quick, secure artistic strokes, indicating a perception of line, space, and perspective unusual for his age. He painted a covered wagon, which reminded him of his father, who had lived out West. A second painting had four trees on a green landscape (a definition of his family?). A third was of an empty house, painted in black with red curtains. He drew the sun shining while wind blew outside, and his name appeared twice in outlined squares. Adam became increasingly anxious about me, showing obvious affection. His favorite music, which he shared, contained the line "how good to be free with you and me." He offered to trade rings with me; continued to ask, "Why do you like kids?" (now without ridicule); and inquired as to my religion.

At about this time, he shared his first dream: "I had a strange dream last night; I was in a covered wagon with my best friend. We reached a secret country called The Great Walled Country and saw a bunch of little kids, no grown-ups. Oh my God! I couldn't wait to see the king's crown with diamonds and rubies, so I went down. They saw us, and the great war started. They were shooting cannons, with gunpowder. My friend got out, and they tried to kill him; they put him on a cross. I got out and punched the kids and made my way through. I picked up the cross and put it in the wagon. My friend fainted. The wagon stopped. They seized us and took us to a castle, but I had a bright medal. Girls were guarding us. I said, 'Well, hello, honey [with ridicule]. I'm going to get out of this place and you can't stop me!' I pried up the window and rode through the town. I slapped the horse so hard, he went zooming down. We took all the diamonds and all the children from the great walled country back to America. I loaded up forty-nine wagons carrying children and food. I had to take care of all the children. [Obviously imitating in girlish voice]: 'Now stop being like that or I'll put you in school. Stop that ladies first junk.' "

I was struck by the intensity of feeling and the free expression. Inhibition had disappeared, and we seemed at last to have a trusting tie, which led to the unraveling of further inner thoughts. Adam is clearly a hero in this story, in which identity is macho and strong. He saves his martyred best friend (who also represents part of himself) and the other children, as well as the treasure of diamonds. Jewels seem to have taken the place of the sweets he formerly sought so greedily, a selection more appropriate to latency. Astride the galloping steed, a strong phallic image, he is in control of his impulses, an aggressor who rescues and cares for children. I wondered what association this self-image might have to earlier, more primitive wishes and the grandiose description of me as a "miracle worker." Interestingly, religion—in particular, the concept of suffering and salvation—played a prominent part in his muddled sense of who he was and what he valued. He definitely saw himself as superior to girls, whom he subdues in the dream, and at last he expresses his virility, albeit defensively. I wondered if his painting of the wagon and the association with his father were the significant symbols that inspired the creation of the dream.

Closer examination reveals Adam's dream to be a rescue fantasy, in part a condensation of many things he learned in school (the Great Walled Country, the great war, jewels). One must ask: Who is being rescued? Who is the rescuer? What is the danger from which they are being rescued? The persons being rescued include his friend and the children. His friend represents the martyred, damaged aspect of himself, that part of himself—his penis—that was damaged from birth and led to his relinquishing his maleness. Because Adam's sense of imperfection was compounded by fear of castration, the necessary foil, or defense, against these lethal threats would need to be strong and fearless. Adam uses many classic phallic terms—*shoot, punch, seize, pried, slap, load, zoom*—to conjure up a strong male image capable of a successful rescue. The dream expresses a desire to be reborn as an undamaged phallic male, an allusion to the wish to be rescued by the therapist. He is searching for a royal couple, parents who will nurture and protect him and give him a safe home. Adam needs protection not only from external threats but from his own aggressive impulses as well, his anger toward his mother, who gave birth to two children, and his anger toward his passive self, who submitted to being assigned a feminine identity.

Adam's overt expression of directed aggression was becoming obvious both at school and in therapy. He increasingly used his feminine voice and gestures as indicators of ridicule. In school, he was getting into physical fights. In addition, he became more vocal in his complaint that his teacher gave all her attention to others. Feminine gestures were still occasionally obvious in school, however, and his constant demands for gratification were vociferous. With parental assistance, a behavior modification program was worked out between home and school for both boys, and it proved an effective control. In session, he referred to our time together as "the pits" and wrote me angry, sealed notes. Along with testing me with his anger, he shared new secrets: "I want a castle more than anything. I am making a king's crown for myself and am looking for a queen." He took great pleasure in minutely describing the crown he was making. He confided dreams of being a king in "a little kids' world," where he owned everything. Attachment to me, as well as reality testing, was increasing steadily, shown in a strong curiosity about my identity and an obvious wish for kinship: "How come you get to go to Florida and I don't?" "Do you have a Christmas tree this year? We have both" [a Christmas tree and Chanukah lights]. "Who would you pick for a prince if you were a queen?"

MOTHER

As Mrs. A became increasingly trusting, she shared with me her frustrations in controlling the boys as well as her extensive use of physical punishment ("I use a belt like my father and a lot of screaming and yelling"). Although we enjoyed good rapport, I sensed her uneasiness with me and her continuing anxiety regarding criticism. She claimed to enjoy Adam a lot more than she had previously. She described her relationship with him as still very close: "He cleaned the tears from my face as he comforted me, just like my father."

Mrs. A was less preoccupied with herself during this phase of treatment and focused more on Adam, noticing with pride and interest the changes taking place. She noted that Adam seemed to be more daring physically: He was climbing logs and playing ball, "feeling better about himself." On the other hand, he put down "stupid women, people who don't know their own mind." She reported that Adam verbalized, "You love Andrew, but not me." She acknowledged to me, "In a sense I liked Andrew more—even I turned against him" [Adam]. With time, Adam was getting along better at the bus stop with the other children, whereas the previous year he had hounded the other children and was himself ostracized. At that time, he had tried to convert all the children in his class, claiming to be a "super-Jew, one of the chosen few." (Mrs. A's father was Jewish; the family celebrated both Christian and Jewish holidays.)

During these weeks, the boys accepted separate bedrooms and settled into the new arrangement. The father was doing most of the housework, catering to his wife while she took her general examinations, and Adam wanted to be with his father constantly. Instead of pouting and stamping off in anger, Adam could now verbalize, "I'm mad at you." To his parents, he seemed a little different in character, less babyish and whiny. I encouraged the family to eat meals in the evening together (previously the boys had been dining in front of the TV). Some limits were set on the mother's absences from home in the evening. Privacy, as well as curbs on nudity, continued to be enforced. The transition to the ending phase of treatment was marked by Adam's increased security in being a boy and his interest in courting members of the opposite sex.

ENDING PHASE OF TREATMENT: EMERGENCE OF TRUE OEDIPAL CONFLICT

ADAM

Adam continued to pursue his interest in royalty. He wrote a letter to Queen Elizabeth and wondered, "Why doesn't she answer?" When a response finally arrived, he was unhappy. "I wrote her a nice letter. I thought I'd get a crown. It was not the queen who wrote back, but one of the queen's letter people." As dissatisfaction increased, he planned to write a letter to Prince Charles. "He'll write back; he's not busy," he said. Disappointment with his own family was alleviated by independent activities. Complaints about women—real and symbolic—multiplied. On his return from a trip to New York, he volunteered, "I just don't like the Statue of Liberty" and went on to detail his reasons for distaste for this dignified lady. A bit later, "I don't like my mom; she doesn't pay attention to me."

Adam began to care for his physical self independently, for example, brushing his teeth and straightening his room without being reminded. He took an increased interest in nests of all kinds, especially hornets' nests. During sessions, he drew these nests. By now, however, less attention was being paid to drawing and more to the collection of real objects in nature and the gathering of information about them. He recounted being stung by a queen bee in trying to get a nest. He killed it but not the other bees, because it was the queen bee who became angry with him. What an intermingling of fantasy and reality! The queen bee is the mother, who stings with her love and whom he must in turn kill in self-protection. Aggression and nurturance are fused in his efforts to find security. At school his behavior improved significantly. He became more self-aware, reporting that he was still interrupting because he did not get his own way.

A drawing of his grandmother was accompanied by the following story: "This is the house my grandmother was born in. It makes me feel really good when I'm out there. It's almost 100°. That's why I want to stay out there. I wanted her to sleep with me. I really do love her. One night when I was 7 years old, I slept right in her bed. She must have picked me up and taken me into bed with her. But I like [said emphatically] my granny. I make more love than my grandpa. Nobody loves her more than I do." He was unabashed at this sharing of feeling, and we talked together about his feelings of warmth, closeness, and love for his grandmother, as well as his desire to win over his rival grandfather. She made him feel 100 percent, or perfect; that's why he liked to stay with her. The oedipal conflict was a double one, with the loving feelings shared for mother and grandmother.

Along with nesting and oedipal themes, Adam now became even more physically daring. He stood up in the rocking chair and climbed high on the desk to hang his hornets' nest. There were occasional outbursts of aggression ("tornado season") that resulted in paper cups being smashed or a threat to a hornets' nest. As we collected the pieces, I reflected on his wanting to build up and then tear down his beloved treasures.

MOTHER

Significant developments with Mrs. A included her confiding that she had been eavesdropping on sessions. Separation was intolerable for her, and she needed to know what her son was confiding to me. With support, she was able to accept waiting down the hall, behind a closed door. One afternoon, she was 20 minutes late in meeting her son after his session. Adam became extremely anxious and, for the first time in many months, picked up a doll and began to fondle its hair. I interpreted his actions to him, and he accepted the explanation with little defensiveness. We shared how difficult it was to wait for his mother's return. On reunion, Mrs. A responded well to her son's needs: She put her arms around him for reassurance and explained where she had been.

The main issues with Mrs. A at this point remained her trust in me as a therapist and the need for her not to intrude on the relationship that Adam and I had formed in therapy. "Is he really telling you everything? I'd like to know what's going on. He promised me he'd open up." We probed for reasons for this anxiety, and Mrs. A became increasingly open about her feelings. She discussed having responded more pleasurably to Andrew. She was troubled by Adam from the moment of birth and traced her concern to the undescended testicles. Mrs. A went on to relate that when she picked up Adam, "he cried like a cat," and she knew in her heart that something was wrong. She felt unable to cope with the presence of a birth defect, and her father was apprehensive lest she not take Adam home from the hospital. Mrs. A's recognition of the emotional impact of Adam's imperfection was a crucial event in therapy. At about this time in treatment, Adam confronted his mother at home, saying, "Would you give me up?" She reported having him come and sit on her lap and telling him, "If I hadn't wanted you, I wouldn't have had you."

In the following parent session, Mrs. A confided, "I was a mistake." She claimed to have learned this fact in her brother's presence in conversation with her mother. Interpretation was unnecessary; she was able to form the links herself to her rejection of her son and his "imperfection." It was striking that, with the imposition of confidentiality, mother and son simultaneously gave material parallel in content and meaning, unfettered by fear of contamination through intrusion of one on the other. I reflected that each one was dealing with the central issue of rejection individually, with therapy as the protective barrier. What had been effected was both the separation of mother from son and the mother's assumption of a true caring maternal role.

ADAM

In Adam's therapy, the themes of acceptance and caring were mirrored as well. In his role as a performer, Adam dramatized from a book titled *Nobody's Perfect* and insisted, "I'm always perfect." This play enabled him to demonstrate a direct connection between being perfect and being a male; being imperfect was being a female. He showed increased caring and concern for animals of all kinds. In puppet play, the king hit the queen, saying, "I kind of like you, but get away from me sometimes," a reflection of his love for, yet yearning for separation from, his mother. The king puppet then dressed as a woman and said, "This puppet's not me, it's me playing." In an aside to me, Adam said, referring to the king puppet, "I hate this puppet so much, it's dumb." Adam continued to speak for the king puppet, saying "I want to be a girl, yes, I do want to be a girl, I'm so pretty." He put down the puppet and said directly to me, "I'm not so sure I want to be a hairstylist when I grow up. For sure I'm going to be a teacher, and I will be nicer than Mrs. K." As he said this, he was making a hairstyle with pencils. He continued, "I used to style every girl's hair at school. Mrs. K caught me and told me to stop it. Oh, these dolls are boring."

He continued to recount how he used to dress in girls' clothing and wear wigs, and said emphatically, "No, I don't want those things anymore. I almost learned to swim. Dad goes into the pool with us." At this point, Adam was clearly reformulating the internal rules that he used to guide his gender behavior. The support of his father was crucial to this important growth in development. In psychosexual terms, he had entered the phallic-narcissistic stage, was increasingly confident of his phallic nature, and was exhibiting it and beginning to obtain positive feedback about his masculinity from others.

During these weeks, Adam demonstrated an enhanced resolution of his conflicts by sublimation into intellectual pursuits, increased mastery of the environment, and coherent definition of self: "I don't want to be treated like a baby; I'm a man; I want to be treated like a man!" He continued his strong interest in nesting and was always in search of a "good nest." He would bring in nests that he gathered with increased physical daring, climbing trees, walls, and other high places. He asked me, "Dr. Chazan, can you find me a nest?" I interpreted to him that he wanted me to find him things and do his work for him. At the end of the session, he expressed his appreciation: "Thank you, Dr. Chazan." At home he began sleeping in a lot of blankets, burying himself "like a hamster in a nest," his mother remarked. In therapy he expressed his happiness with himself and with his discoveries, stuffing paper in a hole to repair a nest. The drawing of the hanging hornets' nest with holes evoked associations within me of injured testicles.

At about this time, Adam began discussing body parts and differences in relation to insects. With support, these discussions were continued at home, much to his mother's initial consternation and embarrassment, which later turned to mastery of sexual communication and feelings of parental pride. It was the hummingbird feeder and nest ("the little one") that enchanted him the most. Feminine behaviors and gestures were completely absent. Adam began to identify clearly with his father, spending more time with him and sharing such activities as building a bird pond in the yard. Although Adam denounced feminine mannerisms, he continued to express a preference for some activities that are considered feminine in our culture, such as art and games usually played by girls. These were not compulsions or obsessions but expressions of preference. Family activities expanded to include bike riding, swimming, and ball playing. At about this time, we uncovered the fact that Adam had been given a girls' bike. The mother rationalized that it would protect the damaged testicles. Mr. A protested at this point that this reasoning was unacceptable, and Adam in turn refused to ride the bike. The purchase of a new boys' bike gave him independence in the neighborhood. Mrs. A was now less protective of him and able to let go of some of her fears. With general examinations accomplished and preliminary data collected for her dissertation, she displayed a new air of serenity.

Two significant events occurred during this period. The maternal grandparents came to visit for the first time in 3 years. Adam used the occasion as an opportunity to confide in his grandmother and declare his new identity, venting some complaints of suffering in his parents' care.

The second incident involved Mrs. A's continuing desire to use me as an intermediary "good object" between herself and her son. Although her ego initially needed an ally in this respect, we were approaching a point at which this function was no longer necessary. Adam sent letters of declaration of love to his mother, who in turn mailed them to me. After giving thought to the matter, I decided to reveal to the child that the letters had been sent to me. Initially he was hurt and angry at this breach of confidence. I reflected on how natural these warm feelings were for his mother and wondered aloud why she had sent them on to me. Perhaps she had not felt she was good enough to receive them. Perhaps she needed reassurance that she could be "lovable." Perhaps Adam could help her gradually to accept these feelings of love. I explained that I would talk with his mother about the letters, and Adam took them back. Mrs. A progressed from bewilderment to acceptance and delight, especially when she realized that these were normal feelings of a male child for his mother. Later, Adam again gave the letters to his mother with the admonishment that she was never again to share them with me "or anyone else." This event was a major turning point and was followed by the ending of treatment.

The role of the transference unique to simultaneous treatment was critical in this interaction. Because of the mother's positive feeling for the therapist, who also cared for her child, the mother was able to perceive herself as capable of nurturance and love for her child. This therapeutic caring filled a void that had been experienced with her own mother. Simultaneous treatment facilitated Mrs. A's capacity to respond to her loving son with affection.

KEY PSYCHODYNAMIC ISSUES IN ADAM'S CASE

The data from this case report clearly support a hypothesis of conflict (Person & Ovesey, 1974) rather than a preconflictual model (Stoller, 1966). Adam struggled to maintain integrity of self against multiple developmental interferences (Nagara, 1966), given a constitution vulnerable to stress. His taking on of feminine characteristics was a defensive position against a fear of loss of self blended with castration anxiety on a preoedipal level (Roiphe & Galenson, 1973). Each of the factors contributing to the conflict is described below, followed by an analysis of the effects of specific therapeutic interventions.

The underlying conflict was an interactive one that involved a specific family context and Adam's particular personality structure. Mrs. A was perceived by Adam as aggressive, seductive, and overstimulating. Her close attention to him was not experienced as attention, because it lacked the quality of being in response to his independently experienced needs. Rather, these interactions were perceived as overwhelming attacks on his efforts at individuation. Taking on feminine characteristics was the ultimate surrender of separateness, through identification with an aggressive maternal object who wanted him to be a boy (Esman, 1970; Fischoff, 1964). The alternative would have been to fight against intrusiveness and kill the queen bee. These active impulses did find expression in treatment, along with new phallic strength, when he saved his passive friend, the children, and the jewels from the female enemy guards.

Andrew's alternative solution in dealing with Mrs. A was to distance himself from her. Mrs. A attributed this distancing to the pain associated with Andrew's hernia surgery at 10 months (both twins had hernia repairs). He maintained this mode of relating until after 2 years of age, adopting aggressive masculine characteristics, the active side of his mother's personality. For Adam, competition with Andrew further determined the choice of symptom. Avoidance of rivalry strengthened his defensive feminine identification and widened the gulf between the brothers.

Avoidance of competition also stemmed from the powerful position of Mrs. A in the family. Edith Jacobson (1950) and Ruth Mack-Brunswick (1940) have asserted that the wish to have a baby develops earlier in the young male child than the pride of having a penis. The little boy develops rage, jealousy, envy, rivalry, and helplessness about his inability to have a baby and grows violently aggressive against his mother. Thus Adam felt powerless to win against his mother and against his brother. Instead of perceiving himself as capable of winning his mother's love, he protested, "You love him more than me" and "you are more powerful than I am." By losing part of his independent self and sharing in his mother's gender identity, he could become powerful. These feelings were counterbalanced by Mrs. A's inability to renounce Adam; she continued to perceive him more or less clearly as part of her own body, a penis substitute and also a damaged "girl." Adam's undescended testicles, which labeled him as damaged in the mother's eyes, probably accounted for her distortion in continuing to perceive him as an extension of her own body. To win, therefore, the boy in Adam's dream needed tremendous strength and a powerful horse. He needed to prove that, although he was born imperfect, he could become a male.

Adam's many complaints against his mother and his greediness not only for her attention but also for her achievements were confided to the therapist. He was angry that his mother had another child (his twin brother), yet he felt helpless to prevent this occurrence. He was too frightened to tell her these things; he feared she might not want him because he was so furious. His defensive feminine posture was an avenue of protective identification as well as an expression of rage through ridicule. When he could begin to tell his mother to stop intruding (not listen at the door) and there was no retaliation, he could begin to show his affection (Fischoff, 1964). Jacobson concluded that creative work is a main channel for sublimation of feminine reproductive wishes in men. Interestingly, Adam was described by his parents and teacher as extremely creative. In therapy, artwork was a regular means of self-expression. In addition, the collection of nests, which he actively searched for, was a representation of feminine wishes. Adam was especially interested in the nest of a baby sparrow.

Mr. A's physical presence had no effect on the psychodynamics of the family. He played a role secondary to his wife, performing household duties that were devalued. Emotionally, he was a lost child in search of a natural mother, whose identity he never knew. His search had led him on extensive travels, at times at personal risk, locating paleontological treasures. His search also led him to adopt his in-laws as substitute parents. Adam was aware of his father's searching and sense of personal loss. The image of Dracula may reflect Adam's awareness of his father as a potentially destructive rival. Mr. A lost his adopted father at age 5 years, the height of the oedipal period, which might have intensified further these rivalrous feelings (Neubauer, 1960).

The grandparents filled an important emotional void in the family unit. They related directly to the children and provided a protective barrier to the mother's aggression. Thus Mrs. A perceived her father as helpful and dependable. Adam perceived his grandmother as someone who loved him very much. He had no doubt he could love her even better than his grandfather could, a clear sense of oedipal victory. The separation from the extended family unit during Adam's second year probably was the immediate factor that prompted the emergence of symptoms.

Adam was vulnerable to regression owing to anxiety aroused by differentiation. This vulnerability was one facet of an unusual sensitivity to his mother's psychological state. It was as if he understood the nature of his mother's unconscious bisexual conflicts and therefore behaved like a girl and believed at times that he had a vagina. He incorporated the castration wish as a means of avoiding rejection, but it was a choice of symptom that engendered its own anxiety and evoked hostility. The deficit in ego functioning, a permeability of ego boundaries, may have been determined partially by a constitutional predisposition that might have remained latent given other environmental conditions. As I have noted, although motor milestones were achieved within normal limits, a clumsiness in gross motor movements developed at approximately 3 years of age, along with a reluctance to engage in active sports. Other muscle weaknesses that required surgical intervention included a double hernia and a strabismus. In contrast, fine motor, verbal, and fantasy skills continued to develop at a precocious rate. Both twins were ranked as intellectually superior by their teachers; Adam was reading when he entered first grade. Although Adam clearly possessed the cognitive capacities necessary for resolution of conflict (Kohlberg, 1966; Kleeman, 1965), his adoption of defensive internal rules to guide his gender identity and behavior resulted in maladaptive self-socialization (Zucker, 1982, 1985; Zucker & Green, 1992).

Therapeutic interventions occurred most markedly within the transference relationship and within the family context in the changed role of Mr. A. The therapeutic relationship afforded Adam the opportunity to ameliorate the effects of a pathological symbiosis. He was able to express aggression, envy, ridicule, and greed without fear of retaliation. The therapist did not encourage masculinity; she remained a neutral object allowing Adam to work through his gender identity conflict within the transference. By actively engaging in the therapeutic process, Mr. A became an increasingly potent figure for gender identification and a role model of appropriate activities. Adam was able to use his support to facilitate individuation and reach gender identity. Sublimation of preoedipal needs became apparent in Adam's productive artistic endeavors, interest in birds, and related search for nests, as well as his desire to lecture and teach.

CASE SUMMARY

This case history is encouraging in providing evidence for the effectiveness of simultaneous treatment in gender identity disorders. Because the basic processes underlying identification—projection, introjection, and projective identification—are a major focus of simultaneous treatment, it makes sense that in many instances it is the method of choice. This case also indicates a capacity for resolution of gender identity confusion during the grade school period. It provides data to support a conflict model and the possibility for growth within a transference relationship. It confirms the value of early recognition of gender identity symptoms and treatment of the underlying disorder, as well as recognition of pathological interaction within the dyad.

Therapy with Adam and Mrs. A began with conflict and parallel process as both mother and child experienced separation anxiety. Adam evidenced disorganization and chaos in his perception of himself and the therapist. His mother was threatened by the therapist's attempts to create a sense of personal coherence with Adam. Gradually, Mrs. A overcame her fears and formed an alliance with the therapist, although she maintained a vigilant attitude well into the middle period of treatment.

In another instance of parallel process, as the mother was able to reveal her insecurities to the therapist, Adam was able to discover his own strengths and complete the process of individuation. Both within his family and in school, Adam was accepted in his role as a boy. Similarly, Mrs. A was able to clarify her role as a parent and her career aspirations. Finally, resolution of the oedipal conflict was achieved indirectly through Adam's relationship to his grandmother and the transference relationship. The therapist then acted as intermediary for the dyad by being supportive to Mrs. A, enabling her to accept directly Adam's expressions of masculine affection.

In this case, simultaneous treatment was able to address the shared issues affecting mother and child in a focused way. Individual treatment by separate therapists would have encountered two barriers to resolution. First, the mother's treatment would have been prolonged and could have lacked the necessary focus on gender issues. Second, the child would not have felt sufficient support to risk change; even if change were achieved, he would be living in an emotional environment that had not changed along with him. These residual effects at the end of therapy are minimized in simultaneous treatment, in which both parent and child change in the process. Progress by Adam and Mrs. A reflected the efforts of both mother and child to overcome limitations imposed on them by past relationships and to create their own secure bonds of affection.

CHAPTER 5

David: A Case of Narcissistic Personality Disorder (Part I)

D SM IV (AMERICAN PSYCHIATRIC ASSOCIATION, 1994) cites as criteria for personality disorders "enduring patterns of inner experience and behavior that deviate markedly from the expectations of the individual's culture" (p. 275). These differences must be manifested in two or more of the following areas: cognition, affectivity, interpersonal functioning, and impulse control. The enduring pattern is inflexible and pervasive across a broad range of personal and social situations, leading to impairment in social adjustment and academic learning. DSM IV notes that these patterns have an early onset, at least going back to adolescence.

The diagnosis of narcissistic personality disorder has been found useful by clinicians in working with children, even before adolescence (Abrams, 1993; Bleiberg, 1984; Egan & Kernberg, 1984; Kernberg, 1989; Ornstein, 1981; Rinsley, 1980). In the cases of the children observed by the clinicians cited, the enduring pattern began in childhood, with its roots in infancy. Although DSM IV does not mention narcissistic personality disorder in childhood, it suggests that the category called other personality disorder may be used with children if the pathological traits are stable.

In these instances of early deviant patterns in personality structure, it is clear that the context in which the child lives is implicated, as well as his constitutional disposition. Simultaneous treatment permits intervention at the level of the individual patient as well as the dyadic context within which he functions. In many children in whom pathological patterns of personality are held rigidly in place because of intractable interpersonal relationships, simultaneous treatment is the intervention of choice.

David, the 8-year-old child discussed in this chapter and the next, presented with many features that put him at risk for the later development of narcissistic personality disorder. In children, the most outstanding characteristic of the narcissistic personality is a grandiose sense of self (Abrams, 1993; Kernberg, 1989). These children expect immediate success in school and do not invest effort to improve performance. Typically, the law of all or nothing prevails, making for either very good or very bad grades. Other characteristics may include antisocial traits, such as lying, and paranoid anxieties aroused by fears of retaliation. Unrelenting envy destroys the capacity to depend on others and to experience a sense of fulfillment and gratitude.

Other defenses aimed at maintaining the grandiose self include devaluation, primitive idealization, omnipotent control, and narcissistic withdrawal. Both peer and family relationships suffer from the effect of these maladaptive defenses.

NORMAL AND PATHOLOGICAL NARCISSISM

Psychoanalytic theorists (O. Kernberg, 1975; Kohut, 1972; van der Waals, 1965) define normal narcissism as narcissism that reflects the libidinal investment of a normally integrated self, which includes both libidinally and aggressively invested components. In normal narcissism, tension between actual and ideal representations leads to realistic acknowledgment of the external object and progressive integration of the ideal self and other, with superego precursors, into the superego. The actual self representation is distinct from the ideal self representation and the idealized representation of the other. In pathological narcissism, the actual self representation may become fused with an ideal self representation and an idealized representation of the other.

Paulina Kernberg (1989) described the differences between pathological narcissism and normal infantile narcissism found in age-appropriate fantasies, demands, and attachments. Small children normally have grandiose fantasies and make angry efforts to control the mother and be the center of her attention. Fantasies of great power, wealth, and beauty are normal during the preoedipal period. Unlike pathological narcissists, normal children do not need to be universally admired as the sole owner of everything that is enviable and valuable.

In pathological narcissism, the demands are excessive and can never be fulfilled. They are secondary to an ongoing denigration and even destruction, out of envy, of whatever nurturance and love are given. The chronic intense envy, devaluation, primitive idealization, omnipotent control, and narcissistic withdrawal are all defenses aimed at protecting the grandiose self.

PRESENTING PROBLEMS

The dyad discussed in this chapter, a boy and his mother, were enmeshed in an ongoing, relentless cycle of fear and anxiety. The child suffered from periods of depression, with suicidal ideation. These affective storms were indications that his underlying defensive stance of omnipotence was at risk as he sought a sense of connectedness with others. Because of these extreme measures to protect his grandiose self, the presenting symptom of depression masked the underlying basis for his anxiety. The hopelessness was a signal of his beginning struggle to establish a new foundation for forming relationships. It was at this juncture that he came to treatment, where a fuller appreciation of the deficits within his personality, and how these weaknesses "fit" with those of his mother and influenced family dynamics, unfolded. David had been a "perfect" baby, healthy and beautiful despite the doctor's concern he might be malformed because of inadequate weight gain from the 7th prenatal month. Developmental milestones were all within normal limits. David met his parents' expectations until 18 months of age, when he suddenly became unmanageable, engaging in demanding behavior that they resented. David's experience of rejection was heightened by the birth of a sister when he was 3 years, 8 months. The siblings never got along well, in large part because of David's haughty, disdainful attitude toward his younger sister.

The struggle that ensued within the family pitted son against father, mother against son, and husband against wife. The frustration in dealing with their son led both parents to feel that they were dealing with a "monster" child. Although she once felt adequate and self-assured, the mother came to feel overwhelmed by the demands of her child and guilty about his difficulties. The father's inability to satisfy the needs of his wife and their child enhanced her feelings of outrage and self-rebuke.

David's sense of self-esteem was compromised as he experienced, first, overidealization and then devaluation. He found no refuge in friendships and turned instead to solitary fantasy play. His school-work suffered as he struggled to function autonomously and was unable to meet class requirements.

He failed to complete homework assignments, his work was disorganized, and his grades did not reflect his level of native intelligence. Psychological assessment revealed no specific learning disability, only a minor problem with fine motor activities and a minimal amount of restlessness.

The central organizing feature in David's development was the affective response he received from his parents. At first, he evoked intense love; then, hate and rejection. These ambivalent parental feelings remained unresolved, leaving David with parents unavailable for emotional referencing. He remained encased within his isolation, fearful of intrusion. Some of this parental reactivity was in response to David's temperament, for example, his sensitivity, irritability, and restlessness. These temperamental traits predisposed David to becoming the focal point of intense parental feelings of joy and depression. The intensity of the parental reactions to their child, however, suggests unresolved trauma within the parents as well. Children like David are subject to patterns of depersonification (Rinsley, 1980), in that the parents do not acknowledge the child as a person in his own right but cast the child as a representative cf their own world.

David experienced these ambivalent parental feelings as frightening, and the safe haven within the home became a source of threat to his psychological survival. The parents' own fearful reactions to their child's behavior provided the link for the affective continuation of intergenerational emotional trauma. David's grandiosity was an attempt to retain the feelings about himself as "wonderful and good" and to fend off the bad feelings brought on by parental devaluation. In the process, he devalued others—his friends, teachers, parents, and therapist—to protect himself from being perceived as meek, scared, and vulnerable.

RELEVANT MATERNAL HISTORY

Mrs. D, age 42, described herself as having been precociously autonomous as a child, forced to pull away from dependency on her parents and to make no mistakes. She listed parental errors she did not want to repeat with her own children. Most important, she wanted to be able to support her children's autonomy. Mrs. D described herself as having suffered extreme anxiety when she was not functioning as an extension of parental needs and wishes. She feared that they would die, she would kill them, or they would kill her. Her own need for approval and acceptance by her parents was more important to her than financial reward.

According to Mrs. D, whatever happened to David would hurt her.

If he had a tantrum, she felt that his anger was targeted directly at her. She could not deal with his hanging on her; his whining was draining, and he disgusted and revolted her. She used David to highlight features of her husband she did not like, such as his consuming neediness for attention and care. Mrs. D felt that she was a different parent with her daughter. She thought that David had been a happy child until the daughter was born and he was forced to share.

Mrs. D shifted to a discussion of her own sibling, a brother 6 years younger, whom she had parented. On the one hand, she adored him, because she had been lonely before his birth. On the other hand, she resented him, because her parents shunned her after his birth. She was scrawny and unappealing; they refused to pick her up and carry her any longer. Her childhood ended abruptly in this way.

Mrs. D described her daughter as a source of security for David, who slept in her room when he was fearful. Mrs. D immediately associated to her own fearfulness as a child. She was always afraid someone would take her from her family. She felt her own mother had been impatient and would "dump" her into bed to be "rid" of her. Her father, by contrast, was understanding and tried to protect her from her fears, saying, "Daddy's here now, don't worry." Her extensive fantasies as a child dealt with scary, powerful figures (Dracula, Frankenstein) who would take her away from her family. She described her father as relieving her by fighting off her demons, yet she would feel remorse for needing this special attention as well as gratitude. "I did everything in my life in spite of myself . . . a constant struggle."

Mrs. D's relationship to her mother was also intensely ambivalent. She hated her, and yet she felt she resembled her in many ways. Her maternal grandmother had died when her mother was an infant; her maternal grandfather had been a gambler and unstable. Mrs. D felt she always had to meet her mother's needs and was very much a parentified child. She stressed the exactness with which she had to be pleasing to reach her mother: "I was the goodest little girl, that's how much to the letter I was made to follow her." Efrain Bleiberg (1984) claimed that children reared to compensate for their parents' shortcomings lack an inner core of secure self-identity. They are permanent role-players seeking external cues on how to be good. These children learn early that they are acceptable only through a proper performance and adopt a false self; they reach adulthood deficient in an inner core of a valued self on which to depend.

An elderly maternal aunt was the closest to a maternal figure Mrs. D experienced. Mrs. D was a young girl when the elderly caregiver became chronically ill. Mrs. D was fearful of being alone with her, because she was terrified her great-aunt might die. "If she were to die,

I would be left alone. What would I do with a dead person?" In her relationship with David, he came to represent a parental failure—both her own and that of her parents—as well as something offensive, like "dirty laundry." She was aware of her feelings of disgust for him and felt they were damaging to her child.

BEGINNING PHASE OF TREATMENT: IN SEARCH OF RELATIONSHIP—GRANDIOSITY AND ALIENATION

Treatment began for David on a twice-weekly basis; parent counseling sessions were held every other week. Mr. D was impatient with the progress in treatment and did not feel he benefited from our sessions. His impatience barely concealed how overwhelmed he felt by the family difficulties. Denial and avoidance were the strategies he used to relieve himself of stressful family relationships. When these attempts to cope were inadequate, he would erupt in intimidating rage. These outbursts eventuated in his seeking his own individual treatment. In times of crisis, a parent counseling session was sought to diminish tensions.

Mrs. D's inner conflict was depicted many ways as she began to perceive me as receptive to her difficulties. She was extremely articulate about her own issues and able to describe how they intersected with David's experience. The contrast between her capacity for verbalization and her helplessness was striking. The troublesome issues concerning David kept recycling and led Mrs. D to understand she would need help, as David would, if there was to be progress. Her husband gave tacit agreement to Mrs. D's request for simultaneous treatment.

DAVID

At our initial meeting, David, who was 8 years, 6 months, listed his ideas of what he would like to become. It was a long list of possibilities, ranging from the practical—"an architect, a paleontologist, a farmer"—to the fantastic—"make my own supermarkets, be a nightrider and take hostages." His list of what he would not like to be included "a wrestler, because you get hurt; a lumberjack, it's too dangerous; a space cadet, the *Challenger* blew up; a basketball player, you could get your eye poked out." He seemed to be an outgoing, grandiose child, both lonely and scared. Nonstop talking made him appear extremely pressured.

David's conversation was accompanied by restless movements and frequent posturing. He was of average height but very thin, with dark hair and intense blue eyes. He was neatly dressed and wore large glasses, which made him appear serious. He said his reason for coming to treatment was "to help him make friends." David quickly began to talk of his interest in wild animals, contrasting huge and tiny creatures. He told of a battle between sharks and described the monstrous size of a prehistoric shark. In describing the terror evoked by these monsters, he elaborated, "If sharks ate a man, they wouldn't have to chew. A cupcake would be as small as this hole. An ant they couldn't see, because they have such bad eyesight. But sharks can smell blood from far, far away. If they want to, the big creatures can be as silent as an ant. Like the nightrider, a man who pretends to be good but is really evil."

As David shared with me the terrors of his fantasy, we bonded together, experiencing the intensity of his fears. David's alliance with me led him to share his interest in building, and he constructed a grand mansion and peopled it with dolls. In the house, a father queried his son, "What will you be upon graduation? You need to go out into the world." The son asked, "Can't we stay together?" The father replied, "Maybe." The son volunteered, "I'm going to be everything." In an excited tone, David quickly returned to his favorite subject of sharks. He reported they even devour whales for food but that they are really "dopes," as their eyesight is not very good.

David's stories barely concealed his preoccupation with parental demands and his feelings of vulnerability. His father was legally blind from a congenital defect. David's father was the only child of wealthy parents who had always been controlling and exerted pressure on him to achieve. The hungry sharks were "dopes" because of poor eyesight, a devaluation of his father, and at the same time a reminder of his threatening presence. The relationship between father and son was severely stressful. David depended on his mother almost exclusively, because he was intimidated by his father and lonely for companionship.

David told me what his favorite TV shows were and asked if I would watch them. He listened as I responded that it would not be possible for me to watch them all but that it was good we had the times we did have together. I assured him I always would be available to him at our regularly scheduled times. Despite separation anxiety apparent at the beginning and end of sessions, David seemed to accept my benevolent limit-setting comments with equanimity. He confided that he really loved Peanuts and, especially, Peanut's small monkey friend.

The next few weeks brought elaborated stories, usually told with mounting excitement with some disorganized themes, expressing blame for stupidity and fears of dismemberment and annihilation by being bitten and swallowed. An example of this type of frightening story was the description of an encounter between a fish and a dinosaur: "He's swallowing him. He's saying, 'Boy, this is a mouthful.' Then, he goes directly into his mouth, the fish into the dinosaur, and he bites all his head off. The end."

His stories became longer and longer and always included an extensive list of characters, usually peers and a parental figure. These tales had an endless quality. They were often confusing to follow and conveyed the excitement he felt at our being together. He began to play with themes of war and power, and he repeatedly abused and killed me. I expressed the loneliness he felt when he killed me: There would be no one there for him to play with. I conveyed to him my understanding that only when we were very different in a certain way—when he was strong and I was weak—could we play together. This comment directed David's attention to the defense used to make playful interaction possible. The outcome had to be predetermined, with his grandiosity fully in control of his fate.

A hopeful note to the ambivalent feelings developing within our relationship was expressed in a story he wrote and gave to me. It was entitled "Star War":

> When men died out, stars gave birth. At first they were friendly, but something started a war. The stars used beams of light to attack each other. Usually stars would be blown up by war. Usually big stars would be blown up. The small stars would dodge better. One day a star had an idea. He moved. The stars moved after him. He said, "If you follow me, you will have to make peace." That is what they did.

This story reflected David's longing for companionship. It barely concealed a scene of family struggle. It is the small star who has the idea that quiets the celestial battle. David was clearly communicating his willingness to enter into a practicing stage relationship (Mahler, Pine, & Bergman, 1975) with me, as long as I followed him and did not threaten him. When people loom large and powerful, they resort to destruction. With little people, David could feel safe. In later sessions, David often found expression for his deepest feelings of alienation and longings for affiliation in the celestial metaphor. Even the smallest star suggested an outstanding luminescence that shines from above, an effort to balance his feelings of low self-esteem and rejection by ordinary mortals.

Four months after the beginning of treatment, the course of therapy was full of reversals and contradictions. As therapy proceeded, David's play activity became increasingly complex and less concrete, and there were fewer loose associations. The play activity spoke profoundly to me through metaphor, with an arresting openness, and invited my participation in the drama of his deepest thoughts and feelings. However, David continued having anxiety over separation from his mother during sessions. He complained that he was being jailed in having to come twice a week, yet he played at being a therapist. He was full of verbal abuse, calling me "stupid" and a "mental." His grandiosity barely concealed his neediness and feelings of vulnerability. His feelings often became confused: He wanted a connection with me, but his difficulties with affect and impulse regulation made him unable to address me in a positive manner. Instead, he attacked me and became disorganized. At these moments, David was in constant motion and turmoil, unable to focus on sustained play.

MOTHER

A key connection between David and Mrs. D was through feelings of fear, worry, and guilt. Early in our work together, after Mrs. D had accepted the role of patient, she dreamed that David had brain cancer. All his unacceptable behavior (rudeness, foul mouth) could be attributed to the physical illness, and she was helpless to make things better. Two and a half years previously, an uncle of hers had had a misdiagnosed brain tumor and subsequently died. The combination of catastrophic illness and unreliable medical care was experienced as traumatic by Mrs. D. She had a history of morbid preoccupation with sickness and lack of trust in doctors. The children were aware of the details of the uncle's illness. This illness as a metaphor within the family represented dread and fear, an omen of impending death. It also came to represent for Mrs. D and David a threatening destructive feeling from within the body.

Mrs. D worried that David was going to be a lonely, miserable child. This negative previewing led her to elaborate on foreboding expectations for David. She felt guilty because David was her "mistake," the mistake of her marriage. Every time she looked at him, she cringed, feeling "I don't like him." She hated that about herself; she was the mother and felt hate for her son. Early in our work together, Mrs. D began to explore why she rejected her son. She described her feelings of hatred as alien intrusions within her, experienced as a "malignant growth, something that could kill."

Fears of annihilation and death were repetitive themes in the treatment of both mother and child. It was as though I were hearing an echo, as one member of the dyad revealed inner thoughts and feelings that so closely resembled those of the other. The metaphors were parallel: One was more suitable for an adult, the other for a child, but both sets of experience reflected the long-standing frustration of being unable to calm the unending terror of emptiness and loneliness.

When Mrs. D observed David to be engrossed in a world by himself with his fantasy people, she reacted with horror and physical distress, "wanting to throw up." It was as if he were saying, "You can't reach me." It led her back to the early trauma of hospitalization at 22 months when she regressed and became fearful of anyone in white. Her parents recalled the nurses inquiring, "Doesn't your child ever smile?" She became terrified of strangers, thinking they would kidnap her and separate her from her family, a fear she had retained during her childhood. "Why do I relate to him as if he were me?" was a poignant question Mrs. D asked as she realized how she equated her son's solitary play with her own state of regressed withdrawal.

As Mrs. D expressed a desire to explore her own issues, she associated to the image of "dirty laundry," as if her concerns were always being shoved aside, relegated to second place after her son's issues. Dirty laundry also referred to secrets. She was finding it hard to keep from me the feeling that she was less attached to David than she appeared to be. She was fearful of what I might think and how she might become depressed if she admitted the extent of her own personal concerns, as though she did not have the right to a separate existence. Revealing her anger and the extent of her envy were beginning steps for Mrs. D toward acknowledging her true concerns.

DAVID

David often accused me of causing him to feel as though he were in jail. He would take a toy gun and shoot me, while giving me directions on how to play dead. He began to play at messing with clay and potions. When gratification was delayed, he would explode and threaten to leave. Along with the messes, he continued sporadically to play at shooting me dead, still instructing me how to die. He called the game "The Wild West." Each time he enacted this "dead" sequence, he seemed a little less terrified, although the play was chaotic and tense. I followed his play directions and by mirroring and participating in his script, we were able to play out his worst fears. I talked about the loneliness of being dead, being totally cut off from one's friends and family and all that is alive. I played at calling out when no one would answer. He became anxious at moments when the play became too real. The play activity would be interrupted, and he sometimes left the room, but he always returned. I shared with him how upset he got when things got wild and out of control. He became distraught and shouted at me, "I hate you . . . you are dumb . . . my parents think you are smart, but you are stupid."

David acknowledged to me that the reason he got so wild was that he wanted to kill me; he then became afraid that I would kill him. He would rather not be with me and have these feelings. He envied his sister, who did not have to come. I agreed with him that things could get scary and wild sometimes when he felt those murderous feelings, but I noted that somehow in the play we kept coming back together. These comments summarized our sequence of play activity and were encouragement to David that his worst fears did not materialize and that we did survive these affect storms together.

Although play sessions continued to be chaotic, David demonstrated a nascent capacity to reflect about himself and was becoming aware of his fantasies. He claimed that most of the time he was at home he was in make-believe. In school, he dreamed with his eyes open. He said that he dreamed about his toys and that when he was younger, he dreamed about his parents.

MOTHER

Mrs. D continued to talk about herself and her child. She freely linked his experience with her own and, at those moments, blurred boundaries between them. These projections intruded frequently in daily living; Mrs. D was flooded by personal memories evoked by David's behavior. These memories heightened the shared experience of mother and child and undermined David's attempts to individuate. For example, Mrs. D reported that David could not sleep at night and that he said he wished he could die. She recalled how much she adored him as an infant and did not leave him alone until he was 3 years old. At that time, her husband was verbally abusive. She recalled she could not allow herself to be angry with him and experienced suicidal ideation. She remembered thinking, "My son would never know how much I love him. No one else could convey that if I were not there. I pictured my own funeral."

Mrs. D's further associations to David's suicidal ideation led to memories of the deaths of two relatives. David was present at both funerals, because Mrs. D had no one to leave him with. She also recalled having to embrace an aged grandparent in the nursing home and being terrified. "I had to get closer and closer, it was my duty." Again, she recalled her great-aunt, who cared for her and whom she feared might die. At age 4½ years, David did not want to attend a birthday party because he did not want the magician to make him disappear. Mrs. D claimed that she had the same fear as a child but could not express it. I reflected on how many things Mrs. D had done in her life that she really had not wanted to do. It was as if she would disappear and exist only as an extension of someone else's wishes. It became clearer to both of us that David had become a vehicle for Mrs.

D to reexperience many of the troubling aspects of her childhood.

Mrs. D dreamed that she was tutoring at the end of the year and that there was a substitute teacher in the room. A student told her that the regular teacher was attending a meeting about a group of orphans who were coming to the school in the fall. At the end of tutoring, the substitute teacher offered Mrs. D a lift home. On the way out, she informed Mrs. D that the regular teacher really had not been at meetings but was out of school with a bad back. The substitute teacher came to Mrs. D's house for lunch. Mrs. D was surprised to find herself not in her house but in an apartment, and everything they did revealed something wrong in the apartment. Finally, the substitute teacher had to change her clothes, and Mrs. D confirmed that this teacher had stolen some of her jewelry. She confronted her, and the substitute teacher confessed without remorse. Then Mrs. D left the apartment. She was not sure if the teacher kept the jewelry or not.

Mrs. D was upset about this dream for 3 days. She felt that she had lived it, and it left her with a feeling of disappointment and heaviness. She expressed surprise that there was a substitute teacher and found her to be frightening, like her mother, who was bitter, angry, and always critical. She was also surprised to arrive back at an apartment, the dwelling of her childhood. Everything that was wrong was pointed out; what had seemed right before was shown to be unacceptable. There was a sense of betrayal. She had trusted and had been lied to, and yet the woman showed no guilt or remorse at the theft. That astonished her; if their positions had been reversed, she would have been mortified. The substitute teacher was an intruder who reversed the familiar and was untrustworthy. Something was being taken away from Mrs. D.

This dream revealed to both of us the extent of our beginning relationship. She was trusting me, despite her misgivings, and the relationship was taking away her sense of isolation. It was as if by caring for me, she had been robbed. Clearly there were many surprises in the dream, but there was no terror. History was not repeating itself exactly; there were changes. The unexpected substitute is not the person Mrs. D expected her to be, although the surroundings seem the same. The atmosphere of tension is somewhat diminished by the outrageous actions of the intruder. I commented to Mrs. D that perhaps it was significant that the substitute was not a duplication of Mrs. D's expectations; she was not the same, she was different. And that difference made the dream intriguing.

Mrs. D had been unable to relate to David in an intimate and meaningful way. Her attachment to him was marred by anxiety and repulsion. She commented that "the abyss is when flaws in me cause something bad, within myself." Because of these negative feelings about herself, Mrs. D could not allow David to idealize her as "the perfect mother" and have a full positive experience. Because of her intensely aversive feelings about herself, which constantly intruded, and her idealization of David, David's sense of differentiation had been delayed. In the dream, disappointment in the form of marred expectations did not harbor guilt or rejection. The dream reflected a budding tolerance for negative feelings toward the self and others within the therapeutic relationship.

Mrs. D related these negative feelings about herself to her parents and their marital relationship. She clearly had experienced oedipal victory and felt that her father loved her more than he loved her mother. There was a role reversal in the marital relationship, with her father the more maternal and involved parent. He was an intellectual who never realized his potential and vicariously valued Mrs. D's academic achievements as if they were his own. He suffered from severe debilitating bouts of depression, which rendered him helpless despite years of treatment. Mrs. D also felt as though she had served in loco parentis as her younger brother's mother. Rather than having good feelings about her successes, she felt guilty and depressed, barely concealing her wish for revenge and retaliation against her parents.

In light of these feelings concerning her family of origin, it was significant that Mrs. D could share with me not only her burdens but also the successes she was having in her professional training. She seemed to find her work an avenue of connection and positive identification with me, because it also involved children and families. Her work was now a source of pride, reversing the experience she described with women supervisors—"If I win, I must die"—and with male supervisors—"If I fail, I die." Failure in turn was associated with a fear of being an imposter and of making mistakes. Mrs. D described herself as constantly preparing for bad outcomes to avoid being overcome by chaos and always pleasantly surprised when outcomes were positive.

In public, Mrs. D appeared competent and self-assured; privately, she felt fallible and vulnerable to "being found out." Her ultimate need for protection was against the fear of dying and losses, such as the loss of her front tooth as a child and her grandmother's deficient hearing. These memories were constant reminders of the dread she carried within her. They were the feelings of a parentified child whose role was to gratify parental needs for accomplishment at the expense of her own development. Every divergence from perfection was a threat of personal annihilation. She subjected others to the same scrutiny and would be enraged at being left in the care of someone less than perfect. I commented that she must often be enraged by her accurate perceptions of my shortcomings!

DAVID

Seven months of treatment passed. David's vulnerabilities became more evident, alongside his defenses. He reported feeling "weird." He strutted around, provoked his sister, and was overbearing and obnoxious. He felt sad and inadequate and was becoming more distant from his parents. If his father got physically close in roughhousing, David claimed he was being hurt.

In play activity, David's sexual impulses were confused and rampant. In one session with the dollhouse, David reported that all the children were "peering" at the nude mother; the boy doll "farts like a child"; the family "boots him out" and he "flies back in" and is "booted out" again. The baby is "flushed down the toilet." The children "tickle the mom's ass and feel her vagina." The "motorcycle men" (to whom he gave names of his friends) come in through the glass window and the oldest ogles the mother along with the other children. They push the father doll away and then throw him out. While making these comments, David was looking at me furtively to reference my response. Voyeurism enacted in the play activity was accompanied by chaotic excitement and loss of control. He boasted and bossed me around. None of the play activities satisfied him.

David's sensitivity and feeling of personal injury were revealed in a litany of complaints: None of his friends paid attention to him; he did not win a prize at a party; all but familiar foods were distasteful; other kids were making fun of him. Along with these complaints, David was isolating himself increasingly from his peers, demanding special foods, being easily insulted and threatened, and taking every remark personally as a token of rejection. He confided in his father that he had no feelings, that he was just a machine; and then, before his father departed on a trip, David hugged him and told him he loved him very much. David was demonstrating both ambivalence and anxiety. He had difficulty controlling sexual and aggressive impulses, but he was increasingly vocal about his strong desire to be socially accepted.

As the winter holidays approached, David made presents for all the members of his extended family. My enabling him to make gifts for the family evoked in him sustained positive feelings for me. Also, David made reference to not liking himself; making presents helped him to feel better (reparation). I responded that he cared a lot about his family and that it was a special gift to have such caring feelings. David accepted my compliments about his gift making. He came early and asked for extra time. I limited him, acknowledging the difficulty for him and inquired whether his loneliness was any better. He said no, but he was willing to listen to my suggestion that we talk about it without retaliating. When I engaged him in conversation, he drew a fighter plane, and he listened when I commented, "When I don't let you do what you want to do, it's a battle." He was reluctant to leave at the end of the session. He slammed the door and apologized, "Oops, I forgot."

The next several months in treatment were marked by an upsurge in self-observation and diminution of blaming. Projection and reversals of affect persisted, especially in play. Play activity contained projections, with outbursts of loss of control arising in response to separations. Persecutory feelings and desire for revenge against the self and others often became extreme. Hypochondriasis appeared as a corollary to more advanced object relations; David used concerns about his body to seek out caring. His helplessness could be extreme: He perceived himself to have a malignant brain tumor that needed to be excised; his attacks on me at those times were virulent and derisive.

As a compensatory defense against these intense feelings of being persecuted (by his malignant part), he had feelings of alienation from humans, of being a kind of robot/machine superior to human beings. These states of alienation doubled back and reconnected with depressive affect, this time associated with loneliness and thoughts that suicide was the only workable solution.

At home Mrs. D was constantly besieged by David's demands for attention. She felt overburdened by her routine responsibilities and unappreciated by David. Recently she had returned to work, and David begged her to remain in the home. He burst out crying, saying he would hurt himself and wished he were not alive. Despite his desperation, Mrs. D remained firm and maintained an empathic connection with his plight. Following a visit to her school, David had nightmares about spiders that were all around him. His mother capitulated and let him sleep in her bed. This victory did not appease David. He remained despondent, and it was impossible to please him. He hid from the family and said it was not fair that they would not put him up for adoption. He wanted to change his name. His negativity had a playful quality rather than being grim or foreboding. However, David was not yet ready to relinquish his anger and remained peeved, although he was also proud of his mother's new accomplishments.

At our next meeting, David intruded into my office before his scheduled time. He was eager to share with me some thoughts about an ancient pyramid he had built. The pyramid was surrounded by a fortress. This elaborate structure from the past also had futuristic guns and tricky steps, so that whoever climbed them kept falling. If you got to the top, you had a chance for a good life, or even better, you had to be small like an ant to get there. I commented on how it is sometimes helpful to be small. David wanted to know what the other children had said about it. Who had seen it? He asked to take the pyramid home with him, and I limited his request. The pyramid is the ancient pyramid of darkness, he said. Every time it falls down, it rebuilds. Dinosaurs try to climb up and destroy it.

DAVID: If you get to the top, you need a parachute. You might fall if you don't have one. Cats always land on their feet. The cat tried to get into the pyramid. It got inside, but the pyramid blew him out. The cat's name is Tantrum. When he gets into a tantrum, he gets this big; he gets gigantic. Everyone says, "Uh oh." Tantrum says, "Don't do that, don't smash me." He knocked out their window-pane—I really did! [Note: This was David's confusion, confabulating himself and the cat. He barely managed to conceal himself within the narrative.]

THERAPIST: You really did have a tantrum. It's part of growing up. When you have a tantrum, you feel bigger and stronger than anyone else. That can be scary.

DAVID: Triniac [the dinosaur] is bigger than Tantrum, even when he's mad. Triniac can run through 3 million tons of iron, rock, silver, all at the same time, plus shields. His horns help him to move the shields. In a battle, he can lift up anything on the planet. Triniac is wrecking the pyramid a lot. He has magnetic feet that lift him up.

THERAPIST: These are very destructive animals.

DAVID: Tantrum really wants to destroy the pyramid. Talk about Dad's anger, he's never afraid. He's always giving Mom a hard time.

The pyramid became a good pyramid. I commented on how the building and guarding of the pyramid brought us closer together; he adamantly denied this observation. I noted that sometimes his feelings played tricks on us and turned into the opposite: from good to bad, from happy to sad. He was annoyed at the comment and called me "stupid and dumb." He experienced any "look at" comment by me as threatening. I could gain agreement only by mirroring him at the moment. However restricted this relating may seem, mirroring was an affirmative, shared experience and represented progress over negation or denial.

Despite David's efforts toward integration, the threat of our growing closeness triggered a period of increasing loss of control. He brought in the cutout of a woman, whom he described as "half robot, half human, a killer girl." He was fearful I would intrude into his play space and divided the room in half. I must keep to my side of the room. This intolerance toward me seemed to reflect David's anxiety concerning losing his own world to an intrusive other who could not tolerate his constructions.

David's depression deepened once again and this time was aggravated by an episode at school concerning school achievement difficulties. David was full of rage, disparagement, and destructiveness. He replayed the dollhouse scene in which the baby is flushed away, like a piece of "poopie." At the next session, his mother informed me that David had told people in school he wanted to kill himself. David became full of rage at her disclosure. We negotiated that his mother would tell him before she informed me about events. He did not have the right of veto, but he would know her intentions in advance. The next three sessions were marked by anger and attempts to destroy the room. When I limited him, he waited outside the room for his mother.

At David's request, I purchased the toy robot Hot Rod, a transformer who has a smaller son. While playing with this toy, David was able to talk to me openly about his wishes to die and commit suicide. He claimed he always had had these thoughts. He wanted to die so that he would have no thoughts and no feelings. Dad's anger was only part of it; he did not know what the other parts were.

When I explored with David the finality of death, he felt that his death would cause his parents to be angry with themselves (blaming again, this time projected onto the parents). They would berate themselves: "Why didn't we get him everything he wanted? Look what we did." David examined the toy robot I had bought him and showed me Hot Rod's armor. "He hurts more easily than most robots, like bad mosquito bites. All people have these feelings when their life is difficult. His life is very difficult." With great warmth, he thanked me for the toy. Hot Rod was even more than he had expected! I encouraged him to note that he usually expected a lot and that this time he got even more than he had expected. I was sharing with him his happiness at experiencing gratification.

David received my gift without destroying it and shared with me his exquisite sensitivity, which made his life very difficult. He could not forgive his parents for causing him pain, and his suicidal threats were clearly attempts at retribution. He wanted revenge by hurting them in the same way they had hurt him. He wished not to be there for them, just as they were not willing to be there for him.

David phoned me late one evening on his own initiative. He could not sleep, and he was distraught. In his closet were ghosts, spiders, and skeletons. He was having terrible dreams, which he could not talk about. He thought of robots, and then he felt better. I asked him to tell me more about Hot Rod, the robot he had requested for the playroom. He relaxed a bit as he talked about this robot. I asked him to put up a sign directing all his scary friends to my house. "I would like to get to know them," I said. David replied, "I've tried to get to know them since I was a baby; [in great despair] nothing can help, I'll see you Tuesday."

In his play, David named Hot Rod "Boss"; the small boy robot was "Little Guy." The action sounded like a distorted replay of past parent-child interaction from a child's perspective. "Boss" got mad with "Little Guy" and wanted to kill him. He had brought him to life, but now "Boss" wanted "Little Guy" to fall to his death, and he would not bring him back to life. "Little Guy" was not impressed by these threats; he replied to "Boss" that he did not appear as angry as before. "Boss" tried to threaten him again with his omnipotent powers, but "Little Guy" remained unfazed. In the final scene, "Boss" is destroyed by being shattered to bits. He asks "Little Guy" for help, but "Little Guy" refuses.

Underlying David's wish for retribution against his parents was the issue of control. It was a struggle of big against little and of an older person against a younger person. It was a struggle for life against death. The adult's omnipotent powers were altered, giving more strength to the child.

Sharing this scenario with me helped David to feel secure in our relationship, and his fear of intrusion diminished. Construction themes resumed. He began building bridges, leading us to explore themes of support, connection, and fear of falling. David's favorite song to sing as he built was "Home on the Range."

As his anger subsided, David enacted the scene of a policeman falling off a mountain in his play. He died, but significantly, he came back to life; his heart was still beating, and he recuperated. He climbed up the mountain and fell again, but he was not killed and recuperated. David told this story as a monologue and would not listen to any comment from me. He checked with his mother several times during the session. This enactment revealed a theme of practicing, a stage in the development of relationship when the young child practices exploring from and returning to a secure base. Separation was no longer life threatening, and the rules of this policeman were sufficiently lenient to permit rebirth. His mother was being used as a secure base to practice separation. I was the other side of the relationship and provided a mooring for his forays into the wider world.

MOTHER

Mrs. D related that the closer her life approximated fantasy, the better off she felt. She was referring to an idealization of motherhood embodied in the television prototype mother played by Donna Reed, a stabilizing, nurturant figure who baked brownies and provided unconditional love. "That's the role my mother fell short of." Mrs. D's vision was of a home that was tidy, where the kids knew when it was time to take out the garbage and "everything flowed." She was strongly affected by chaos; any kind of mess was upsetting. I inquired, "Is that because it mirrors your internal world?"

Mrs. D described her internal world as constant approach-avoidance, a confusion between going and coming back. This description also fits the practicing stage of emotional development, but Mrs. D's description is tinged with anxiety.

Mrs. D said: "If I am a child, my mother is not there for me. If I am a mother, I need to take the place of my mother. I am not replacing a nobody. I'm booting somebody out. It's not an empty slot I could slide into. There is a forbidding something there. You never see the core; something is radiating from it. You don't see the middle, only the stuff around it. You know a presence is there, but you only see the stuff radiating around."

This radiating, amorphous image paralleled David's sense of a radiating core regarding the continued construction of his pyramid, described later in this chapter. There was an emptiness at the core of the self; it radiated from an intense sense of neediness without a clear image of the other. Mrs. D described her state as shuffling back and forth. She goes back again because she is not sure of what is there, yet she is afraid of it.

MRS. D: There is nothing protecting me there, no one more powerful than me. I need to feel that structure, as much as I want to be autonomous. To be a sun with everything revolving around me would be too much for me; I would fall short and crumble. Omnipotence again, full of power, just by myself, I will undo.

THERAPIST: You reach out and there is nothing there, or you destroy something, so nothing is in its place.

MRS. D: They seem the same to me. There's no one there for me anymore, and I'm supposed to be "it." There's nothing inside, nothing worth revolving around, after all, that can meet what has to be met. It's something I've known for a long time. You use all the stickers for approval, and the channels are not leading to the right place. Instead of going in, they just keep circling. It creates energy, but there's nothing inside and there never was.

THERAPIST: Are we talking about you or your mother?

MRS. D: When I think about Mother, I think of a presence; she never loved herself or us being together. [Later] She is still very dear to me. For myself to replace . . . I don't have that dearness for myself.

THERAPIST: You are talking about replacement, not a sense of connection.

MRS. D: Whatever is there can't still be there if I am in it. I don't know if my wanting to be there is a wish for her not to be there. It's an unacceptable wish, because I keep backing away from it.

Mrs. D expressed her sense of conflict with great urgency. She clearly had thought these thoughts before and had been unable to move forward. Her anxiety was palpable, and her thinking concrete. Relationships were organized rigidly around polarities of presence versus absence and the protected versus the protector. At this point, she needed to deny her own existence as well as the existence of her aggressive wishes and feelings. Her need to insist on the illusion of no existence, whether it be the existence of the therapist, her mother, or her self, is a measure of the extent of her defense against aggressive impulses.

In response to my inquiry later in the session concerning whether she could imagine herself and her mother coexisting in any way, Mrs. D made the following comments:

MRS. D: It would be fine. But I become more like her than I necessarily want to be. The week my daughter was born, my mother spent the week with me. I didn't know if it would be horrible or wonderful. It turned out to be wonderful. We were like one person. I didn't need to tell anyone what to do; that drove her crazy. She would take care of it first, and she was protective of me. She was wonderful. I loved it.

THERAPIST: But it was like you weren't even there.

MRS. D: It was like I had never been there before. Like I was the little child I had never been before. There was no buffer; it was getting too comfortable. I would have loved to have lived it.

THERAPIST: And you are sure you never did.

MRS. D: I don't know. Even on my report card it said "sweet, mature child." And my mother would laugh, "Ha ha ha. What they don't know!"

Mrs. D went on to describe going away to college to try to free herself from dependency on her parents and their critical attitude. Paradoxically, however, they remained a source of good feelings she could not give herself.

DAVID

There was strong evidence in subsequent play sessions that David's connection with me was a source of great pain to him. Despite a trip through time back to the Ice Age, Megaton (a robot) still got hurt.

David said about Megaton, "His self and machine are one. He needs a repair. His connections are hurting." Full-blown tantrums at home and in sessions were triggered by sibling rivalry, envy of my other patients, and a growing wish for exclusivity with me. He continued to draw me closer to him and then reject me, refusing to discuss issues in the play or between us. I attempted to put words to his pain and articulate what he was feeling. I inquired how it felt to be so out of touch with his parents, to be unable to play with his favorite uncle, to have his sister destroy his things. Echoing his earlier comments, I said that he must feel like a piece of junk, something ugly or dead.

Despite my efforts to stabilize his emotional states within the play activity, the next several months were full of upheaval, with continuing bouts of depression and suicidal ideation. The fears had receded, but David could not become stabilized and deteriorated into rage, despair, and self-hatred. At times he would run out of the playroom and, when returned by his mother, would require physical restraint to avoid his hurting himself or someone else.

MOTHER

Mrs. D felt "rattled" by her growing relationship with me. She confided that Dracula, Frankenstein, and witches had always frightened her as a child, just as they frightened David. Many older adults who cared for her reminded her of witches. She used to ask her mother to sit with her, and her mother would become irritated and cackle like a witch. The hump and misshapened head of an older woman filled her with terror.

At this point in treatment, Mrs. D was anxious and fearful about her growing attachment to me. These anxieties were conveyed through a dream. Mrs. D dreamed she had moved into a frightening, big old house with no partitions between the rooms. I was in the dream commenting that she seemed to be making progress. "How could I be making progress when my whole world is falling apart?" she asked, describing the dream to me later. "Maybe there is an upside to this, but you seem to have no idea of the extent of pain I am feeling. It is the general upheaval of my life: the old structures, all the supporting structures were not there. Here I was sitting in the midst of debris and still alive, going through the motions."

I addressed Mrs. D's sense of being alone and encouraged her to allow herself to become aware of my presence. "In having hope, you seem to have taken a new perspective on your life and to be viewing the past as all messed up and painful." Mrs. D admitted that she used to live as a nonreflective person. Now that she has a new lease on life, she said, she does not want to go back.

Mrs. D reflected again on David's early infancy. She felt calm then, and she had never felt more competent. It all changed when David started to talk and became resistant. She explained to me in an urgent tone, "I couldn't deal with his defiance. I never confronted *my* parents. It was like he had the rights of royalty. When challenged by a 2-year-old child, I became shook up . . . I never had time for myself . . . I needed some time and space . . . he didn't blend in with other kids. They made the transition more easily; he was clinging. He started to demand more than I wanted to give" [feelings she also had about her marriage].

Everything had been so ritualized in her family of origin that Mrs. D was upset when David did not follow the rules or seemed to be getting out of control. Seeing David as "chaotic," she became frightened of him. Her parents had been strict about rules, defending them as "the way children know you love them." To the contrary, Mrs. D perceived their love as conditional and could not trust them sufficiently to diverge from their clear expectations.

Mrs. D emphatically stated, "As a child, I never took risks. I knew I had almost died from pneumonia at 22 months, which precipitated my father's first nervous breakdown. Then I developed bronchitis and had a T&A, all before age 2. I remember the anesthesia, all the white coats. They looked like a spider, with many legs, that grabbed me and put me under. I didn't stop throwing up at the sight of white coats until I was 4 years old." This traumatic experience of being overwhelmed was encoded in eidetic terms. Mrs. D experienced the untransformed terror of a young child as she recounted her ordeal.

Perhaps it was because these overwhelming, early feelings were condensed in the memory of a life-threatening illness that Mrs. D always associated self-assertion with a threat to her life. She felt she still could not confront people and resorted instead to childish whining. She was easily rattled when David felt rattled. Mrs. D continued, "I can be sucked into another's reality. I lose myself. We both drown together." Clearly, despite her anxiety and pain, Mrs. D had made strides toward feeling more secure. She could now perceive and describe the states of disorganization and disintegration she experienced. She was using me as an auxiliary ego to view and review her past. As she described it, she could not tolerate any mistakes. "One false move, and I will drop the bundle, or I will fall, I will crumble." Because there are no playful illusions of the other person, there are only rigidly organized, idealized, or demonic fantasied relations. Because of these rigidities, Mrs. D never "gets on the road" to object constancy, and she remained mired in her own ambivalence.

DAVID

David had been in treatment almost 12 months when, after a vacation in Mexico, he constructed a pyramid that had "more on the inside than the outside." It had trapdoors that opened and "vines that supported you." Time is warped. His play portrayed a series of deficient relationships from his past: "Egyptians made pyramids for cities, so in the future, things in the ancient world would be preserved. They kept most people out of them; only some people knew about the inside. The mummies don't need anything to survive; they are dead. They can survive famine; they can survive anything. Giant flowers that consume humans—the flowers do not have brains and can eat things which will destroy it. In contrast, the cobras can fight back and are deadly. Like we have tears, they have poison; like tears they come out through their eyes; they do it for protection."

He continued to berate me: "The cobras know what they are doing, they have a brain, like me—not like you." David went on to describe the time warp: "Something created by someone totally by accident, and when that happens the accident of time is that severe that it's a time warp. It brings glory to the people who were first to do it and changes time. It changes time totally. Something happens that is not supposed to happen until the future. They not only change their future, they live something of themselves and of other people."

The work on the pyramid continued for several weeks. It became transformed into a fortress totally made for war. The fortress was to defend the city, which David described as awesome and his own creation. Nuclear bombs intended to protect the city exploded. David invented a power core of radiation for the city and a series of shields to protect the inhabitants from this superintense source of energy. (This image parallels his mother's dream about a radiating core.) Only by "dismantling" the center of the generator could the power core be destroyed. David spent considerable time elaborating types of energy that arose from the power source and describing how the inhabitants could lose energy and become tired. He invented people with no feelings, who could be turned on and off.

Clearly the pyramid-fortress-city construction was an important new effort to communicate his sense of past relationships. The pyramid conveyed David's inner experience of "nonaliveness," with people he experienced as inanimate. This inner world was kept dormant through detachment. He identified with these characters, who peopled a world where relationship implies mutual destruction. The cobra betrays David's longings to merge. David had to defend himself against being consumed, so he created a dangerous phallic figure to deal with these threatening longings. The revival of this inner conflict brings with it an intensification of longings and fear of merger, and then an accident occurs: Time becomes warped, and he is trapped in the struggles of others and forced into the future before his time, stuck and unable to move away and back into normal perspective.

David was a child caught in intergenerational conflict, his experiences warped as they reflected emotions that intruded on him too early and belonged to another time and place. No guilt was ascribed here; no one was held responsible. He was simply the helpless victim of an accidental mishap, and he was trapped in unreality. At this juncture, David's play activity was restitution. He was restoring fragments of his experience as he remembered it. The therapist was a supportive spectator as he worked in her presence.

In sum, the beginning phase of treatment for both parent and child dealt with themes of grandiosity and inadequacy, loneliness and alienation, and murderous rage and suicidal ideation. Mrs. D was the parentified child, who fulfilled the wishes of her parents. David represented the child of rejection, who was remote and detached from his parents. The narrative style of both patients was highly ideational and verbal. Everyday issues were not prominent in the beginning phase. Projective reality and the world of fantasy were the interior arenas within which therapeutic action took place. The narcissistic defenses filtered out everyday concerns and focused attention on the internal representational world. Learning the metaphors of parent and child provided me an opening for communication. This heightened intensity of fantasies was a feature of the pathology common to parent and child.

Parent-child interaction can be a meaningful and joyful duet of mutuality and reciprocity. If the child has had no input into interactions, there is no freedom for the child to discover the parents by finding them in surprising places. The child was denied the opportunity to experience the variability of his perceptions in a playful way. Curiosity was compromised, and the child turned inward for sustenance, having literally fed on his own inner world, experienced as fantasies. The rigid quality of these imaginings paralleled the rigidity of parental attitudes. It stifled creativity and the possibility for further discovery. Both David and Mrs. D were absorbed in fantasy, the result of constricting emotional environments. The middle phase of treatment continued exploration and elaboration of these parallel and shared fantasies. The emphasis on ideation gradually underwent modification, along with shifts in interpersonal relationships.

CHAPTER 6

David: A Case of Narcissistic Personality Disorder (Part II)

MIDDLE PHASE OF TREATMENT: IN SEARCH OF RELATIONSHIP—DIFFERENTIATION AND REBIRTH

THE TRANSITION TO the middle phase of treatment was marked by diminution in tension between David and Mrs. D. She was better able to set effective limits for both of her children and to see beyond the role of motherhood. David's preoccupations broadened to include everyday interests and friendships. Mrs. D's sense of isolation diminished. Her heavy burden of responsibilities within the home lightened somewhat. She became hopeful for her son's recovery. David's grandiosity diminished, and specific phobias developed. He voiced complaints and worries about his physical health. Pervasive anxiety and unrealistic thinking were obvious only at times of stress. David became able to spend time in his room alone and often was engrossed in independent activities. In treatment, he began the process of reorganization of his sense of identity through new self-awareness and the creation of personal narrative.

During the middle phase of treatment, Mrs. D began to sort out her feelings about parenthood on three levels: her parents to her, herself to herself, and herself to her children. Using the therapeutic relationship, she increasingly was able to articulate a difference between a biological baby of her own and her own "inner" baby. This was a creative and productive period of her life. She finished graduate studies and qualified for an excellent professional position. Forging new connections brought renewed awareness of the passage of time, accompanied by sadness as well as the emergence of positive feelings about herself. Having her achievements recognized, she increasingly was able to repress her infantile longings and find satisfaction in an emergent sense of professional identity and calmer family relationships.

DAVID

David's grandiosity began to soften, and he developed specific phobias. Although David was easier to manage at home, his fears could be intense and disturbing. David became greatly frightened of a new character, an intruder named Ralph. He described him to me as very bright, not likable, and not a bum. "Nobody knows him except me." A new conversational tone and openness indicated that David was turning to me for a new perspective on his terror. He felt Ralph was trying to intrude and kill him.

THERAPIST: You seem to feel you've done something so terrible you deserve to die.

DAVID: I don't feel that; I just feel Ralph is trying to kill me.

THERAPIST: Maybe the only way you can talk about your feelings is to have a Ralph to talk about, and so you created him with your imagination.

DAVID: Maybe I did, but not intentionally, definitely not. It happened totally by accident.

THERAPIST: Sometimes your feelings inside are so terrifying, perhaps you could change Ralph.

DAVID: One part of me creates Ralph; it is a stupid part of me I could not control. I did not know it would pain impact on me. Since it is part of me, it would also have a pain impact. Once they [the aliens] create something, only they can take it away. Actually, you know what it is? It is a punishment on them.

Ralph was created by the powerful aliens. He seemed to represent a frightening part of David created by his parents. Only they could remove it. David felt overwhelmed by this introject he could not control and fell into a disintegrated state in which his synthetic functioning was rendered out of commission. The aliens took over, and he was helpless. However, Ralph was empowered to take revenge against the parents and punish them.

THERAPIST: Perhaps you feel these aliens are stupid and out of control. They hurt you without meaning to hurt you. You seem to understand these aliens. They are pained when they punish you.

DAVID: They are trembling. It's like I'm a universe of feelings. So if I'm afraid, what happens is, those feelings are getting shook like an earthquake—trembling and trembling. The bad feelings that created Ralph are just saying their prayers; they hope they won't die. It's a lot like another thing I suffer from most lately—stress. Too much pressure is not good. With too much pressure they just blow up, all those feelings, except the universe can always rebuild itself with the same people.

David referred to his problem with stress in a mature tone. His feelings trembled and threatened the universe, putting his humanity under great pressure. David's preoccupation with vampires returned, and he rebuilt his fortress. He claimed his imagination had different sides: It was not a war. One side created something, and the other side did not know how it would impact on him. David was experiencing a split within himself. In David's narrative, he described how this schism within him threatened his psychological survival. The description of Ralph was the beginning of a self-narrative (Gergen & Gergen, 1983) that was focused exclusively on an internal world representing a set of experienced life events.

DAVID: If they [the aliens] knew he would hurt and upset me, they would never have created him. I can't say to them, "Go chase the guy away."

THERAPIST: They created him.

DAVID: He's their baby.

David seemed to be referring here to the grandiose part of his infant self. We considered briefly whether Ralph could become his friend, and David was uncertain. He then felt he understood something helpful.

DAVID: It's impossible to have bad things happen to him unless he is forgotten. Ralph is a thought, and a thought can escape anything. Ralph is a thought I did not want to make up totally. I did not want to make up Ralph. I did not say, "I'm going to make up Ralph. I'm going to make up someone to haunt me every night." That's not the way it goes.

THERAPIST: Ralph is a thought that stays with you all the time, but the vampires come and go.

DAVID: I can understand Ralph being there, but vampires? That's weird! Ralph used to come every night. I usually don't see him anymore.

THERAPIST: You used to see him more often?

DAVID: Yeah. You bet.

THERAPIST: Ralph and vampires are ideas that come from inside you.

DAVID: That I can't help . . . really.

THERAPIST: One way I might help you is to get to know these characters better. Here's my thought. You may not believe it, but someday you and I may make a strong enough team together to approach these people in your mind and understand them. Then they won't be so frightening.

DAVID: Saralea, that was a stupid idea, because for you to get to know them better, then they'd know me better, they'd know my weaknesses.

THERAPIST: You mean if I get to know them, then it will make you weaker?

DAVID: Exactly. Whew, finally you are getting somewhere!

David was greatly frightened of diminishing the frightening images in his imagination. If he did not have these powerful, fearful ideas, people would know him for the weak, helpless person he really was.

THERAPIST: But David, the ideas come from inside you. I'm on the outside, separate from the ideas. If I know more about them, it will help us. If they get weaker, will you get weaker too?

DAVID: Finally you're getting somewhere. If they know about me, then I'll be giving myself away. It's like a scene in a battle. You don't want the enemy to know about you; you want to know about the enemy. The thoughts are the enemy.

Here David seemed to indicate he was hiding and protecting something, something he feared to disclose to me and to the aliens. The powerful omnipotent thoughts were the source of his intense fearfulness. Yet he could not give them up and hope to survive. He had to remain constantly on guard against his enemy from within.

THERAPIST: Where do I fit in this? I'm not in the battle.

DAVID: You don't have to be in the battle. You're just like a referee. He doesn't belong to any side. He refs the game—says who wins and loses.

THERAPIST: Who are the two sides?

DAVID: Me and the Ideas.

David wanted me to be the referee to settle the battle between himself and the ideas. In this metaphor, there was a clear delineation between the grandiose self and the normal self, with a sense of conflict between them. This was an either-or formulation that reflected David's upbringing in which, as an infant, he had served as an object for his parents' idealization. David created Ralph to protect himself from paranoid feelings. He was in need of protection from his own frightening ideas. When I understood this, I commented that he seemed to be longing for a referee. This referee was clearly an auxiliary ego. David described a referee as someone higher than the others, who settles disagreements and does not cheat.

I said to him, "It's like there are two boxers in a ring. I think you are scared inside because the two parts are going to cause a lot of hurt, and you are looking to me to see no one gets hurt. Wars are settled by understanding; war gets out of control when you don't understand. Right now, it's hard for you to understand these ideas. Maybe someday we can gradually build up hope to our side."

I was previewing for David the possibility of conflict resolution in the future. At the time, his personal narrative was conceived around a split framework that could depict only conflict. This inner conflict reflected conflicted interpersonal relationships within the family as well as conflicted expectations of him. I was encouraged to learn of the hidden self that could engage in dialogue with the unmodified, omnipotent self of infancy.

Phobias emerged again in relationship to this vulnerable sense of "me" that David could now share and wanted to protect. David's new capacity for differentiation of self from infantile-self reflected his experience with me in the therapeutic relationship. His fears were specific to persons outside himself who threatened him; the fears targeted emerging aspects of himself that were threatening as well. These personifications offered me a means of connecting to David's inner thoughts and feelings in a direct and lively manner. The more specific and vivid his fears became in his imagination, the more possible it was to forge a connection to his hidden wishes. When we examined together the wishes underlying his fears, they could be experienced as benign. By enabling David to observe his parent also in the role of patient, simultaneous treatment facilitated self-observation. In simultaneous treatment, this parallel process was in the service of individuation instead of pathological replication.

MOTHER

Mrs. D developed a set of sadomasochistic fantasies organized around the notion of victim. These images paralleled David's fears of Ralph, "the intruder." When David succeeded in terrifying his mother, he won a conflict of wills, and she became as helpless and vulnerable as a young child. David used his capacity to evoke fear to control her. These situations led to almost constant efforts on David's part to gain omnipotent power and reverse roles, leaving him with no source for security outside himself. These associations were a further elaboration of Mrs. D's perceptions of herself as having no one to depend on for safety and strength. The fluidity and constancy of this polarized push-pull conflict seemed to both therapist and parent to be the source of parent-child states of terror.

Mrs. D said, "Maybe he's my Ralph. He's so oppositional, he gets you to the point where you want to kill him. Increasingly I feel cold rage, not terror. I was revolted; 'Don't turn it on and off and control me that way.' I wanted him not to be there."

Mrs. D was getting closer to the recognition of her own "killer" feelings. Calling David "her Ralph," she meant to convey that he could become the embodiment of all the hatred and horrible feelings she feared. She was surprised by her own fury, and her eyes filled with tears as she realized that she was never able to allow David to make amends for his actions; she wanted only revenge. Mrs. D felt she had wanted to kill her "baby" (David). She did not want him to be so different, so ill.

Mrs. D: I want a healthy baby. That's what my mother used to say about me. I was so hard for my mother. She was such a rigid, methodical person, she could do no wrong. When she was cross, I used to think of her as a witch. She would say, "I can see you are sick. I can tell when nobody else can."

Therapist: She seemed to know before you knew.

Mrs. D did not want to see the part of herself she perceived as sick, the baby part. I said, "These might not be sick feelings at all, just feelings a normal baby has when it yearns for its mother. As long as the baby is called 'sick,' it can be outside of who you are, rather than just another aspect of you."

In these comments, I was reflecting on the early failure of empathic relationship that resulted in a split within Mrs. D's experience of self. The rejection of infantile feelings as sick feelings reflected her early assumption of pseudomaturity in the role of parentified child. As our alliance strengthened, Mrs. D assumed active participation in her own treatment. She began transcribing her dreams and sharing them with me, often including her associations. She recently had passed her professional examination and was feeling like a "new person." She was holding her own with David and had been able to push away her mother's devaluing comments.

Mrs. D recounted a dream that contained a personal narrative of her own psychological gestation and birth. She was confused at first concerning whose story she was telling, hers or David's. She identified the story as her own because of the associated affects experienced. Thus her sense of self was emerging linked with specific feeling states rather than polarized images. In this dream, Mrs. D was on vacation and standing in line at a buffet breakfast:

"Like a farmer's market. I chose an egg, still with the shell on it. I lifted it out of the basket, and it felt funny. It was a cracked-open egg, with a half-born baby chick. It had two eyes; it wasn't fuzzy; it was too small for that, with no beak. I discarded it. I was very sad rather than disgusted. I wasn't really pained by it. I was mourning this baby chick. It pulled at me. It reminded me of children who are not right, discarding children who are not right. Was the chick David, or was it me? I see him as my stigmatized child. The baby was half-formed, which connects up with premature. I was premature birth weight. The chick had no beak; I did not talk; I never said what I wanted. I wish I knew who the chick was . . . probably would go with David, still not good enough. The role of the mother is to be there, to accept, not to reject. I clearly couldn't close the egg up again and let it grow. It was a fait accompli. The chick in the dream is probably me. No beak equals no pecker equals a baby girl. Not yet ready to be born equals a preemie equals I was premature in birth weight.

"You mentioned last week you thought I was grieving for the baby in me, who never had a chance to be. That would seem to fit the dream. If the baby were David, and I had to reject him because I had no hope for his recovery, I think the dream would have left me with a terrible feeling of despair rather than the ones of resignation and melancholy. Despair is a pervasive feeling but not as intense as those this dream left me with."

Mrs. D wondered about the chick. "Why was it not nurtured?" The only way she could get her mother's attention was to be sick. She remembered her mother's crying, "I don't know what to do for her." "That's one of the times I felt my mother's love for me, instead of her sense of duty, the only time she related to me humanly. I could let my armor down and feel a surge of compassion for my mother. I never felt my mother wanted to swallow me—the egg that wasn't eaten. But I know she felt that connection, devotion. I used to cry a lot. My father told me, 'We were not unaware. We just didn't know where to begin to help you.'"

This dream afforded Mrs. D a beginning rapprochement with her parents. It marked a new therapeutic beginning as well as a new self-awareness in which she differentiated herself from her perceptions of infantile David.

DAVID

For the next several months in both the play activity and in conversations, David shared his deep sense of loneliness and longing for contact. In David's imaginary world, Ralph died climbing up a ladder, and Dracula reappeared as well as the eerie stones of Stonehenge. He reached out to me through his play to share his need for connection with another person and to share human feelings. We talked about how Dracula was a brilliant man who dealt with his loneliness by imagining things.

I said, "People sooner or later need other people. If you hold these feelings back, they pop out all over. Dracula was such a lonely man, at night he would go out and bite beautiful women in the neck. He couldn't just sit and talk about his feelings."

David began to enjoy his peers. At home, family conflicts intensified, and the marital differences seemed to be irreconcilable. At this juncture, David's father requested a referral from me for his own treatment.

Perhaps because of the difficulties at home, David became unsettled and his fears intensified. He called me at night for comfort. Yet in sessions he maintained his distance. In place of Dracula, a skeleton appeared to frighten him, turning up when David least expected him. He said, "You look in the mirror and you see something behind you."

In those scary moments, the familiar image of the therapist became frightening, and David refused to listen to interpretations. He continued long monologues about struggles between good and evil. Following these battles, the aliens returned—hundreds of them, and they would not go away. In his play, his toys became very important to him. He wanted to reserve certain of the robot figures and the Lego constructions exclusively for himself. The toys seemed to have a life of their own, and they filled a void that words could not yet reach. The toys were under his control and responded to his omnipotent thoughts and feelings.

The play sequence that began with paranoia and fear of intrusion in the image of Ralph reached its climax in a session that revealed his own unique family romance fantasy of rejection and alienation. Underlying this fantasy were traumatic disappointment in his parents and an idealization of otherworldly beings. This fantasied account of his origins reflected progress in organizing his emotional life around our therapeutic relationship by creating a cohesive sense of personal history. It also paralleled the description by Mrs. D of the baby chick in the cracked egg; significantly, both were creating their own saga of origins, exploring conception, gestation, and birth.

DAVID: About the aliens—they come from me, from my imagination. They don't represent anything.

THERAPIST: What does alien mean?

DAVID: Alien to me means a being from a different planet; it also means illegal entry.

THERAPIST: Someone that doesn't belong.

DAVID: I don't feel part of my family. I do feel loved. I don't feel like I am really part of the family—they didn't have me, somebody else did who I don't know.

THERAPIST: You must feel very different.

DAVID: Much.

THERAPIST: That "much" must hurt a lot.

DAVID: It's a little frightening, but that is all.

THERAPIST: Do you feel like you don't belong?

DAVID: I feel like I belong with somebody, maybe human, maybe not human.

THERAPIST: A part of you feels . . .

DAVID: Not human.

THERAPIST: Like a robot?

DAVID: Nothing that people know now. I feel myself I am like an alien. Jason got suspended. He is not allowed to go to school.

THERAPIST: It's like saying you are not part of the group. We do not want you here.

DAVID: He was disrespectful to Ms. Green. He said shut up to her. Usually the reason I have these alien fears is sometimes I think the aliens want to bring me back, and I don't want to go. I don't even know them. They left me here. There was a war, and they scattered people all around the star system and galaxies. When I see stars blinking on and off, I think that is their aircraft waiting and watching me, figuring out how to get me.

David's narrative of personal origins placed him outside the human domain. He belonged to an alien culture that existed in space and had evolved out of battle. David was powerless in the face of these alien creatures he knew were the product of his imagination. It was a story of a mental birth; he was conceived by ideas and now was at their mercy. He feared they would come to retrieve him and kidnap him back into space. David's fearfulness belied the nonlinear process of treatment. Although he had become more self-aware, because of the split in his self structure, he was also more aware of the forces organized against him. In contrast to his mother's fantasy organized around affect states, David's experience was dominated by the characterization of fearful images. In his personal narrative, there was a pervasive mood of doom and inevitability.

MOTHER

As Mrs. D sought out new colleagues and friends and renewed family ties, she suffered from fears of exposure. She did not want to let others see the bizarre aspects of herself. She yearned for connectedness, but desired to go back. This was another instance within the treatment of mother and son of doing and undoing, progression and regression, going forward and then backward. Each cycle seemed to bring about a more authentic expression of her feelings. The following excerpt from a treatment session integrates infantile longings for admiration and love with mature collegial acceptance:

"I want to go back to where I'm the fair-haired child, where I am perceived as special and I am in situations where I really feel I am special. When I'm out of them, I don't carry the specialness with me. I don't mean distinct specialness, where I'm set apart. I don't want my specialness to alienate me from people. My specialness is where something can be expressed to me, and I can convert that into love. For example, the faculty don't love me, they accept me as equal. I could sit with them, and they would value my input. I know they look at me differently. I know it's not love, but I can equate it with that. I really don't want to be loved for weakness. I want to be loved for strength. And yet I seek their approval. [I want them to] pat me on the head rather than shake hands, although I always shake hands. I am always appropriate. It's always difficult for me to express my feelings so I can encapsulate it into a package; my feelings are so intense. I don't see that as healthy."

Mrs. D had a strong desire to be an individual in her own right, but it was still extremely painful for her to exist autonomously. She was using therapy to grow and to confront not having been helped by her parents to individuate as a child.

David reminded Mrs. D of the "bizarre" parts of herself she did not like. She wanted to hide and not be connected to him at all, but it was no longer possible for her to do this, and she feared exposure; everyone would be aware of those parts of her that she tried so desperately to hide. She had always defined herself in terms of the expectations of others and lacked a sustaining core. She felt like a cold-blooded animal; whatever environment she was in, she took on that self-concept. She was full of self-recrimination and guilt. Harshly blaming herself, she referred to David as representing her failures. Mrs. D felt she had not fulfilled her mother's expectations. As a teenager, she was obese, and she was never athletic as her mother had been. Despite her mother's best efforts, she had made her feel like a failure. Mrs. D's feelings of guilt and self-recrimination were projected onto David, who in a parallel fashion had not fulfilled her expectations.

As Mrs. D increasingly was able to disclose in treatment, she gained the confidence she needed to assert her own wishes in her marital relationship. Disclosure was linked to positioning within the family. She experienced this "disloyalty" as a shell that was cracking; the shell of isolation that could no longer contain her. In her dream, she had selected the egg that was cracking and found that it wasn't "just right." It was fragile, "like having yourself on the line, an inner fanatic wanting everything perfect, not being able to handle anything going wrong."

Mrs. D's growing desire for relationship, coupled with a terror of disclosure, was a continuing theme for several months. She was particularly fearful of the dependent side of a relationship, favoring "doling out, rather than the recipient role." Her dilemma was expressed in a dream she had had several months previously but "forgotten" until this time.

She said, with some embarrassment, "It involves you. I was either here with David or on my own, and I forgot something and came back to retrieve it. I wanted to come here, retrieve it, and leave as inconspicuously as possible. I was upset at having to retrieve it and felt like an interloper. I couldn't do it inconspicuously; your family was in the garden. You weren't there, but all the trappings were there of your family life. You were in the midst of doing something that had nothing to do with me. You weren't even there, unless [with puzzlement] you totally ignored me. I was getting it on my time, not our shared time. I felt terrible having to go through this. If I could have tunneled . . . I felt awful, humiliated . . . exposed."

The dream was Mrs. D's way of reaching out to me; it was a transition into sharing more intimate feelings of connectedness. As usual, she returned to a place she had been, this time to retrieve "something," a dream she had "forgotten." This dream was essential to the transference and found her reworking several themes at once: longings for intimacy and exclusivity, wanting to have more than her share, feelings of humiliation, being in the wrong place, the threat of disclosure, and the intrusion into my privacy.

The themes in Mrs. D's personal narrative were becoming better integrated as Mrs. D recognized boundaries and became aware of her desires. It is useful to compare this dream with Mrs. D's early dream of the teacher-therapist who intruded and robbed but, surprisingly, was not ashamed when confronted. Mrs. D had progressed in her capacity to accept these longings for closeness as her own.

At about this time, a parallel event occurred in David's dreams. He dreamed that the aliens were having a picnic. They were no longer simply robots but required sustenance and nurturance for survival. This rescripting of the aliens as having redeeming human features was noted by me. I decided to remember this benign transformation for future interpretive work.

Mrs. D's style of self-expression continued to be indirect, through metaphor. Only infrequently would feelings be expressed more directly, such as the exuberance she felt on achieving her professional position. More complex feelings of disappointment and personal injury toward herself and others would take longer to reach. She gradually was gaining a capacity to be alone in my presence. (David had acquired that ability sometime earlier.) She was able to understand that our perceptions of things could be different. This difference often caused intense hatred when I did not agree with her.

Feelings of hatred were particularly intense when we were dealing with her parental role and responsibilities. She needed to accept the illusion of herself as a competent and loving parent. In a paradoxical way, if she could not be perceived in this way, she felt like a nobody, "like nothing at all." The experience within the therapeutic relationship was beginning to help her to realize the limitations of her personal omnipotence and accept the separateness of the therapist. The cost of these gains seemed at times life threatening, and as rigid boundaries gave way, the experience was one of radical transformation. Gradually it seemed more probable that what would emerge would not be a retraumatizing experience with the therapist as the dreaded "dead" or "absent" parent but transformation of herself into a real and genuine person.

DAVID

Six weeks following the family romance fantasy play, I received a phone call from Mrs. D. They had had new kitchen chairs delivered and had put the old ones in the garage. David had become upset and was crying. He felt the inanimate chairs had life and were dying. It took him several hours to resolve his dilemma: "I know they are not living, or real. But in my mind, they are." His mother was threatened by his experience of loss but welcomed his confidence in a dignified way and dealt with the situation with restraint.

A few days later, David called in great excitement. He reported having seen three aliens, who arrived on a flying saucer to abduct people when they were alone. He was quite anxious and gave a detailed report of the appearance of the spacecraft and of the intruders. He had nothing to hold onto to comfort himself and help him feel secure. He reported being unable to feel safe since he was very little.

When he came to session, David did not want to talk about the aliens but about the chairs. He said they had nothing to do with the alien feelings. He described the chairs as made out of metal and orange vinyl. He did not talk to the chairs, but he could "sort of just tell how they were feeling." He would think a message, and they would know it. He felt sad and thought they would miss him. They would be unable to sleep at night because they missed him.

DAVID: Nobody thinks of the chairs as people, and therefore that makes them dead. As long as their owners think of them as people, they will live lively lives. But most people don't think of chairs as people.

THERAPIST: David, you have a special understanding about these chairs that makes them live. You must miss them very much. [David agrees.] This sadness over something lost must be a new feeling for you.

DAVID: It probably is, and it probably isn't, maybe, maybe.

THERAPIST: The chairs hold memories for you.

David remembered how the chairs had held him, as his parents had held him: They were therefore part human and part not.

THERAPIST: These seem to be two sides of you—the human side and the nonhuman side. Maybe when someone lets the aliens in, they are testing you to see if you are human.

DAVID [rejecting this suggestion]: No, they are testing to see if I have a brain. They wouldn't want to go for feelings. All they want to do is to see if the humans are less powerful than themselves, and the planet earth is ripe for taking.

At this point, David interrupted the dialogue and began his play activity; again, it was a battle. I interpreted: "The bad guys are lonely, isolated humans, with something inside them that makes them not want to be alone. The good guys are aliens trying to enter into a walled-off area." This interpretation was based on David's earlier observation that aliens could be hungry. I was reversing roles in the script, making the aliens good guys and giving them a humanizing purpose. David volunteered that the bad guys were weaker than the good guys in this case. David could not trust the good guys (or the therapist) quite yet and had the aliens appoint a leader who created destructive evil droids who plotted to kill him. As his construction play and monologue continued, it became clear that the city he built was inhabited by humans who were related and lived as a group. The humans then banded together to kill the evil droids.

During the next several months, David was often extremely anxious over the warring forces within him. He would experience himself as having two sides, with one wanting to kill off the other. His vivid imagination created many aliens and good guys, both part of himself. I supported him by observing that a new part of him seemed to want to come to life. The aliens wanted to come in and become some part of him. At times he was extremely threatened by our closeness and again berated me as "stupid and dumb," calling me always by my first name.

Letting the aliens "inside" could still be terrifying, and the boundaries between everyday reality and projective reality were often compromised. I worked to diminish the alien, weird experience of his intense longings. My purpose was to propose outlines for a new structural framework that could include these parts of his personality as benign and human. This empathic understanding was aimed at lessening his anxiety and enabling integration to occur.

Vampires reappeared in David's fantasies, and this time he felt he was turning into a vampire (an involuntary transformation), a thing that could be killed only by a stake in the heart or by going out into the sunlight. This was a startling instance of identification with the aggressor, a defense used against fear and anxiety in which the person believes he has become what he fears the most. The purpose of my interpretation was to place the vampire feelings within an understandable human context. This time it was not a split within his personality; he felt he was being transformed in his entirety. I commented slowly and at length, as he appeared receptive:

"It is only natural that you enjoy our time together and want to take me inside you. Wanting to eat something you like is very natural, and in a way we are all vampires. We are always imagining people we like inside of us. You seem to need to make this into something terrible, but in the realm of imagination, we can all be vampires. We should be; it helps us get good feelings. There is something about being in the warmth of the sunshine that helps us to open our hearts to other people. You are so afraid that if you open up your heart you will die, and so you have to keep your feelings a secret."

In his dialogues with me, David frequently mentioned real worries about life at home and with his peers. At these times, he seemed increasingly able to limit his instinctual wishes and fears and reinvest them in daily pursuits. He worried that because his parents often fought, they might be getting a divorce. He seemed oriented to my upcoming vacation and inquired where I was going. He confided to me some plans he had for moneymaking projects with his friends. He expressed a strong desire to be better and free of fears. David wished that his father spent more time with him and that he, David, did not fight so much with his sister. He talked about how much he missed his extended family and made plans for a family reunion.

MOTHER

One of the earliest indications of a positive outcome to Mrs. D's increased activity was her recognition that someone else could care for her child; correspondingly, she gained the insight that she could get help from others. Simultaneous treatment, in which insights obtained in the parent role can be applied freely to the self, played a role in facilitating these understandings that were conveyed in a dream.

"In the dream," she said, "I am commenting to my husband about the dream; I see myself in the dream, but I am not a participant. In this dream you were me—the nurturing Mommy—wearing a robe like mine, but it was your own, you didn't take mine. I had come over to comfort David and offered to sleep with him. He said no, he would like to sleep by himself. He wanted his own space; he'd rather sleep alone. I/you didn't feel rejected: 'It's okay if I can't comfort you in that way.'"

The I/you confabulation in the dream was an example of primary identification (Sandler, 1993). It was not a confused percept; rather it was an early form of empathy, in which roles easily can be reversed, "where I am you and you are me." This twinning was in the service of identity formation. When reversibility in roles was experienced as frightening in Mrs. D's past (for example, I/you equals I/spider), pathological defenses were used, such as splitting, to insert a barrier between herself and the other person. Instead of a flexible growth-producing process, a constricted and rigid set of maladaptive defenses was used to ensure security. The I/you percept was encouraging in that it indicated that our therapeutic alliance and empathic under-standing of each other were contributing to growth.

The second part of the dream had a broader focus: "My home was overrun by teachers; it was much larger. We were having a pajama party. I commented to my husband, 'There's Ms. . . . and Ms. . . . ' I acknowledged these were important people in my children's lives other than me. It was okay, no remorse, no regret. I would have antic-ipated those feelings seeing you in David's bed. There was no partic-ular satisfaction when he rejected you. It was alright."

The transference in Mrs. D's case had many layers. Because simul-taneous treatment dealt with both parent and child, the therapist evoked direct empathic responses from her patient emanating from all stages in the life cycle. The therapist was experienced by her patient in diverse patterns of relationship. The variety of empathic responses to the therapist resulted not only in diverse identifications, but also, even more important, in a flexible process of identification. The to-and-fro, back-and-forth motion to mutuality was restored.

Once restored, this process generalized to other caregivers, providing the background of trust and security so lacking in Mrs. D's history. It is interesting that acceptance or rejection by the child was not an issue for Mrs. D. Outcome was no longer important, because there was newly found comfort in the process of relating.

In addition, Mrs. D clearly had made the transition to the triadic level of relationship and was no longer tied to exclusive one-to-one relationships. She now realized she could get help from others and did not have to be isolated. Her emotional and social activity had loosened up the rigid dyadic focus of her relationships.

DAVID

The middle phase of David's treatment drew to a close as the bad guys lost to the good guys and the sadomasochistic fantasies were replaced by a retelling of the myth of Medusa, which he was studying in school. David used this myth to begin to deal with triadic issues, specifically his experience of oedipal victory and the dangers posed by that triumph. He began to complain of severe headaches, which he attributed to guilt feelings because he was not completing his work. His mother had confronted him the night before about his lack of organization and then had called me, feeling guilty about the "terrible" blowout. "Although I was aware I was hurting his feelings, I could not stop." In fact, from David's perspective, her anger seemed to validate that he had committed a terrible act.

This is the Medusa myth, according to David: "There is a guy named King Apollo, who had a daughter named DeDe. When DeDe was born, Apollo went to the oracle and asked, 'What is the future of my child?' 'The child will bear a son, and the son will kill you," said the oracle. So King Apollo locked DeDe up in his chambers. Zeus looks her over and has a baby with her. King Apollo takes a very big chest, puts DeDe and her son into the trunk, and throws them into the sea. He means for them to die. They don't die—they get washed ashore in another kingdom, and a fisherman finds them and opens up the trunk. He and his wife adopt DeDe's son and let DeDe live there. When Dede's kid grows older, the king of the island asks, 'Who lives there?' 'My mother.' 'Is there a father?' 'No.' Dede's kid gets invited to a party. He did not know he had to bring a gift for the king. He said he would do anything the king would want. The king asked DeDe's child to bring him the head of Medusa. 'If you look at her, you turn to stone. There are snakes in her hair that spit out venom; if one bites you, you die.' DeDe's child sets out to get the head of Medusa. He gets Medusa's head with the help of the gods. He makes the head into an island and by mistake hits King Apollo with a discus. It's an accident."

The Medusa story was told in a whimsical way, with good humor. David protested that the headaches were not because he was scared: "It's schoolwork, and work alone. The book [of Medusa] is not scary, it is funny." He was angry with me, insisting that it was not the book that was causing him problems, but the work. He demanded to end the session (it was time to go) because he had homework to do. He would call me if he needed me.

In his rendition of the Medusa myth, it was clear David was making strides toward triadic relationships. He had defeated the oral sadistic mother and the preoedipal father in an effort to become his own person. He seemed fearful of success, however, and would not recognize his own competence. Schoolwork was laden with latent issues of guilt and fear of success. In the transference relationship, he was caught in a rapprochement dilemma: He did not want to go too far away from the therapist and become lonely, but getting too close could transform him to stone.

THE ENDING PHASE OF TREATMENT: IN SEARCH OF RELATIONSHIP—DISCOVERY OF THE SELF AND RECOGNITION OF THE OTHER

Two years had passed since the beginning of treatment. Both partners in the dyad were experiencing new ease in relationships with each other and others as well as an inner security. Gains gradually were consolidated, and mother and child reached beyond the dyad with increased self-awareness to group involvement and individual pursuits. Mrs. D indicated a desire to continue to work with me. David proceeded to work toward the goal of ending treatment.

DAVID

The ending phase of treatment continued the theme of mythology, often involving Greek characters or, alternatively, current powerful political personalities. These grand-scale dramas were the vicissitudes of David's grandiosity told with good humor and charm. They were integrated stories, affording me new insight into David's perspective on family relationships. In telling me these tales, often experienced as dreams, David took an increasingly active role in defining his sense of reality. The therapeutic relationship seemed to afford him the security to explore different roles, reverse roles, and take charge. Although he would resort to grandiosity to diminish me, he did not appear to require my annihilation. The relationship in treatment provided a ballast for the reintegration of longings for connection with others in more human terms as the cast of characters grew to include mythological creatures as well as robots and aliens.

David informed me that the Medusa story no longer bothered him—an oedipal victory of the son. In fact, it gave him good dreams, which he would not elaborate on. Another dream explored homosexuality: "Ching Chang and Dan Aykroyd are making love. They kiss and go to the White House where they talk with Gorbachev. Aykroyd refers to Ching Chang as 'Bush,' and Ching Chang calls Dan Aykroyd 'Ronald.'"

This dream clearly balanced David's earlier preoccupation with the maternal-child dyad and seemed to give some weight to his father's affection and authority. He taught me to play Monopoly by his rules, as he played with his father at home. He avoided winning and devised a debt system that kept me alive. He told me a reassuring story of how he once lost the game after owning everything. This effort to reassure me and keep me active revealed his own anxiety over being overly confident and losing because of one failure. The Monopoly games continued in each session, as did his advice to me— when to mortgage, when to buy, and when to sell—and his admonishments not to give up. His message to me was clear: He wanted to beat me, but he wanted me to survive.

As we continued our games, he eventually came near to winning and exhausted all his strategies for me to follow. I interpreted to him that it seemed to me he would not let himself win, just as he did not want to share with me how good he was feeling. David grinned widely, and I continued, "You might be afraid to win because you might need me again, and you might wonder if I would be here."

David asked me to copy for him the scores for the day and made a paper airplane of the score sheet to show me how he could fly it. I commented, "You are feeling so good, you are ready to fly."

MOTHER

With Mrs. D's return to work, the marital balance shifted, and she became more assertive. She explored the meaning of the threatening spider image that had so frightened David as it applied to herself, her son, and her therapist. She associated to her anesthesia experience as a young child: Seeing all the people with hands outstretched seemed like one large body reaching out to grab her.

It was typical of Mrs. D to condense her experience of terror into one threatening symbol, such as white coats. She visualized this threatening hospital experience as rendered passive by a large devouring creature. Her relation to me in the transference became more flexible to include both magical demonic and idealized components. I became both the good witch who grants children their wishes and the bad witch who steals children to devour when hungry. Most important, she was able to perceive me as an aggressor and to share these perceptions with me. She complained that before this time, I had heard only half of the story—how David perceived her—and not how she perceived him. Sharing her perception of her child as threatening and devouring was a manifestation of her trust in me. She could confide these threatening thoughts without fearing judgment, ridicule, or retaliation. This was a significant step forward in our work together. Mrs. D was revealing ambivalent thoughts not only about me but also about her child. Permitting me access to her infantile reactions to her child was not without risk. The representation of me as a critical, devaluing person was always in the wings, to be called out at the behest of stressful anxiety.

Mrs. D began an in-depth analysis of her relationship with her own mother. She (Mrs. D) felt guilty that she had been a threat to her mother. Her mother had been overburdened when Mrs. D was an infant, lacking in social and emotional supports. Earlier in the treatment, Mrs. D had shared some of these feelings regarding her mother; she now explored them in greater detail, also probing more of the complexities in the transference relationship. Although David was still one focus for these associations, she was shifting to emphasize her own personal narrative.

This narrative began with her birth. Mrs. D's mother returned from the hospital without a baby; Mrs. D had been premature in birth weight, which probably was the origin for her feeling of being defective. A series of events followed that added to the difficulties of her infancy. The baby nurse put too much silver nitrate in Mrs. D's eyes. Three months later, she had congestion and a cold. At 15 months, she had pneumonia and was hospitalized for 14 days because the fluid in her lungs did not recede. All of these details were etched in Mrs. D's mind. When Mrs. D was 2 years old, her mother planned a party because she was happy to have a child who was alive. Her mother heard her sniffle, Mrs. D developed bronchitis, and the party was canceled. This story was clearly a family myth.

Mrs. D also felt sorry for her mother, because as a young child she threw up everything she ingested. She felt she had given her mother just cause to be angry with her and was filled with remorse.

Mrs. D experienced her mother as angry and frightening, always yelling at something. Reversal of affect was the only way Mrs. D could feel affection for her mother—by being concerned and caring, at the cost of surrendering her own initiative and separate identity: "I couldn't express anger toward her. I had to protect her from any more of it. Instead, the anger went inside, toward myself and [later toward] my children. I was the cause of much of my mother's anger."

The omnipotence and distortion of this perspective are notable. Mrs. D perceived herself to be the center of her mother's world and the cause of all of her distress. "The interface between me and my mother was not loving and nurturing. It was terrifying and malevolent. My mother had an uncanny sense of when I would become sick. Even though I felt okay. [To her mother] You're like a witch. You say I'm sick and I am."

In the transference, feelings of negativity toward me surfaced as disgust at my passivity in not giving her more personal attention. Mrs. D linked her complaints about her mother to wishes for an exclusive relationship with me. These thoughts and feelings were unrelated to David and were focused on the therapeutic dyad. She expressed the conviction that I cared for her only as an extension of David.

Confronting me in this direct manner evoked intense anxiety for Mrs. D. In her anxious state, Mrs. D felt I perceived her as malevolent and that I did not understand the factors that justified her behavior. She needed to justify herself as though in a court of law. This was a complicated defense strategy. Rather than continuing her litany against me, which was uncomfortable, she attributed to me her own judgmental feelings. She could not own her rage but was wedded to her need to feel guilty. Within the dyad, heightened anxiety or terror had resulted in a reversal of percepts. Mrs. D's persistent need was to perceive herself as unjustly victimized, not only in childhood and within her own family, but also within the treatment relationship. The complementary percept was of herself as the perpetrator of suffering in others; this perception rewarded her with the familiar feeling of wrongdoing and guilt.

DAVID

Increasingly, David expressed the desire to solve problems on his own. He confronted me, and battles continued between the good and bad robot forces. He wanted me to watch him play, at times wanting to obliterate me and then wanting me to reappear. This ambivalence toward what constituted a safe distance in our relationship was expressed in his play activity. For instance, twin robots could understand each other without talking, by sending telepathic messages; they also could switch bodies. Later, they lost their ability to communicate in this secret way. Early empathic states were depicted in this play as magical. The twin robots not only could read each other's thoughts, they also could enter each other's body at will. I commented that it must be both reassuring and sad that twins had lost their special powers. Now they would have to use language to share their feelings, but they also would have their privacy. David seemed to be describing through symbolic activity the experience of porous boundaries that left him vulnerable to intrusion. Perhaps it was early experience of this type that overwhelmed him and resulted in the creation of grandiosity as a defense. In his grandiosity, David had become both self and other, incorporating all power within himself.

By this time, almost 3 years had passed since the beginning of treatment. David's fears had diminished significantly. In play activity, his hero transformer became less frightened that the plants would eat him up. The scary plants receded and were "really far away"; the child hero was protected by an adult figure.

MOTHER

In her professional situation, Mrs. D became more assertive; at home, she became firmer with her husband and children. I was able to share with her that she seemed freer to be assertive with me and less afraid that I would put her down. If she lost me, she could now feel she had lost someone who had taken care of her; she also was losing her capacity to retreat into sickness.

It became clearer to Mrs. D that the creation of the spider had been a dual representation of herself and the other person in the dyad. Perceiving the spider, she also had perceived aspects of herself. In being overprotective, she related to malevolence within herself as well as to external threats. She could become overwhelmed by dangers from the inside and the outside. Although she always had viewed herself as the victim, she was also a parasite. If the host died, she would die too. David had identified with this overwhelming state of terror and replicated her feelings by experiencing her worst fears as his own.

The next several months brought increased recognition for Mrs. D in her professional work. Treatment was extending beyond David to other family issues, her marital relationship, and work conflicts. She and her husband agreed to David's leaving regular sessions of treatment in the fall. Mrs. D would continue her individual sessions for another year. The remainder of this chapter focuses on David's last months in treatment.

DAVID

Several sessions before our separation for the summer, David revealed the existence of an Early Warning System, which the Good

Guys had had for a while and the Bad Guys had just acquired. It was a warning used against a cloaking device, which could render the enemy invisible so they could penetrate their opponents' defenses. Using the Early Warning System, the intruder could be destroyed through a computer programmed to destroy aliens who got inside.

David's representation of the intruder may be understood on several levels. Clearly, the intruder referred to oedipal desires to intrude on the dyad who excluded him, but it had preoedipal implications as well. The intruder was his mother, who invaded his personal boundaries without consideration of his need for autonomy. The intruder also represented the therapist, who had come from the outside to enter his inner world.

Signal anxiety is a psychoanalytic concept that refers to anticipation of a possible trauma that occurs through response evoked by a symbol. Thus a person is warned and may be prepared for the unknown. The Early Warning System was a representation of this capacity for preparation. It enabled the opposing sides to be aware of intruders. The capacities to anticipate and make preparations are mature strategies for coping with risk and anxiety. David was experiencing a resurgence of separation anxiety as the summer vacation approached. He also was aware that he would be finishing regular treatment sessions in the fall. As this metaphor for signal anxiety appeared, so did a recurring symptom, severe headaches. David rejected any connection between his headaches and his inner world. At one session, he declared that the head pain was none of my business and left tearful and angry, saying, "I'll be in the hospital in brain surgery, while you are swimming at your country club."

David's headaches continued to increase in number and severity as the time for my vacation neared. He feared he had a brain tumor, something that had invaded his brain and would destroy him. He became ill at camp and wanted to remain at home because of his pain. His mother was frightened by the headaches; they reminded her of her cousin's illness. She was extremely ambivalent about keeping David at home because she felt he might be malingering. We arranged for an additional session, and David complained bitterly of his head pain, saying that no one was taking him seriously.

It is important to note that David's symptom triggered a triadic meeting. It was an intense session that brought out no clear cause for David's complaints aside from my anticipated absence on vacation. I suggested a rule-out visit to a neurologist. Mrs. D reacted bitterly, saying I did not have confidence in her parental competence, and became extremely angry. She perceived the suggestion as a threat to her perspective on David and felt I was critical of her because she had not followed through on an earlier suggestion that she seek a medical opinion. The lines were sharply drawn, in her view, between physical and mental, as they were between her competence as a parent and her feelings of inadequacy.

On the way home from this triadic session, an enactment of reversal of roles occurred as son comforted mother and tried to calm her rage so she could drive. David later scolded me for making his mother angry. Reversal of roles within the dyad enacted in response to an intervention by the therapist usually signifies a significant therapeutic event. In this instance, the event was traumatic for Mrs. D for several reasons. It raised the possibility of life-threatening physical illness; she felt it undermined her confidence and authority; she was enraged by her son's persistent complaining; and she was anxious about the impending summer vacation and ending of her child's treatment in the fall. In response to her anxiety, she felt diminished, dependent, and needy. The tables were turned, and this time David acted as caregiver to support his mother through the crisis.

This enactment of role reversal was recounted to me later by an enraged and humiliated Mrs. D. It was a turning point in treatment. The dyad had felt sufficiently secure to unmask and share their secret with me. Appearances had been deceiving. The true parent in this dyad had been the child; in many ways he had carried the burden of his mother's anxiety. His pathology had developed in response to his parent's unresolved infantile needs. To ward off being overwhelmed, he developed the sense of omnipotence and grandiosity that became the core of his personality. David's fears represented a breach in this defensive structure. Because conflict was allowed to develop between the struggling forces within him, David's development was renewed. The dyad now was able to enact for me their hidden shared reality so that I could understand the extent of their progress.

Despite the upheaval my suggestion caused, while I was away on vacation, the consultation was carried out. A neurological examination ruled out migraine; magnetic resonance imaging (MRI) was conducted; and a titer was taken for Lyme disease. The consultation concluded that there was no evidence for neurological disorder underlying the headaches.

On my return, David's head pain vanished. In its place were myriad complaints about the condition of his life. His father was considering relocating the family to improve his job opportunities. David exploded with worries about this possibility and claimed his parents did not consider his needs. This lack of parental concern was a repeated refrain in David's complaining. He finally had a good social life, and now his life was falling to pieces. He was fearful of his own rage and felt that he was falling to pieces. In a barely concealed displacement of feelings for the therapist, he worried about his paternal grandmother, who if left alone would miss the family so much she would not be able to survive.

David's play activity was engrossing and dealt with bringing the forces of good and bad closer together. Both forces had Early Warning Systems but did not need to use them. David's schoolwork varied from being organized to being disorganized. David began to link his distractibility to his engrossment in daydreams. He seemed to be entering a preadolescent upsurge of preoccupation with fantasy. He claimed the robots had memories and that this is what kept them alive. I commented that when we ended our work and did not meet regularly, our memories would remind us of our time together.

In the fall, David continued his playful rejection of me and my ideas, although clearly he remembered them and related my comments to himself. For example, on Halloween he drew a picture of a vampire that resembled his mother. He rejected the idea that vampires suck because they lack supplies or need nurturance, as I had interpreted previously. He used the past tense—"when I was really scared"—to emphasize the lack of appropriateness of this interpretation, especially in his current state.

David had a dream that terrified him because it involved transformation. He shared the dream with his mother, who wrote it down and, with his agreement, gave it to me. Mrs. D's serving as an intermediary reflected the strong positive alliance that supported ongoing treatment. Despite her feelings of being intimidated by me, she was able to regroup and make good use of me. This expression of good faith was extremely significant at this point in treatment. Without his mother's support, David would have remained overburdened with feelings of mistrust and persecution.

David did not want to associate to the dream or discuss it further. He claimed it no longer frightened him and that he had returned to sleep with no difficulty. The dream contents acted as a communication on different levels. The dream expressed a trust he had undermined earlier and expressed his perspective on the course and outcome of treatment. It showed clearly that he had come to view his mother not as an extension of himself but as a person in her own right.

The dream began with David in math class. The teacher announced that something weird was outside on the lawn. Everyone looked out. "There was this huge thing that looked like the Apollo moon-landing module, but it was fifty times bigger and thirty stories high. These guys came out and looked human enough, but all the guys had mustaches and were wearing cosmonaut uniforms (with big things on their ears)." They came through and shattered the classroom windows and jumped into different things and bodies (one jumped into a table and one jumped into David's science binder).

In this part of the dream, therefore, as the aliens come inside and make themselves belong in the classroom, David places himself among other children. He is coming out of being "crazy" (the gigantic space station) and is joining the human group.

Later in the dream, David, Mom, his sister, and his friend were driving in Brooklyn. They drove over a bridge over the highway. Mom turned into his teacher, and her face got red hot. David saw that the bridge was about to fall, so he got out of the car and so did his sister. His friend threw a bucket of water over his teacher/Mom. The spikes (huge nails) that held the bridge together were breaking off.

This scene seems to describe David's experience of his mother's state of emotional disintegration. Clearly, he and his sister are safe, whereas his mother is getting assistance. The bridge seems to be an attempt to bridge two states, possibly his feeling of getting better and his reflections on his mother's disturbance. Perhaps it also represents a wish to be rid of the unhealthy mother and to build new bridges to connect to a healthier state.

David began to deal with the paradox of life and death. He decided it was alright to die if it meant you got to live. His attitude was less pompous and more conversational than previously, treating me as his confidante. His imaginary world became peopled with human characters: One dyad was Mr. Red and Mr. Blue, who were partners and friends. His schoolwork improved, although he still required assistance with homework. He undertook the initiative to get tutorial services in school. He no longer had attentional difficulties and was able to concentrate without restlessness. David could still be cantankerous, rebellious, intense, demanding, and grandiose. But he had come to terms with the human condition.

CASE SUMMARY

In simultaneous treatment, the therapist is in a pivotal role for both members of the parent-child dyad. In David's case, it was possible to follow the flow of projections and introjections that contributed to his grandiosity and narcissistic character. His arrogance was counterbalanced by his mother's feelings of inadequacy. David's attitude of superiority camouflaged deeper feelings of alienation and rejection.

Simultaneous treatment allows the therapist to observe directly how the defenses of the child mesh with the parent's needs. Typically the parent values the child not for himself but as a representation of an ego ideal. Alternatively, the parent rejects the child because the child personifies an unacceptable aspect of the parent. David first was idealized by his parents and then was rejected as he began to move away from them toward independence.

In the course of treatment, I was able to observe many parallels in the thematic material that emerged between parent and child as they reworked their personal narratives. At the beginning of treatment, neither of them had achieved the practicing stage of development in object relationship. Within the security of the therapeutic relationship, each achieved the practicing stage and went on to attain object constancy. Because parent and child were seen by the same therapist, it was possible to analyze the shared issues that underlay their manifestly different attitudes and problems.

David's and Mrs. D's pathology resided in their linked internal representations. These representations were the basis for role constriction, maladaptive coping-defensive strategies, murderous rage, and suicidal wishes. Instead of adapting to each other flexibly, the parent-child dyad was mired in rigid relationship patterns. I worked on clarifying, expanding, and elaborating on these rigid relationship patterns. David and Mrs. D could not have achieved their gains in individual treatment, because neither therapist would have had access to the representational worlds of both parent and child. Only in simultaneous treatment could David's grandiosity be traced back to its source in his parents' unconscious representation of him and treated there as well as in David's own therapy. Being capable of empathic understanding of both mother and child, I was able to facilitate the formation of a healthier parent-child relationship. This renewed relationship would sustain the gains of treatment.

CHAPTER 7

Sammy: A Case of Pervasive Developmental Disorder (Part I)

M Y FIRST GLIMPSE of 28-month-old Sammy was as a small bundle, nestled in his mother's arms. To my surprise, my gaze was met briefly by his, an intent hurried look. He eyed me and shrieked, and after many loud screams returned to the refuge of his mother's body. He clung tightly to two objects, a plastic baseball bat and a stuffed dog. I initiated a conversation with him using two hand puppets, a turtle and a squirrel. Sammy seemed to take it all in, remaining huddled and attentive. He continued to mold his body to his mother's, his protests mute, and he fell into a deep sleep from which he could not be awakened, even by a whistle or a song.

I spoke with Sammy's mother about her situation; when it came time to leave, she said she would return to meet with me with her husband. Having already pursued several treatment options, Sammy's parents wanted to work with me. Sammy's arms and legs twitched in a spastic way. His mother was close to tears and said, "He never falls asleep like this." But as we said goodbye, Sammy awakened, leaped down to the floor, and picked up a toy train. He said, "Choo-choo," smiled, and started to play. I saw that Sammy was average in size, walked with an awkward gait, and had an unusual facial expression, appearing unfocused and constantly scanning. Mrs. M disentangled him from the toy, and as they left, he sucked relentlessly, randomly in the air.

Sammy's mother had confided that Sammy had no tolerance for delay of gratification, and she felt unable to place limits on him. There was a split in their relationship. Sammy alternately avoided her, making her feel rejected, or molded with her body as if they were one organism. I commented, "It is as if you had two different babies." The mother replied that she found these fluctuating states unbearable and had experienced murderous rage.

REASON FOR REFERRAL

Sammy and his parents were referred to me by a senior analyst who had been treating Mr. M for 2 years. The same analyst also had consulted with the family concerning Sammy's older brother, Michael, who had experienced persistent nightmares and toilet-training problems the previous year. Sammy had been evaluated by the diagnostic team of his local school district when he was 26 months old and was given a diagnosis of pervasive developmental disorder with autistic features. Sammy's parents were shocked and overwhelmed by this diagnosis. Reportedly, Mrs. M became nonfunctional for a week, with suicidal ideation accompanied by guilt feelings and depression.

Subsequently, Sammy was seen in independent consultation by three other professionals to gain consensus on the diagnosis. There was some disagreement on the nature of the problem; for example, one consultant felt it was inappropriate to jump to diagnostic conclusions, because she had observed Sammy orienting to his mother for assistance. All three consultants agreed that Sammy manifested significant receptive and expressive language delays, delayed play skills, withdrawn and bizarre social interaction, hyperactivity, and a short attention span. Treatment was started but was stopped abruptly when the therapist suffered an incapacitating injury. Sammy was referred to me so that therapeutic intervention could be resumed.

At our first meeting, Mrs. M presented as diminutive, attractive, articulate, and distraught, unable to cope with the many family demands and intense personal conflict she was experiencing. She was a highly trained professional who until recently had been employed in a demanding position and was highly esteemed by her peers. She longed to remain home with her children, however, and despairingly felt she had lost time with them that could never be made up. She perceived Sammy's difficulties as evidence that her absence had damaged him. Her main concern at the time of referral was that Sammy did not play. Other problems were that he communicated by single nouns, was motorically driven, and had virtually no frustration tolerance or attention span. The interpersonal connections between Sammy and herself and between Sammy and others seemed abnormal.

Meeting with both parents gave me the opportunity to hear two different perspectives on Sammy's difficulties. Mr. M was robust, assertive, somewhat caustic in manner, highly articulate, and obviously concerned. He was employed in a high-level profession and worked long hours. He emphasized that from his perspective, Sammy had a mild problem. He described his son as "very athletic—he throws, initiates contact, and does what he wants to." Mr. M felt Sammy was persistent, and he did not like to limit him. For instance, Sammy loved climbing, and Mr. M would keep boosting him higher and higher to try to gratify his insatiable demands. Both parents viewed Sammy as an oddball and laughed nervously when they described him, a response that seemed to be a defense against feelings of helplessness.

RELEVANT FAMILY AND DEVELOPMENTAL HISTORY

Sammy was the youngest son of Mr. and Mrs. M. The firstborn, Michael, was 20 months older and developing normally, except for fearfulness and toilet-training problems within the neurotic range of difficulty. The parents were both skilled professionals, but Mrs. M was currently a full-time homemaker, having left an excellent position 7 months earlier. Mrs. M had returned to work when Sammy was 8 months old and continued working until he was 21 months old. It was when she stopped working that Mrs. M became aware of Sammy's troubled development and began to seek assistance.

The extended family offered little support. Maternal grandparents lived a short distance away and visited once a week; their visits were often tense, with Mrs. M feeling a need to meet parental expectations. A paternal grandmother visited twice a year. Her regular telephone calls were remembered by the children. The paternal grandfather lived out of state and was not an active part of the family. The mother's younger brother visited occasionally. Her older half sister went to live away from home when she was 13 years old because of behavioral problems.

Sammy's conception was unanticipated. The mother conceived when her first child, who had been a colicky infant, was 11 months old. She described herself as prone to having an unplanned child because she had been fatigued by her daily routine and emotionally drained by concerns about her marriage. The pregnancy was uncomplicated. There were concerns regarding insufficient weight gain, but five routine sonograms revealed a normal embryonic course. Delivery was spontaneous; epidural block was used. Birth weight was 7 pounds; Sammy was born head first, in good condition. He went home from the hospital with his mother.

Breast-feeding was attempted for 1 month but was not established successfully. Sammy did not relax during breast-feeding and cried after sucking for a minute or two. He was more relaxed after bottle-feeding but often threw up afterward. Mrs. M was deeply hurt and disappointed by his rejection of breast-feeding. She told me tearfully how she still longed for the perfect merger experience of a nursing mother with her infant and felt extremely deprived. For the first 3 months, Sammy was fussy in the evening. He generally was unfocused and seemed uncomfortable or unhappy. Mr. and Mrs. M reported that it was difficult to read Sammy's signals and to understand what he wanted. It also was difficult to elicit smiles or laughter. As an infant, Sammy awoke many times during the night. If he could not be comforted by a bottle, he would cry or vomit. During the beginning of the second year, he often would cry through the night and wake up for the day at 5 o'clock in the morning. At 18 months, he settled comfortably into a pattern of sleeping from 8 in the evening until 8 in the morning.

Motor milestones were within normal limits. Sammy sat up without support between 7 and 8 months, crawled at about the same time, and walked alone at 14½ months. He was extremely active, moving and climbing all the time. This compulsive movement diminished at approximately 2½ years, within a few months after the beginning of treatment.

By contrast, language development was significantly delayed. Reportedly, Sammy said mama/dada by the middle of the first year, single words between 14 and 15 months, and two-word phrases at 2 years. An audiological examination conducted at age 2 years was normal, but a tympanogram was abnormal. Sammy had a history of five episodes of otitis, the last when he was 2 years old.

The parents' concern about Sammy's social and emotional development was that he was "not attached enough." He reportedly pushed his parents away during the first year of his life, when he was attached to a plush dog. At a year old, he became attached to his father and also to a warm and caring housekeeper. Sammy first began to show affection for his mother at 18 months. His brother, Michael, was someone Sammy always sought out. In addition to the dog, Sammy clung to a hammer and a baseball bat, objects he used for hitting. These were the objects Sammy brought with him to our first meeting.

THEORETICAL BACKGROUND

Clearly Sammy presented a therapeutic challenge. He manifested several of the characteristics described by Donald Meltzer (1975 [1991]) as common to the autistic state. He seemed intelligent and to process the world about him in an instantaneous way. He was acutely sensitive to sensory information and to minute changes in the environment. He was capable of dismantling his attention, so that it scattered and wandered from object to object without sustaining focus on the self or on the other person.

From our first meeting, it was clear that Sammy controlled his experience in a profound way. For example, in response to encountering a new person he fell deeply asleep. Only at the time of separation did he manifest interest in an object in my room, the toy train. This directed attention, accompanied by a vocalization, was one of his highest functioning responses. It seemed to be an effort to sustain the continuity of the place he was experiencing at the moment.

In our meetings, Sammy demonstrated the use of what Frances Tustin (1990) described as autistic sensation objects. He carried with him a plastic hammer and baseball bat. According to Tustin, autistic children carry hard objects around with them, or try to stick themselves with hard objects, in an attempt to feel hard and strong. For such children, the hard sensations engendered by these objects are more important than the functions for which the objects were intended. For Sammy, these hard sensations were experienced in his activity of banging. In sessions, when he was frustrated, Sammy was observed to bang with his head, his arms, or his whole torso, as he would bang with his hard objects.

According to Tustin (1990), the child feels that these hard objects are part of himself, an extra bit of his body that will help him to feel safe, because in the child's mind they are associated with parts of the body that were used for protection. They are "me" objects, in the sense that they help the child to feel he exists and that his "going on being" is ensured. These "me" objects shut out distressing flashes of awareness of what is felt to be the dangerous "not me," which seems to threaten both the child's safety and his existence. They are not to be confused with D. W. Winnicott's (1951) transitional object, which is a combination of "me" and "not me" and helps to link the two. The transitional object is a bridge to the "not me"; autistic objects are a barrier to it.

Sammy also demonstrated the use of what Tustin (1990) referred to as autistic sensation shapes. These arise from soft bodily sensations, such as the flow of urine from the body, bubbles of spit from the mouth, diarrhea, or vomit. They also can be engendered by holding an outside object loosely or by pressing gently against it, by rocking or spinning, and by hand and body stereotypic movements. The shapes thus engendered are felt by the child to have no separateness from his own body, nor are they related to the shape of any particular object. Like autistic objects, they are idiosyncratic to the individual child. They are "tactile hallucinations," and because they are soothing and calming, they are a bodily form of tranquilizer. Sammy's soft shapes included his saliva, produced by voluntary bubbling, sucking, and drooling; his bottle, which he kept dangling from his mouth; his plush dog; and the soft contours of his mother's body.

Mrs. M felt unending remorse and hopelessness over Sammy's condition. She had felt overwhelming frustration at being pressured by her husband to return to work when their first son was 7 months old. She experienced a deep longing to be with him and rejoiced that her second pregnancy might mean she could return home. When her husband did not share her anticipation, however, she felt lonely and depleted by the demands of motherhood.

Mrs. M reacted with intermittent panic to her sense of loneliness and her experience of being alone. She had looked forward to the pleasure of nursing and was disappointed when Sammy did not take to the breast well and because he was so different from Michael. She felt irritation with Sammy and continued to be preoccupied with Michael. She felt there was something unusual about Sammy's development, and this worry became an obsession. Sammy's difficulties loomed larger and larger, precluding the possibility of enjoyment in his growth. She could not interest Sammy in objects; he did not focus. He seemed dazed, unhappy, and unconnected. Mrs. M felt angry because he was not relating to her, but she could not understand the source of her anger, annoyance, and deep distress. She blamed herself for his difficulty; it never occurred to her that something might be amiss with Sammy.

Mrs. M's panic reflected her own deep sense of insecurity as well as her discomfort with Sammy. All her family relationships were discomforting, but she had hoped to be at peace with her baby. She was longing to experience him as a source of comfort and protection from anxiety. Akin to his mother's desires, Sammy also was seeking contact and comfort, which proved to be elusive and unavailable. Tustin described the crux of an autistic child's difficulties as the inability to mourn for loss, in other words to deal with situations in which gratification is not available. Instead, the loss is filled with sensation objects and shapes, which are palliatives and do not deal with the problem in a fundamental way. In coping with experiences of loss, Sammy could not provide comfort for his mother, and there was no comfort for Sammy.

Tustin (1990) described the dynamics of a mother who suffers from a situation of loss resorting for comfort to the baby inside her body. When the baby is born, therefore, she feels she has lost a vital part of her body. Such a mother will not be able to help her baby when he discovers that the sensation-giving nipple is not part of his own mouth. The baby's unbearable rage and panic about the seeming amputation and loss of his own body will seem too much like her own. In this situation, the child feels helpless, vulnerable, and desperately at risk. This description seems to fit the dynamics operating between Sammy and his mother.

During our first consultation, Mrs. M was able to articulate clearly for me her multiple disappointments in those she trusted for sustenance. She sustained misgivings about her marriage and her parents. She had endured hardship and guilt following the abrupt loss of her older half sister, whom she idealized and her parents vilified. She had been a precocious child who very early was parentified and intuitively met the emotional needs of her depressed mother. Her intellect had served her well as protection against deeper longings for protection and security, until the birth of her first child. These longings were never fulfilled but remained in the background of her experience. They seemed like a dream, beckoning toward an idealized fulfillment attainable through motherhood but remaining beyond her grasp.

BEGINNING PHASE OF TREATMENT: FROM BEING LOST TO BEING FOUND

The method of intervention chosen was simultaneous treatment, addressing the problems of dealing with loss that both mother and child had experienced. Because Mr. M was continuing twice-weekly analytic treatment, contact with him would consist of monthly parent meetings focusing on issues of parent management. Mrs. M was receptive to the suggestion that she and Sammy meet jointly with the therapist twice a week. At times, Sammy's brother, Michael, would be present as well. With the parents' consent, all joint mother-child sessions were videotaped. In addition to play therapy, Sammy received 45-minute sessions of language therapy four times a week in his home. He also received help from a consulting physical therapist and occupational therapist. These services were part of a treatment program provided by the county for children with disabilities.

My approach to Sammy's difficulties followed Tustin's (1990) view that the autistic child compensates for earlier psychological deprivations by overvaluing tactile physical contacts and sensations. Only what is tangible and physically present is felt to exist. Memories, images, fantasies, and thoughts are intangible, and therefore imagination is blocked. These children are protected from experiencing loss and so are never stimulated to evoke absent people or objects by means of pictures, images, language, or memories. Their incapacity to use symbolic thought is reflected in an inability to play imaginatively and an incapacity to identify with the feelings of others.

The purpose of simultaneous treatment was to allow the mother and child to experience each other in a nonthreatening way. The mourning, or longings, would be tolerated so that protective thinking could diminish and symbolic fantasy could emerge within the dyad. Because of Sammy's young age and the overwhelming intensity of the dependency feelings evoked in both members of the dyad, it was necessary to have parent and child physically present in the therapy room together. Tolerance for separation increased gradually during the first 9 months of treatment. The presence of both mother and child in the therapy room elicited the expression of intense feelings and the gradual transformation of sensory experiences into images, which became part of their separate representational worlds. These gains were consolidated during the ending phase of treatment, which typified the usual course of children in treatment who have attained a measure of individuation.

MOTHER AND SAMMY

The first therapeutic session with Sammy and his mother was marked by multiple tantrums. Sammy brought play tools and used them to hurt his mother. When they were taken away, he persisted in trying to retrieve them. Throughout the session, he demonstrated the recurrent pattern of perseverative, goal-directed behavior described by his father. When he became frustrated, he threw a tantrum, and his mother would attempt to comfort him. Sammy would return and try again to obtain the weapon-object. He was unrelenting in pursuing his goal; his assertive efforts almost overwhelmed his mother and me.

Following a tantrum, during a quiet time, Sammy established momentary eye contact with me, seemingly oblivious to his mother. In response to frustration, he began head banging, which seemed deliberate. He also wished to bang other things. Some garbled efforts at communicating with speech were heard. Some of these utterances sounded like "go" or "let me go." In addition, there was a great deal of inarticulate babbling, rooting, and random sucking. When his mother withheld his bottle from him, Sammy showed some rudimentary interest in a toy train and then threw it away. He continued his tantrum, ended abruptly, said "car," and went to get the toy car across the room.

These behaviors suggested Sammy's use of objects as an extension of his own body. He indiscriminately banged on his own body, the bodies of others, and other objects, without being aware of the effects of his actions. His persistence seemed to indicate some primitive sense of efficacy obtained from sustaining the experience and making it recur or, as Winnicott described, "going on being." It was for the purpose of maintaining a rudimentary sense of existence that he was so goal-directed. This sense of purpose also accounted for his extreme frustration and desperation when his goal was obstructed or unobtainable. Interestingly, he was able to make fleeting eye contact with me, whereas he seemed oblivious to the existence of his mother, repeating the momentary visual contact of his first glance at me during his initial visit to my office.

One month later, in a joint session, Sammy came in without his bat. His mother said that it was lost and that he missed it. This statement was an example of projection on his mother's part. Sammy did not miss things: He missed something more rudimentary than an object, namely, a state of continuity in being. His mother, on the other hand, clearly was dealing with feelings of loss, searching to retrieve a state of being that was no longer present.

Sammy was attracted to a new dump truck in the office. I noted that he readily took stock of what was different in the room. He emptied and filled the truck. He made it go up and down. This kind of exploration of a new object was promising. Sammy seemed able to discover sustaining activities in the therapy room. His curiosity was clearly different from the aimless, demanding states observed earlier and described by his parents.

Sammy showed interest in another toy, a container holding objects of three different shapes. He clearly was intrigued by this toy and was distracted from his absorption with his mother's body by the sound of the shapes dropping into the canister. His mother dropped the shapes into their respective slots and they played together at naming them: "Mommy, Sammy, and Michael." Sammy's articulation was poor, but he imitated his mother's naming of the shapes. Sammy then designated me as Michael three times during the session. I clearly had a name and seemed identical with someone familiar. It suggested to me that Michael did exist for him as a separate entity, one who could be duplicated in his absence through the vehicle of naming! Perhaps my attribution of reasoning was too advanced, however, and Sammy was simply perseverating at mimicking and prolonging an utterance. Perhaps both factors were somehow at play in tandem.

My hunch that Sammy was capable of sorting things into categories was demonstrated to be correct in this session by a focused and prolonged episode of play activity. Sammy became absorbed in putting colorful balls on pegs. Occasionally he seemed to be sorting the balls by color, although the result might have been accounted for by chance. It was difficult to know how to classify what we observed. His mother and I seemed to catch glimpses of Sammy's awareness of a world outside the immediate senses in which he was absorbed. We shared and confirmed our perceptions and experienced the pleasurable excitement of having begun a joint venture together.

Sammy was active and enjoyed exploring objects in the room. I observed Sammy's mother hold him in a chair to keep him from climbing on a table. I made a note to myself that treatment was giving her the strength to limit him. Sammy was enjoying rolling a toy back and forth and expressed his glee in making dancing movements. He examined trucks that were on the table from different perspectives. He climbed on the dollhouse roof and wanted to walk on the dollhouse stairs. He did not seem able on his own to perceive himself in proper relationship to the size of objects. Playing with his mother helped him to process the size of objects. He needed her to be close and, without her, was fearful of size and proportions of objects. His mother's presence seemed to help him regulate between states of grandiosity and being overwhelmed. In this role, his mother functioned for Sammy as a secure base. The leave-taking at the end of this session was smooth. Sammy waved and threw me a kiss; there was no disorganization in mother or child.

MOTHER

Six weeks had passed since the beginning of treatment. Mrs. M reported that Sammy was not as frenetic as he previously was. He was beginning to show interest in toys at home. He also was able to interact with his grandparents in his mother's absence.

Mrs. M was still trying to rationalize the need to set limits for Sammy. She was conflicted because of a nagging fundamental conviction that children needed to have all of their needs met to feel loved. She described being fearful of her own greed and the greediness of her children; she had a fear of giving less than was demanded because of the rage it aroused. She recalled being conforming as a child; she had always accommodated to her mother's demands.

Mrs. M took an intellectual perspective and viewed rage as destructive because it taught children the culture of assertion and self-absorption instead of passivity and total giving. (Note the sharp division between polarities of possible outcomes.) Mrs. M's unspoken assumption seemed to be that one needed to give in to children or they would be damaged for life. I recalled to her a previous discussion in which she had agreed it was better for Michael if she did not give him everything.

Mrs. M remembered our discussion, but she needed to defend against acting to meet the realistic needs of her children for limits. With this reminder, it was possible but still painful for Mrs. M to place some boundaries on gratification. She seemed annoyed and at times angry with my reminders. At those moments, she was identified closely with the infantile needs of her children and needed to struggle with herself against giving in to their demands. It was as if by limiting their behavior she was somehow depriving herself. This experience of deprivation was not a rationale one. She was well aware of the parameters that needed to be enforced by a parent. However, there was a strong undertow of emotion, which led her to feel antagonism toward this parental role and created a strong pull toward collusion with her children's wishes.

Mrs. M claimed that as a child she intuitively understood the need for limiting disclosure to protect herself and had kept secrets from her parents. She did not want to inflict this barrier of privacy on her marital relationship. She had an ideal of merger, which meant perfect sharing and surrender to her mate. Mrs. M felt that merger was part of the kitten game she played with Sammy. The kitten teases and is vengeful and spiteful, purposively destroying. (In the guise of a game, Mrs. M used projective identification.) Mrs. M expressed the meaning of the kitten play as the following: "Do you love me?" "Who am I?" "Can I exert power?" "Can I share power?" She felt that Sammy had an intuitive understanding of the power structure within their family. She felt he was like the kitten, teasing and vengeful. Mrs. M felt Sammy was expressing his hostility with pounding and hammering. (Note the negative attributions toward the child.) My understanding was that Sammy's hammering was a sensation-driven experience. Mrs. M experienced it as an expression of anger and conflict of wills.

MOTHER, SAMMY, AND MICHAEL

Mrs. M's comments concerning Sammy's intuitive understandings proved to be partially correct. In a session that was attended by his brother, Sammy demonstrated his highest level of social understanding. Within the sibling system, Sammy was more interpersonally aware and protective of his territory. Within the parent-child system, he was more diffuse, less assertive, and more infantile. I was intrigued by these observations and turned to research conducted by Judith Dunn (1988) on sibling relationships. I wondered whether the sibling system had afforded Sammy an alternative pattern of relationship that protected and nurtured him. Would this alternative pattern of relating be tapped by the parallel process operative in simultaneous treatment? Moreover, could the kitten game reflect the mother's participation with Sammy on a sibling-child level? If that were the case, perhaps Sammy's dilemma was that he was engaged by his mother in two conflicting patterns of relationship concurrently. Simultaneous treatment would be the method of choice to address each of these conflicting patterns as they coexisted within parent and child.

Dunn has observed that one difference between sibling-child and mother-child conflicts is that children's interests are far closer to each other's, and therefore children are likely to compete for similar goods. Moreover, each child knows well what the other particularly likes and dislikes. By the first half of the second year (14 to 18 months), the younger sibling shows an increasing ability to provoke the older sibling by teasing. Behavior at this age reflects not only an understanding of what will annoy the sibling, but also a growing grasp of what is and what is not sanctioned within the family. Between 24 and 36 months, children begin to use reason in their disputes with their siblings, as they do with their mother. The social rules of possession are central to most conflicts. During the third year, the younger sibling begins to draw the mother's attention to misdeeds of the older child.

These observations are crucial to our understanding of Sammy. Dunn's (1988) argument, substantiated by considerable data obtained in naturalistic settings, is that in situations of sibling conflict and threatened self-interest, the child's growing understanding of the social world is not only revealed but also fostered. Although Sammy did not express it verbally, in this session he enacted his grasp of possession and territory. He clearly was attuned consistently to his brother and constantly aware of Michael's whereabouts and activities. He preyed on him without limits, within the social understanding supported by his mother, that he was the baby and that Michael must relinquish things to him.

In his own self-interest, Sammy exploited this social rule to the utmost; he remained outside the orbit of social contract, negotiation, and compromise. Sammy actively enjoyed confronting Michael, teasing him, and exerting his infantile power within the family. I wondered, Could this be the same child described as withdrawn and autistic? These family politics did not further shared play and amusement but supported a system of parasitic enmeshment. Sammy did not even need to use language to exert his power. He could impose his will and get his way through active interference and overwhelming infantile affect (screaming, yelling, and crying).

Because Michael was home from school, he accompanied his brother to session. As Sammy entered, his loud, piercing, continuous wailing was heard, like a young infant's cry. Sammy walked over to Michael and took the fire truck from him, and Michael pushed him down. Mrs. M intervened: "You have to take turns." She was sitting on the floor next to the boys, running her hands through her hair in despair; by now, both children were screaming. Sammy was focused relentlessly on the fire truck, menacing his brother with looks and holding on tightly to the toy. Mother prevailed on Michael to relinquish the fire truck and play with the toy train. She explained to the older boy that her request was not fair but that she wanted Sammy to quiet down. Michael refused a succession of toys and finally settled for the dinosaurs; Sammy was happy with the fire truck.

To my surprise, Sammy clearly referenced his brother, wanted what he had, and stood his ground to obtain what his older brother possessed. Sammy took the truck, put it on the table, and rolled it back and forth, all the time watching his brother put together the train tracks. He called my attention to himself, saying, "truck," and initiated a game of rolling the truck back and forth to me. We played this game while the mother played with Michael.

In the next episode of play, Sammy was engrossed with a peg toy, sitting with his mother, while Michael and I continued the train play. Mrs. M's gaze was continuously on Michael; Sammy was engrossed in the task of pegs and did not regard his mother. This interaction pattern was prolonged. It was broken by Sammy's dropping some pegs. Otherwise, the mother sat with her head in her hands focused on Michael and me. Sammy returned to his repetitive task. In contrast to the active interaction in the beginning play sequence, here Sammy was withdrawn into himself, referencing no one. Mrs. M was either completely absorbed with regarding Michael or despairing.

Sammy's absorption changed when Michael turned from the trains to pick up a hand mirror. Sammy darted over and grabbed the mirror from his brother's hands. His mother restrained him (with assistance from me), and Michael went on to play with something else. Sammy immediately reached for the mirror. I intervened because Sammy wanted to use the mirror to bang things. I introduced Sammy to a game, "Look who is there." Sammy was resistant, then relaxed a bit and complied. He returned to hammering with the mirror; I limited him; and he wailed. Then he responded to my invitation to see his reflection in the mirror. Sammy continued to play with me and the mirror, disregarding his mother and brother, who were engaged in playing with the railroad tracks. In this episode, Sammy profited from his brother's initiative. Because his brother had been playing with the mirror, he became interested. At first he used it for sensory activity, but at my initiative he was able to respond to structured interaction and regard his own reflection for the first time.

After this interlude of play, Sammy wandered over to his brother, made a beeline for the tracks, and started scattering them. Their mother limited Sammy and held him, saying no. Michael cried, and I helped him to rebuild the tracks. Sammy watched Michael intensely from his mother's arms. Clearly, in this episode, Sammy benefited from his mother's setting a limit, and there was intense referencing of his brother.

Michael began to play with a truck. Sammy continued to cry, struggle, and scream in his mother's arms. Their mother suggested to Michael that he give Sammy a turn; he relented, and his mother thanked him. Sammy went directly to the truck and pushed it back and forth, imitating his brother. This was the first clear instance of imitation by Sammy that I had observed.

Michael went to rhythm instruments and began to play with a toy drum and triangle. I showed Michael how to use the instruments while Sammy pursued the truck. Mrs. M continued to watch Michael intensely. "Ding" sounded the triangle; Sammy immediately turned to Michael, ignoring the truck, and scooted over. His mother commented, "Here comes somebody who likes that ring." Sammy regarded Michael and then reached out. Michael gave him the triangle, he took the cymbals, and they played music together. Sammy learned from me how to use the triangle, listening and then doing what I demonstrated.

In many ways, this detailed account of play activity seems mundane, because it describes patterns of interaction familiar to anyone watching preschool-age siblings. Given Sammy's pathology, however, the level of social interaction observed was most surprising and encouraging. Most remarkable was the wide variability in behaviors observed in both Sammy and his mother. Mrs. M's responses to her children ranged from despair and withdrawal to effective intervention. Sammy's behaviors included tantrums, withdrawal, aggression, referencing, and modeling.

Sammy's highest level of functioning since the beginning of treatment was observed in the dyad between himself and his brother. Sammy clearly referenced his brother, imitated him, and showed interest in objects his brother chose. He did not spontaneously demonstrate this level of interest in his mother's activities, nor did his mother in his activities. At the end of the session, mother and therapist worked together, making it possible for the brothers to join in a shared activity. It was a dyad being regulated by a dyad: The shared objectives of mother and therapist, working in unison, acted to regulate the activities of the children.

MOTHER AND SAMMY

The next session, 1 week later, detailed the more regressed interactions characteristic of the mother-child dyad. It is significant because of the awakening interest between the two partners demonstrated in visual referencing behavior. The therapist is an observer of these dramatic interpersonal developments occurring within an infantile dyadic realm. It was as if parent and child had begun to restore together what had been lost.

Sammy came into the session wailing, carrying his plastic hammer in one hand. I offered him a dump truck, but he could not be pacified. Sammy continued to scream and yell; he wanted his bottle. He sat by his mother on the couch, who gave him the bottle. He clenched the nipple between his teeth, with the bottle dangling from his mouth, his plastic hammer in one hand. He then got down on the floor and played with the truck with the other hand, not relinquishing the hammer or bottle.

Sammy turned to regard his mother, looking up at her from the floor and holding his bottle with one hand. There was a prolonged episode of mutual gaze as he sucked from his bottle and his mother met his gaze and sustained the mutual regard. With the bottle as intermediary, mother and child looked deep into each other's eyes. The mother reached out to caress Sammy's hair and came down from the couch to sit by him on the floor. He reached out for a toy. Never letting the bottle out of his mouth, he watched as I put shapes into the openings of the toy and listened to the noises they made. He imitated my actions, and his mother applauded. He hammered with the plastic hammer and indicated an interest in a music box. His mother turned the knob for him to make music, and he tried to turn the knob, all the while clenching the bottle between his teeth. Together, we listened to the music box for some time. Sammy hammered on the music box and other objects. He removed the bottle, wailed, reached for it, and returned it to his mouth. This time, as he drank, he looked up to gaze into my eyes. His mother lifted him up and sat him on her lap, cuddling him as he nestled into the warmth of her body.

The harmonious activity of therapist and mother had tangible results in initiating a calming duet between mother and child. This transfer of good feelings was palpable in the room as child and mother reached out, touched each other, and set in motion a "dance" of connectedness, with gains in mutual sustenance.

Sammy was clearly a reactive child. In joint sessions, he became more playful as his mother became calmer. He was increasingly happy and responsive, playing mirror games with his mother and imitating her play with a dump truck (loading and unloading; filling and dumping). He played a ferocious hugging game in which he was "eaten up" by his mother. She claimed he would not respond to gentling. I pointed out that he tended to follow our lead when we interested him in objects. His focusing was improving.

When his mother limited his behavior, Sammy hugged my chair for comfort; this gesture brought to his mother's mind a missing person or toy. She felt that Sammy missed other people but not her. He came to her only when he missed his bottle. She got depressed and angry as all day long he asked for what he did not have. She referred his behavior to herself and criticized herself for not providing adequately.

As a parentified child, she had experienced an overwhelming need to take responsibility for her parents and to fulfill their expectations. Mrs. M told her story in a tearful, complaining voice. I said she seemed to be complaining about these pressures in the same way she complained about Sammy and his demands. Perhaps she had taken responsibility too early for the regulation of chaos. Sammy may have been doing something similar in using avoidance—by holding on to the chair when he was angry—to shield her from harm and protect her from despair. His hyperactivity might be a strategy to deal with pain; by running away from the source of discomfort, he was searching for boundaries that could contain him. Similarly, his negativity, which was to be expected at this age, seemed to connect into what caused her pain. In these comments, I was linking Sammy's behaviors with affective states, both his own and those of his mother.

MOTHER

Mrs. M continued the theme of Sammy's sensitivity in her individual sessions. She described how Sammy attuned early to her own states of helplessness. He seemed to pick up on her anxiety and become more chaotic; she experienced being overwhelmed by him when a loss of boundaries, "a mushiness," would occur. Mrs. M felt Sammy perceived his role as trying to rid himself of helplessness instead of seeking comfort from her. When he was clinging to her, maybe he was giving her what he perceived she needed; her terror became his terror—a fear of helplessness with no one to depend on.

Mrs. M continued to overwhelm herself with blame. She saw herself as the cause of all of Sammy's difficulties. She thought she must have communicated to him a fear of separateness, by coercing him: "If you don't depend on me, you won't survive." Along with these guilt feelings, Mrs. M's sense of having been deprived in the past and being deprived within the treatment was great. Just as she could never satisfy Sammy, I could never meet her needs. As she left, she complained bitterly that there was never enough time during sessions; she had so many unanswered questions. Abruptly, on the threshold, she turned to me dramatically and blurted out that she wanted Sammy to be dead. It was not qualified by "sometimes" but was expressed as an absolute sentiment. She could not satisfy his hunger for objects, and it caused her endless frustration. This was her malevolent wish under-lying the immense feelings of responsibility she carried inside her. She shared these feelings on leaving, probably not yet able to explore them comfortably within the session.

Sammy's mother's feelings of overwhelming frustration reflected the rigid dyadic focus of parent-child relationships within the family. I observed that Sammy split triadic groups into dyads: For example, he clung to his mother to avoid me; he clung to his father to avoid his mother; and he clung to Michael to avoid either parent. In a parallel pattern of relating, Mrs. M was always dissatisfied in her relation-ships. She wanted to hold onto and merge with the other for nurtu-rance and survival. This rigid dyadic pattern resulted in a lack of per-sonal freedom and overweening sense of responsibility, barely concealing malevolent controlling wishes.

MOTHER AND SAMMY

By confronting and venting her own inner dissatisfaction, Mrs. M became able to relate more fully with what she did possess in the "here and now" of daily life with Sammy. The following excerpts from several sessions indicate Mrs. M's growing capacity to focus on Sammy and to pull him into playful interaction. She became more active in the parental role, maintaining exquisite empathy with Sammy's feelings.

1. The mother introduced a game, putting on a colander as a hat and asking, "Where Am I?" Sammy reached out to hit her and knocked off the hat. She stopped him. She put the hat on her head and said, "Mommy's hat." She slouched down under the hat so she could not be seen. With a triumphant grin, Sammy pushed back the hat and repositioned it on her head. "Want me to hide?" she asked. "Where's mommy? Here I am!" He ran to her and threw himself on her. She hid again, he found her, and she enfolded him in an embrace.

2. The mother and Sammy were playing together with the dollhouse. The mother said to Sammy, "Show Saralea how Daddy sleeps." Sammy made snoring sounds. We all laughed. Sammy played with the daddy doll. He put him in the bed, and everything fell down. We resonated with his response of "oh-oh-ooo." Sammy showed me a small light and gave a matching small light to his mother. He had us give the lights back and forth to each other. (Note that this is an early example of triadic focus.) Sammy began to zoom cars. His mother took a miniature car and zoomed it all over his body, laughing with him in play. He smiled back at her, took the car, and

ran it along the table. I commented, "It is like you are visually holding him, focusing him. It takes a lot of effort." Mrs. M reached out to touch her child warmly and continued the play.

MOTHER

At one session, the mother entered with her face glowing, in sharp contrast to her affect at previous sessions. She reported that all of Sammy's bizarre movements and climbing had stopped. Sammy did not even want to watch TV. Mrs. M immediately associated to memories of herself as a child. She always had felt a black cloud was following her. She had tried to lighten her mother's burden and brighten things for her. She always had resented her mother's sadness and felt "life does not have to be this way. When I marry and my husband moves, I'll be okay." (This was a reference to her family's move to a new city and her mother's subsequent depression.) Recently, Michael also seemed much better; he was sleeping well and was not as fearful.

At our next meeting, Mrs. M reported that Sammy was more socially aware; for example, he brought play food to his father. He also seemed peeved at being excluded from his brother's play date and began to interfere. (His mother felt it served Michael right for excluding him.) Formerly, Sammy would have remained alone in his room. The mother described a collusion within the family to keep Sammy a baby. They called him "the Beast of the East" and "Master of Disaster." She often felt this way about him. "Sammy is like an alien, unknown. I'm so nervous with him. I don't feel a merger like I felt with Michael. It's hard to fill time with Sammy; you have to roughhouse to feel a connection. Sitting at the table, he pushes my patience to the limit."

In contrast, Mrs. M felt Michael was a lot like herself. At 2 years, he was no longer doing a lot of unacceptable things. "You did not have to teach him not to run in the street. He was never antisocial. He explored; he was not destructive." She used to negotiate with Michael. "He's reasonable; he's able to hear you." Mrs. M described herself with Sammy as always having questioned, "Am I doing it right?" Now that she was asserting more authority, she did feel it was right. Michael was testing her more also. In turn, Mrs. M tested me by questioning the time of our meetings.

In subsequent weeks, Mrs. M continued a critical attitude toward herself despite recognition of her child's progress. She became preoccupied with what she did not do and highlighted similarities between herself and her own mother. She reflected on how her mother felt inadequate and always made her feel inadequate (probably a statement also of her feelings about me). These ambivalent feelings were probably in part a resistance to recognizing progress, because Sammy was taking big strides forward in the regulation of affective states.

The challenge to Mrs. M at the close of the beginning phase of treatment was to accept that she no longer could perceive herself as solely responsible for Sammy's development. We observed together how he initiated imitating facial expressions with me (eyes, mouth, tongue) and ended the play when he was ready, by giving me an embrace. He was emerging as sweet at times and explosive at other times because of the need to release tension. His vocabulary grew as two-word phrases appeared (for example, "buy ball") and many new words. Focusing on the "here and now" of Sammy's developmental progress, Mrs. M slowly was becoming able to free herself a bit from the burdens of responsibility, criticism, and despair and bask in the warmth of parental pride.

CHAPTER 8

Sammy: A Case of Pervasive Developmental Disorder (Part II)

MIDDLE PHASE OF TREATMENT: DEVELOPMENT OF THE DYAD WITHIN SYMBOLIC PLAY

As SAMMY AND HIS MOTHER continued treatment, the therapeutic focus continued to be on improved regulation within the dyad. Mrs. M's depression had two sources: states of panic and anxiety that came from a sense of being overwhelmed by responsibilities, and unrealistic expectations of herself as a mother and of her child's development. In therapy sessions, I encouraged her to initiate rewarding activities for the family, to establish a daily routine, to become less demanding, and to set limits on unacceptable behavior. In addition, I used every opportunity to enhance Mrs. M's understanding of Sammy's strengths and weaknesses.

The most consistent indication of progress within the dyad was improvement in social referencing, the process of using another person's interpretation of a situation to formulate one's own interpretation. The other person serves as a base of information and facilitates one's efforts to construct reality (Bruner, 1983; Feinman, 1982; Feinman & Lewis, 1983; Klinnert, Campos, Sorce, Emde, & Svejda, 1983). For example, when young children encounter unfamiliar people or objects, they look at their mother to gauge her reaction.

Lev Vygotsky (1978) termed this social sphere the *zone of proximal development*, emphasizing that children first learn to perform tasks

159

within a social context and only later proceed to learn on their own. Sammy had been profoundly delayed in his use of the ecological context. He seemed withdrawn with his mother and more connected with his brother. As Mrs. M began to reach out, both within her community for social supports and within the expanding therapeutic alliance, Sammy increasingly used her as a source of information and as a secure base from which to explore (Ainsworth, Blehar, Waters, & Wall, 1978; Mahler, 1965)

These referencing looks were becoming paralleled by postaction references, in which Sammy looked to his mother to get her approval or to glean her reactions to his initiative. As Mrs. M increasingly was able to embrace her son with love and affection, he began to respond by reciprocating. He would turn to communicate with her, as if to ask: Are you watching me? What do you think of this situation? What do you think of me? A new level of triadic understanding emerged: Sammy would reference me as he played with his mother, as if to ask: Do you see us? What do you think of us?

Despite Sammy's limited expressive speech, he was able to communicate intent and understanding of reciprocity (Bruner, 1977; Stern, 1985; Trevarthen, 1980). Sammy clearly understood that he and his mother could communicate and signal mutual interests (Bretherton & Bates, 1979; Bretherton & Beeghly, 1982; Bretherton, McNew, & Beeghly-Smith, 1981). It is interesting that these understandings, often accompanied by one- or two-word utterances, usually emerged out of an often-repeated game motif. Examples of this type of symbolic play activity included "Mommy Ghost," "Baby Turtle," and "Fire in the House." This shared, playful social reality was ample evidence that Sammy had emerged from his isolation and that his mother had emerged from her state of withdrawal and aggravated depression.

The following vignettes are selections from the middle phase of treatment, which extended over a 9-month period of therapeutic intervention. During this time, frequency of contact was maintained at twice-weekly sessions for the child and mother and weekly sessions for the mother alone. The father attended the parent sessions once a month. The consolidation of treatment gains and the ending of therapy, which encompassed another year of work, are described briefly in the case summary.

MOTHER AND SAMMY

Sammy came to the door extremely assertively, wanting "Sara." He was using his body like a bat, knocking into things. He was unable to contain his excitement and became disorganized, losing focus and acting more wildly. His mother arrived and agreed to let me hold him. I verbalized for him, "Mommy is here and agrees Saralea should hold me. Mommy is waiting, and soon I will feel better." Screaming and crying continued, but his mother endured. She was seeing him in opposition to, not as a part or extension of, herself. She was soothing him with her tone of voice and comforting yet not holding him. It was difficult for Mrs. M; she suggested it might be better if she held him, but I urged her to be patient. Although she consented to the procedure, there was covert disagreement. She later demanded to know: "Why is this necessary? Why can't we soothe each other?"

Despite the mother's irritation, our joint efforts maintained separation in a state of distress; figuratively, Sammy was held firmly by his mother, in her alliance with me. Following this episode, both mother and Sammy played at filling grids from the Connect Four game with checkers. Before leaving, Sammy requested a bottle, and his mother gave him one; it was only partially filled because she was trying to wean him.

MOTHER

During this session, Mrs. M manifested many changing affective states—sadness, anger, humor, and laughter—as she began to elaborate her own personal narrative. She expressed intense longings for connectedness and anger with me for not listening to anecdotes about her mother. She told of being like her mother, who was agoraphobic and afraid of heights. Mrs. M had been traumatized as a young child when, following an accident, she was lifted up in the car by a tow truck. She recalled her motor unsteadiness and the fact that she had been an extremely cautious child, mirroring her mother's anxiety about safety.

At one point, referring to the previous session, Mrs. M burst out in rage, "Why did you hold him?" It had taken Sammy so long to bond with her that she could not turn away from him; every advance was so precious. Michael had been so special to her from the beginning. Michael had been colicky, yet she felt extremely connected and longed for him when she returned to work, as she felt coerced to do. Sammy's restlessness had put her off; he was unable to suck. She longed for him, yet she could not connect with him. Now she was trying to divert Sammy's rage with comfort. She was using the bottle to help build a relationship rather than as a sedative.

MOTHER AND SAMMY

Sammy came well supplied; he brought his hammer and a juice box to this session. He sat by the dollhouse, saying in a singsong voice,

"Aahah, ooohah." He gestured and looked at his mother. She responded, "Who are you pretending to be?" He rubbed his cheek against hers. "You are pretending to be Buddy" [my dog]. Mrs. M smiled at Sammy in a gentle, affectionate manner. "Where is Sammy? I see Buddy, but where is Sammy? Are you being Buddy, or are you just wiping your nose on me? What's going on?"

Sammy continued to make advances toward her on all fours. She was smiling. "What's going on? Are you pretending to be Buddy? Are you eating from my hand? Nice Buddy." She rubbed his neck and put her arm around him while speaking in a soothing voice. Sammy was eyeing her, holding his hammer and watching her as she spoke.

MRS. M: Where is Sammy?
SAMMY: Meow.
MRS. M: You're a cat. Here's the kitty cat [picking up the small plastic toy kitty]. Do you want to say hi to each other?
SAMMY: Meow.

He took the toy kitty and rubbed his mother's hair with it. While advancing on her, he had left his hammer and juice box on the table. He put the cat in front of her face.

MRS. M: Is the cat up in my hat, on my head? The little cat is up on my head.
SAMMY: Meow.
MOTHER [to me]: I like *The Cat in the Hat*, myself. He likes *The Cat in the Hat*.

Sammy hid the kitty on his mother's body, took his juice box in his hand and searched on the floor. Catching Sammy's gaze, Mrs. M said, "Are you looking for your hammer?" Sammy picked up the kitty that had fallen on the floor.

SAMMY [looking intently at his mother]: A-gaire. Mommy scare.
MRS. M: Mommy scared. What am I scared about?
SAMMY [as the kitty drops]: Uh oh!
MRS. M: Uh oh, the kitty got scared and is falling. The poor kitty is scared.
SAMMY: Ooh.

Sammy changed his focus back to the house and tried to put his juice box into the house. The mother took the juice box to save for later. Sammy took his plastic baseball bat and rolled it back and forth as he watched his mother putting the juice box away. She removed the bat and suggested that they both look into the house together. As she named what they saw in the house, Sammy echoed her with various utterances, then closed the house with the mother's assistance and jumped down.

The mother reached out to him and, cupping his head in her hands, asked, "Where did Sammy go? Did a doggie come in here?" She held him in her arms, and they looked out the window together at the trees in the garden.

It was confusing and disturbing to observe this play activity between mother and child. Was Sammy playing at being the doggie or kitty? Or was he somehow transformed into the creature he was playing? Alternatively, was I observing the rudimentary first steps toward identification? Was Sammy on the way to a sense of personal coherence to which these creaturelike attributes could be assimilated?

MOTHER

Mrs. M had been going through her photo album and discovered that she had stopped putting in pictures at the time of Sammy's birth. She now had resumed putting pictures in the album. She described one picture of Sammy as an infant and said, "I kept looking for my face; I knew it should be there. It wasn't there in that picture. It was only his smiling face. I knew he was smiling at me and I was smiling at him, but I couldn't find myself. I was not there; he could not respond to me." Mrs. M described this experience as akin to psychosis—searching for an image of herself that was not there. Could the search for her own smiling face have been a reconnection with a dissociative experience or a memory of an infantile traumatic event that she was recalling through reenactment with her child?

I suggested that the difference now was in herself: She now realized there was someone's image there to search for. Mrs. M related her child's deficit in awareness to her own and experienced overwhelming guilt at having caused it to happen. I suggested that it was an experience within the dyad, involving input from both herself and her child, and from her husband as well, and yet she took full responsibility. Mrs. M replied, as if recalling a nightmare, "He [referring to Sammy—or was it to herself?] was lost to us for so long: He kept going further and further away and looking so sad."

What Mrs. M was describing has been termed by Frances Tustin (1990) *shell-type autism.* The child seems to be in a shell all the time and cannot be reached. It is the experience of "nothingness," a nothingness that cancels out all hope. These children are in a state of helpless despair. They feel out of reach of human aid. Lacking the feeling of being held firmly in the embrace of caring interest, attention, and concern, these children react by surrounding themselves with soft sensation shapes and holding onto hard sensation objects.

Sammy functioned for his mother in much the same way as a soft sensation object when he merged closely with her body. He seemed to fill her sense of inner void and give her a sense of existence. In the photograph, she was confronted with the experience of her own "nothingness" and then associated to the withdrawal of her son. This was an accurate reading of her child's predicament. If he was in his shell, he could not be reached. He was protected from his mother's inner void and his own experience of nonbeing.

In a session 2 weeks later, Mrs. M again recalled the birth of Sammy. Michael was not yet 20 months old when Sammy was born. Michael had refused the bottle at 3 months and finally was weaned from the breast at 5 months, at which time he eliminated the 3 o'clock feeding. He awoke for the day at 5 in the morning. When Michael was 2 years old, Mrs. M went back to work full-time and felt she had abandoned him. In terrible turmoil, she turned her anger against herself in the form of guilt.

Mrs. M described her personal history in her family of origin. Her mother was in her mid–30s when Mrs. M was born. A brother, 2½ years younger, and a half sister, 7 years older, completed the family unit. She described her father as a dissatisfied person who was several years younger than her mother. She recalled that during the first 6 years of her life, her mother was often unhappy. The family then moved to a small town, and her mother did not adjust well. Her mother felt that a career would have saved her. Her father was harsh and put her mother down. When Mrs. M was an adolescent, her mother made her a confidante. Mrs. M tried to "fix" the parental relationship, but her mother rejected anything she offered. In her 20s, Mrs. M did well academically and impressed her father, although he then focused on her social weaknesses.

MOTHER AND SAMMY

I noted gains in signaling (Sammy shared messages nonverbally with his eyes) and comforting (Sammy went to his mother, responding to her offer of hugs). His mother made gains in individuation. She became involved in volunteer work, although she was certain her own parents would consider this activity "crazy."

Sammy's fine-motor coordination improved considerably. He demonstrated strong assertion of aggression in crashing cars and reparation in joining trains together. Sammy was still somewhat daunted by limit setting; he looked hurt and withdrew a bit. However, he sought out his mother for comfort when he was physically injured. For instance, Sammy hurt his eye on a box and signaled his mother by crying and saying "eye," retaining a hurt expression until soothed.

Sammy entered a relatively stable period. He was capable of sustaining play activity for the entire session. His play activity included trucks (placed alongside or parallel to each other; connecting vehicle parts), the house, and puzzles. In his language development, three-word utterances were now common. Communication of limits could take place in a playful way. For instance, a cat on top of the doll house was rubbing against a daddy doll and fell out of the window ("uh oh!"). This exclamation was an early expressive communication shared between mother and child cueing mutual recognition of a trespassed limit. It originated in drawing, when a pencil strayed from paper, marking the table.

As Sammy became more organized, he demonstrated many new nonverbal understandings. For example, he wanted to watch the tree being cut down in front of the house; he concentrated on playing toy musical instruments; he was playful regarding his reflection in the mirror. Repetitive activities were marked by new ventures into symbolic representation. Sammy played with the hospital bed and patient doll; he used food implements to feed himself and the doll; he looked at my pendant and called it a "wheel."

SAMMY, MICHAEL, AND MOTHER

Both children entered the room with a burst of energy. Michael shared his nighttime fears. Sammy buzzed all around happily, playing with this and that. The two boys now played well together, in parallel and cooperative activity, with Sammy sometimes leading the play. Many new behaviors were evidenced. In one particularly poignant episode, Sammy embraced Michael; in a somewhat primitive way, he threw himself into his brother's arms and touched his brother's face, exploring it gently with his hands. As he did so, his brother stood still, tolerating the touch with a smile. Mrs. M labeled the different parts of Michael's face (eyes, nose, mouth) endearingly, in tandem with Sammy's exploration.

Also of interest was Sammy's new consideration for Michael's possessions. For example, he came over to admire Michael's toy train, watched Michael playing, but did not intrude, and he beckoned his mother to watch with him. This shared interest with his mother seemed to allow him to observe boundaries and tolerate envy of Michael's toy.

MOTHER

The themes of this session were loss and death, loyalty, and betrayal. Mrs. M's childhood loss of a kitten foreshadowed the loss of her half sister, who was sent away to live with relatives because she was unmanageable. Mrs. M remembered that her mother said she was sending the kitten to a farm, when the family went off for a sojourn in Europe, but in fact sent it to a pound. A more recent loss of a kitten occurred when Michael was 2 years old. Her husband was allergic to the animal, and the housekeeper did not like it and threatened to leave.

Commenting on the decision to part with the kitten, Mrs. M said, "You would probably side with the parent." This was the beginning of a pattern of attributions she made toward me whenever she experienced a conflict of loyalties. I would typically be cast in the adversarial role, usually representing a judicious, or "mature," but strict and unyielding moral sense. The role would be assigned to me in a playful, somewhat teasing manner. I was given some opportunity to react, usually with dismay as I pointed out the judgmental nature of the attribution.

Mrs. M suggested putting her mother on the stand to testify, so that she could discredit her by showing conflicting opinions. Then, in a rush of feeling, the playfulness vanished and she demanded to know: "What is the difference between what my parents did to me and my setting limits for Michael?" In her interaction with me, the generational dimension had collapsed: "I am like them [the children]. I feel their pain." She wept for "the child" she longed to protect, a condensation of her infantile self, her dependent mother, and her young children. She was able to share with me her exquisite attunement to infantile needs.

There was confusion and rigidity in Mrs. M's response to limit setting for the children, with little room for compassion. Her infantile self and feelings remained eidetic and vivid in her memory, having undergone no transformation. Her moral sense was analytic, judgmental, and vengeful in her desire to discredit and destroy. It reflected a premature conformity to parental demands out of fear of disapproval and as a defense against the experience of her own rage. "I only knew how to be good." She assumed (again, in a projective identification) that Michael was really fearful of "time out"; it was not that he just wanted to be disobedient. Thus assuming the parental disciplinary role was for her fraught with terror.

Mrs. M and I went on to discuss the early choice by Sammy and herself of the toy "kitty cat" to play with together. The cat was both arousing and teasing. Reflecting these themes of loss and revenge, the kitty needed to be pursued and could get into all kinds of "trouble."

Within the context of this game, many different potential outcomes could be explored. The kitty cat referenced his "mother" to discover if the outcomes of his actions would be interpreted as dangerous, amusing, annoying, exciting, or desirable. Depending on the parental response, the kitty cat would design new strategies of eliciting contact and of coping with the ongoing play activity. These roles often were reversed, with mother in the role of kitty cat and Sammy the person who was referenced. I suggested to Mrs. M that these interactive games were attempts within the dyad to construct a coherent sense of shared social reality. Each of the partners was, in turn, both an active participant and a passive recipient in the play activity.

In the next month, Sammy continued to do well. Mrs. M became increasingly introspective. She described two aspects of herself, the harsh judge and the affectionate, loving part. The loving part of her considered Sammy a "gift." She earnestly said, "If he is a truck driver or a construction worker, if he just has relationships, it'll be okay."

She continued to be upset over her "abandonment" of Sammy as a younger child. This was an example of the harsh judge within her. She felt that until Sammy was 21 months old, he did not have a mother. With Michael, the symbiosis was sublime: "You never had to set limits; he just knew." She was that way with her own mother; she always did her bidding and never had to be disciplined. Mrs. M talked about Sammy's progress with delight: "I am a good mother." She then criticized herself and laughed lightheartedly, neither tense nor manic.

Mrs. M named the two aspects of herself the critical-idealistic self and the accepting self. This inner split was reflected in her split perceptions of her two sons. She continued to describe one son in contrast to the other, rather than seeing them as individual children. This split in her perceptions of her children seemed a metaphor for the soft sensation shapes versus the hard sensation objects that pervaded her inner reality; each child was represented as one or the other. Her own sense of identity lacked coherence and cohesiveness as well and was divided into two opposing experiences of herself.

SAMMY, MICHAEL, AND MOTHER

The split perceptions Mrs. M described were evidenced in the next session within the transference. When I intervened to set a limit to her protection of Sammy, she perceived me as intimidating, and our therapeutic alliance was sorely tested. This was an example of slippage, in which Mrs. M identified with the fearful response of her child to the bright light. She experienced my intervention as hurtful and as critical to her role as parent.

Sammy was restless; he came into the playroom and saw bright sunlight streaming in through the window. I moved the blinds to shield him, but he became frightened and wanted to run out of the room. I lifted him up and carried him to the window. His mother approached to comfort him. I encouraged her to let me hold him and let him see her expression full face. He stiffened, screamed, and then calmed in response to his mother's soothing voice. All the while, Michael was building a castle. Sammy got down and deliberately destroyed the castle. Their mother began to cry quietly. I asked her not to do that now, and she replied, "That's not the issue." At the end of the session, as they left, Sammy looked at me directly for a long time, bewildered, and shrugged his shoulders.

I phoned Mrs. M at home, and we agreed to schedule an extra session. The intervention of my holding Sammy had triggered a crisis between us. Mrs. M stated her feelings as follows: "I want to stick this out. I don't want to run away. Is this best for me?" She was manifesting both our strong alliance and her emergent strong sense of ambivalence.

MOTHER

Our collaborative efforts to help Sammy were in jeopardy. Mrs. M wondered whether she could trust me enough to confront me, even though I, her therapist, did not value her feelings. I commented that I had asked her to suppress her feelings just for the moment, that I did value them, and that that was why I had called. For Mrs. M, my limiting Sammy and picking him up had limited her own infantile longings. She felt I had treated her like a child, talked down to her. She often felt adults did not take her seriously. "Why didn't you ask me before you did it? You promised me you would not do it again." (This statement referred back to the episode early in treatment when I helped restrain Sammy during a temper tantrum.)

I responded that these issues were cyclic and would recur in our difficult work together. I inquired whether she felt I understood. Sobbing, she responded, "If you understand, how can you do it? Did you plan it?"

I responded that my actions were spontaneous. Perhaps she thought I "understood" too much, without checking with her first as to what was going on. Sammy gave us an opportunity to check this out. He challenged us with his extreme sensitivity to light. Mrs. M, still sobbing, said, "But, he wanted me." I pointed out that "his wish was also his fear, of too much closeness. He needed to attend separately to the sound of your voice and the bright light. Having you hold him would have brought the two of you too closely together, and the source of security would have become frightening."

Mrs. M confided that she was better able to let her husband manage the kids on his own and deal with them according to his own ideas when he was alone with them. For instance, he gave Sammy a full bottle of milk to go to sleep (in violation of her efforts to wean him). She was laughing warmly, and the tension was dissipated.

Mrs. M went on to share a series of fragmentary recollections from her childhood. They seemed disjointed but shared a common theme of evaluation of self—a valuing of intellectual achievements and a devaluing of emotional life. Her ambivalence was intense: She worried I might leave her, but at the same time, she had strong doubts about continuing in treatment. She vacillated in her attitude toward me between protest (in her role as a child) and rejection (in her role as a parent).

Recollection 1

MRS. M: Do you remember the Daniel Boone Show? My mother deprived me of watching it. She did set limits, but she did not understand this show was my whole life . . . this fantasy. I shared it with my friends.

THERAPIST: Your pain was her lack of empathy. It was not just that specific show. Mother did not understand what it meant to you. Did Saralea understand what having Sammy close means to Mrs. M, how much Mrs. M loves to comfort him?

MRS. M [smiling warmly]: Why should it matter? It's so juvenile.

THERAPIST: You are like a judge devaluing your precious infantile feelings.

MRS. M: I think they are dumb, silly. Why do I remember all of these incidents?

THERAPIST: It's like you are presenting a case, an argument against your own well-being.

Recollection 2

MRS. M: I was an excellent math student. We used to have to add large columns and I would get bored and would fantasize and would not finish. I played hooky from the after-school punishment because I did not feel it was justified. Mom would not listen to why; she just set the limits. She scolded me for leaving without permission.

THERAPIST: Perhaps you feel I am being arbitrary. I am setting limits without understanding you.

Recollection 3

MRS. M: My half sister was sent away to live with our grandmother because she was a behavioral problem. I was 6, and my younger brother was 4. Then the family moved away. We [the children] were sad, not them [the parents]. [Wistful smile] I know my dad must have been sad too; it must have been awful for him. My brother asked me if it could happen to us—he thought of that at 4 years old! I reasoned it would not, because we were Mom's natural children. I think this was the first time I realized this, about my sister. I idealized her—she was older, beautiful. But I was smarter and somehow more mature. She was mean to me but nice to me also sometimes. It was a terrible loss. I somehow felt guilty.

THERAPIST: It sounds as if you fear I might leave you if you tell me you understand things better than I.

That evening, Mrs. M phoned me to say that she was fearful she would forget her anger if she did not call me, and she did not want the feelings to fester until our next appointment. Rethinking our attempt at reconciliation, she did not feel her disagreement with me was rational; also, she felt less alienated from me. She did not feel satisfaction—just angry and puzzled over what had happened between us. Were my actions correct? Should she consult Paul (the analyst who referred her to me)? "I can't let it go. It was so humiliating to be spoken to as if I were a child in front of my children."

Because Mrs. M was experiencing a conflict between her role as parent and her own infantile feelings, it was not surprising that this tension brought about an incident of role reversal with Michael. Mrs. M continued: "Afterwards, Michael came in and wondered why I was so sad. He explained to me, 'You felt so angry Saralea didn't give you Sammy. That's the way it had to be. You can hold me now.'"

In the next session, Mrs. M continued putting together fragments of self-experience. First, she wondered how I felt when she criticized me. She seemed to have no representation of how I would feel. Then she offered that it had been the first time she ever had criticized anyone. She had felt anger, then sadness, then self-denigration.

Her next image was of an idealized self. She had the fantasy of being June Cleaver, the mother in the 1950s TV series "Leave It to Beaver." She wanted to bake brownies, always be in the kitchen, be spotless and cheerful: "Very unrealistic, what my mother was not. In domesticity, I could make it up to myself. But really, I'm like her."

Other pieces of self-experience were linked to merger with her older sister. There were times when Mrs. M felt her sister's experiences were happening to her. It was an intense bond of attunement to her. Mrs. M recalled: "I was 4 years old, and the neighborhood kids were ganging up on her. She was always a troublemaker, for example, stealing money from my piggy bank. She spent it all on bubble gum;

it drove my father crazy. [Laughing] She ate all the frosting on the cake and insisted the mice had eaten the cake.

"Another time, I was younger than 2 years, I don't know how to explain my feelings. I felt it was happening to me. My sister was lying in bed, and my father was hitting her on the face. I didn't know why, maybe it was because of stealing from my piggy bank. She just lied; it drove him crazy. The evidence was always there. He hit her repeatedly, and she wouldn't change her story. It drove him crazy. No one was listening. I ran to the front door and tried to get out of the house. My mother said to him, 'You're upsetting her, stop.' [Longingly] I must have felt so close to my sister. To be sent away—it had such an impact on me." While reviewing this event, Mrs. M became less forgiving of her father, and her bond with her unruly sister was strengthened.

SAMMY AND MOTHER

In our next session together with Sammy, it became clear that Mrs. M had reconciled herself to my actions. Sammy played with hand puppets and was responsive and interactive with his mother. Then he noticed light coming in the window and wanted to leave. His mother comforted him: "It's safe here." I encouraged him to play with the shadow from the light. Mrs. M said that Sammy played with his shadow as a young child and that *shadow* was one of his first words. I inquired whether Sammy had noticed that a change in light could make a shadow disappear. Meanwhile, he tolerated the bright sunlight and looked out into the garden. He became irritable, then calmed and got involved in truck play. He helped to clean up before he left.

MOTHER

As Mrs. M gathered her recollections, she had difficulty integrating feelings about her parents. Her mother was so devalued by her father, it made identification with her difficult. Mrs. M triumphed over her depressed mother, because her father valued her intellect. However, as much as she tried to please them, she felt they were never there for her.

Another source of despair for Mrs. M was her lack of credibility in her parents' eyes. Mrs. M, who described herself as a compliant child, was terrified by her parents' lack of belief in her: "When I was 5, I had an encounter with a child molester. I felt ashamed. They would not listen; later, they called the police. My parents thought it was a story; they thought I had made it up. They never talked to me about my feelings about it. I felt ashamed and violated. There were so many sad things I felt I could not confide in my parents."

•   •   •

Mrs. M recalled that the idyllic period with Michael ended when Sammy was born. To both parents' dismay, Michael regressed somewhat. He was not toilet trained and was still on the bottle. He got a little more demanding, and during nursing time, he wanted attention. By 2 years, Michael had recovered, played by himself for long periods of time, and was quite self-reliant.

When Mrs. M returned to full-time work, both children experienced a big loss. (Michael was 2 years, 4 months; Sammy was 8 months.) Michael started staying up later, and he would not stay by himself. Some of the time, he was terrified of ghosts in the dark. Sammy, who had begun to crawl, became destructive. Mrs. M began to worry that something was wrong with Sammy, because he would not play with toys for any length of time. She could not interest him in anything. His father tossed him around and got him to laugh; they were desperate to see Sammy play with something. They asked Michael to give up his toys to Sammy. "Share, give Sammy a turn." It was easier for the parents to lean on Michael, because he was verbal. Mrs. M was able to give Sammy's early history without becoming distraught. It indicated the maternal depression linked with Sammy's birth was considerably alleviated.

Mrs. M continued her description: "We put all the pressure on Michael instead of restraining Sammy. I remember worrying when Sammy was 8 or 10 months old [after she returned to work]. Before that time I was puzzled, not worried. He did not take an interest in toys, and he was always so unresponsive. I remember I was irritated with him at 1 day old; he was not nursing." Mrs. M described Sammy as a temperamentally difficult child and asked what I thought about him. She seemed to be asking me for some sort of appraisal of her assessment, and I reflected on all the worry and tension that had surrounded Sammy.

SAMMY AND MOTHER

As mother and child became more confident, they began to play games with aggressive themes. A major one was the peekaboo game, including expressions of surprise, pursuit, and avoidance. A second game between the pair involved themes of biting and consuming. Mrs. M wondered if the play was overwhelming. I introduced symbolic objects—hand puppets and toys—to give distance to the feelings. Mrs. M grasped the function served by symbolic referents and was no longer threatened by the instinctive quality of the play activity.

Mrs. M's further concerns about aggression and malevolence were conveyed in an anxious phone call. She had tried to kiss Sammy, and he immediately had turned his head and knocked against her lip and tooth; it felt as though it was not accidental. "How could you do something like that?" she demanded, and she became hysterical. "I thought my teeth were loosened, and I became enraged."

There were several other acts of hostility during the day. For example, Sammy pulled her hair. Her reaction frightened her, and she obsessed: Did he do it on purpose? Was it an accident? He avoided her; she was flinching; he did not seek her out. She was annoyed with him, and the evening ritual was not pleasant. She worried that Sammy would feel "I'm unsafe and unpredictable," clearly feelings she had for him as well.

MOTHER

At the next session, Mrs. M described her anger at the children when they "act like children." She called herself "the Frightening Mother." She intimidated Michael to get him to comply, became locked in confrontation, and then became depressed. She judged herself harshly: "A parent ought to be able to . . . " Mrs. M was unable to confront her own parents and made no demands on them. She felt extremely sad as well as angry, "like there is a scarecrow inside me." She really was frightened about her own malevolent qualities; she threatened her child with precisely what frightened him the most.

Mrs. M reported that the boys were playing together—fire fighting, parallel play, and cooperative play. Michael had discovered that Sammy could be a playmate. Sammy cooperated in fantasy play; for example, he held the fire hose. Michael now used language to talk to Sammy. Michael used to want to play with his mother or a friend, but now Sammy and Michael could be companions for a 3-hour stretch. They also fought. (I reflected to myself, "A person at last!") Sammy had been trying for 2 months to be his brother's playmate; Michael was now receptive.

SAMMY AND MOTHER

Sammy and his mother were putting trains together, at Sammy's initiative. First, they had to fix the tracks.

MRS. M: Do you need help to put them together?
SAMMY: Okay [sits down beside her on the floor].
MRS. M: Sammy, look at this! [Sammy looks away and persists in tak-

ing out more tracks.] Sammy, look at this, look down. Look down and see. [Sammy turns away and persists at taking out more tracks from the box. Mother waits.]

SAMMY: Mom-tracks [garbled].

MRS. M: Push down here, see? [Sammy follows her example and continues to build the track. Mother watches.] Watch this. [She takes his head in her hands and directs his gaze.] That's right, you did it! [She repeats this phrase three times, each time a track is joined, with amplified affect.]

SAMMY: Track.

MRS. M: Here's more! [Sammy joins the tracks.] Yes, you did it! [Sammy continues to join more tracks together and puts a locomotive on the track, joining train cars together.]

SAMMY: Track?

MRS. M: I don't know where the other track is. You know what we could do? We can make a bumper. [Mother demonstrates alternative track; Sammy watches.] Put that in there; here's a bumper track.

SAMMY [Cooperates and mumbles]: Together . . . Mommy, together.

MRS. M: You want Mommy to put it together. We are both building and joining the tracks into a figure eight design.

SAMMY: Together.

MRS. M: Oh, this is great!

SAMMY: Yeah.

MRS. M: Yeah. [They both crouch over the tracks together.]

SAMMY: Tooo-ooo! [He takes another car, joining it to the engine.] Couple.

MRS. M: He coupled it!

SAMMY: Tooo-ooo, couple. [He works at putting two more cars together and turns to his mother.] Mommy couple.

They worked intently for some time together joining train cars. Sammy's attention was riveted on his car. He was unable to attend to two things at once; when his mother called out that she was encountering difficulty, he came around to his mother's side of the track. He saw her, and they exchanged a long, sustained mutual gaze. She grasped his head in her hands and leaned down to kiss him. He quietly sat back, continuing to gaze at her. He pointed, she whispered, he whispered, he crawled away, she followed. In conspiracy, they located a large carrier truck and pushed it along together. Sammy sent me a sideways glance to make sure I was following the action.

Significantly, in this same session, Sammy initiated with me his first elaborated symbolic play. The theme dealt with a train that breaks down on the track. The breakdown train came to fix it, and the repairman fell repeatedly trying to climb the ladder. Sammy entreated him to "hurry, hurry." The train was reinstated on the track and continued on its way.

MOTHER

The mother reported that as Sammy progressed in speech, he was becoming more disorganized emotionally. When he wanted something, he started screaming. He was more impulsive, had become attached to his baseball bat again, and wanted his bottle the minute he got into the house. He and she played a game Sammy called "Bottle Away," it which he repeatedly found the hidden bottle. Sammy annoyed his mother when he refused kisses or made faces. She felt drained when Sammy became more demanding emotionally, whining and fighting battles over ordinary things, much like a 2-year-old going through the "terrible 2s." Outside the home, he was doing well in an informal group program called "Mommy and Me." He learned music and songs and listened during story time in this informal setting. He learned hand motions to songs and could handle group routines.

At home, it was increasingly clear that Sammy was a creative child. He initiated many games. For instance, he liked pirates and played at being "Captain Hook." He introduced Michael to his play and imagined himself in the role of firefighter. In the game of Mommy Ghost, he and Michael would hide under the covers with a flashlight, "camping out." Sammy would say, "Mommy be the ghost!" Mother would make noises and, while searching for them, put spooky things in their tent ("spiders," "octopus," and a "dinosaur"). She would say, "Oh, ghosts are afraid of light," would go away, and then would come back, trying to get them from inside the "tent." She would have to crawl through a tunnel to get inside.

Sammy hated Michael's ghost mask. He was frightened when Michael did scary things in earnest. By contrast, the mother's ghost was a comical ghost. They liked to play the game over and over again, hiding and transforming something scary to something funny.

ENDING PHASE OF TREATMENT:
CONSOLIDATION AND CONSTANCY

As treatment progressed, we encountered fully Mrs. M's rigid expectations and fear of change. She became easily frightened, sensing trouble and being quick to assume the worst. When change occurred, she felt that everything was falling apart and becoming chaotic. This lack of coherence and capacity to remain organized during transitions was her pathology. In her anxiety, she would rush to extreme conclusions.

Sammy had become inconsolable and despairing on parting at the end of sessions. His mother described her own despair and helplessness when she became overwhelmed. She could not tolerate change, and children are changing all the time. She experienced this change as terrifying, because she could not adapt and be flexible. In these states, she was exquisitely sensitive to any criticism, which she perceived as rejection. Mrs. M explained to me the devastating hurt Sammy had inflicted on her when he would not suck: "He would not even look at me." This was the pattern of an avoidant child and a rejected parent. She had turned a critical eye inward on herself and protected herself from harsh judgment by becoming increasingly withdrawn. Before therapy, she could identify her threatening feelings only by perceiving them in others. Now, through her newly awakened playfulness and enjoyment in her children, she could begin to catch glimpses of these frightening, critical feelings as being partly her own.

As the ending phase of treatment came to a close, clarification and differentiation occurred within the dyadic relationship. There was a recognition of boundaries. Disorganizing affects were diminishing, and both mother and child were experiencing a freeing up of energies for the renewal of development and growth. These gains resonated to the family unit as a whole. The father and brother viewed Sammy as a companion and enjoyed spending time with him in various pursuits. The family spent a fun-filled vacation at the beach. There was a significant lessening of tensions within the marital partnership. Sammy entered a mainstream preschool class with children 6 months younger than himself. He made an excellent social adjustment and had no difficulty following classroom routines. His expressive language improved. A significant problem remained in articulation, however, and he continued to receive speech and language therapy three times weekly.

CASE SUMMARY

Dyadic treatment focused on the issues that had stalemated the dyadic relationship between mother and child. Mrs. M carried unresolved issues from her own early childhood that had left her anxious and insecure. Her anxiety was paralleled by Sammy's withdrawal and regression. Mrs. M could not cope with Sammy's response. His isolation reminded her of her own isolation, when she was unable to reach out to her parents for comfort. The therapy relationship offered her support as well as an avenue for connection to her estranged child.

When the distance between them was lessened, Mrs. M revealed unusual capacities for sensitivity and empathic understanding of Sammy's needs. He responded to her approach in a style unique to his exuberant and passionate personality. At times it seemed that Sammy possessed unusual emotional receptivity, depth, and understanding, despite his inability to articulate his understanding in words. Play activity in which symbolic understandings unfolded was a major means of communication within the dyadic relationship. The mother, who had been a parentified child and was a bright and articulate person, benefited from the play as well. She discovered new nuances in emotional meaning and differentiation of feeling states. For both members of the dyad, this symbolic communication brought with it enhanced emotional regulation and control. When Sammy evidenced clear progress, Mrs. M was able to explore in greater depth the issues from her childhood that still produced fear.

The diagnostic question raised by the recovery of this dyad is whether Sammy's diagnosis of pervasive developmental disorder was accurate. The category of reactive attachment disorder seems to be more appropriate. As a secure pattern of mother-child attachment emerged, Sammy's developmental delay became specific to the area of expressive language, with minor deficits in fine-motor coordination. In addition, he preferred to follow his own interests and needed assistance at times to focus on structured tasks.

This dramatic resolution of a profound stalemate in developmental progress could have been achieved only through dyadic treatment. The joint sessions were supplemented by individual therapy sessions for the mother with the same therapist. The simultaneous treatment model used the natural forward momentum of a child's growth and the inherent maternal instinct to repair and heal. The results were a happier mother and child with hopes for a happier future.

References

Abrams, D. M. (1993). Pathological narcissism in an eight-year-old boy. *Psychoanalytic Psychology, 10,* 573–591.

Achenbach, T. M. (1978). The Child Behavior Profile: I. *Journal of Consulting and Clinical Psychology, 46,* 478–488.

———, & Edelbrock, C. S. (1981). Behavioral problems and competencies reported by parents of normal and disturbed children ages four through sixteen. *Monographs of the Society for Research in Child Development, 46*(188).

Ainsworth, M. D. S., Blehar, M. C., Waters, E., & Wall, S. (1978). *Patterns of attachment: A psychological study of the strange situation.* Hillsdale, NJ: Erlbaum.

———, & Wittig, B. A. (1969). Attachment and the exploratory behavior of one-year-olds in a strange situation. In B. M. Foss (Ed.), *Determinants of infant behavior* (Vol. 4, pp. 113–136). London: Methuen.

Akhtar, S. (1991). Three fantasies related to unresolved separation-individuation. In S. Akhtar & H. Parens (Eds.), *Beyond the symbiotic orbit* (pp. 261–284). Hillsdale, NJ: Analytic Press.

———, & Parens, H. (Eds.). (1991). *Beyond the symbiotic orbit.* Hillsdale, NJ: Analytic Press.

American Psychiatric Association (1987). *Diagnostic and statistical manual of mental disorders* (3rd ed., revised). Washington, DC: APA.

———. (1994). *Diagnostic and statistical manual of mental disorders* (4th ed.). Washington, DC: APA.

Anthony, E. J. (1970). The family as a psychologic field. In E. J. Anthony & T. Benedicts (Eds.), *Parenthood* (pp. 153–156). Boston: Little, Brown.

Beardslee, W. R., Bemporad, J., Keller, M. B., & Klerman, G. L. (1983). Children of parents with major affective disorder: A review. *American Journal of Psychiatry, 140,* 825–832.

Beck, A. T. (1991). Cognitive therapy: A 30-year retrospective. *American Psychologist, 46,* 368–375.

Beebe, B., Jaffe, J., & Lachmann, F. (1994). A dyadic systems model of mother-infant mutual regulation: Implications for the origins of representations and therapeutic action. *Psychologist-Psychoanalyst, 14,* 27–33.

Beebe, B., & Lachmann, F. M. (1988). The contribution of mother-infant mutual influence to the origins of self and object representations. *Psychoanalytic Psychology, 5,* 305–337.

Belsky, J., & Nezworski, T. (1988). *Clinical implications of attachment.* Hillsdale, NJ: Erlbaum.

Benedek, T. (1956). Toward the biology of the depressed constellation. *Journal of the American Psychoanalytic Association, 4,* 389–394.

Benjamin, J. D. (1963). Further comments on some developmental aspects of anxiety. In H. S. Gashell (Ed.), *Counterpart: Libidinal object and subject* (pp. 121–153). New York: International Universities Press.

Biederman, J., Rosenbaum, J. F., Hirshfeld, D. R., Faraone, S. V., Bolduc, E. A., Gersten, M., Meminger, S. R., Kagan, J., Snidman, N., & Reznick, S. (1990). Psychiatric correlates of behavioral inhibition in young children of parents with and without psychiatric disorder. *Archives of General Psychiatry, 47,* 21–26.

Bion, W. R. (1962). A theory of thinking. *International Journal of Psycho-Analysis, 43,* 306–310.

———. (1967). *Second thoughts.* New York: Jason Aronson.

Biringen, Z., Robinson, J. L., & Emde, R. N. (1988). *Emotional availability scales.* Unpublished manuscript, University of Colorado.

Blehar, M. C., & Eichberg, C. G. (1991). Effects on infant-mother attachment of mother's unresolved loss of an attachment figure or other traumatic experience. In P. Morris, A. Stevenson-Hinde, & C. Parks (Eds.), *Attachment across the life cycle* (pp. 160–183). New York: Routledge.

———, Waters, E., & Wall, S. (1978). *Patterns of attachment: A psychological study of the strange situation.* Hillsdale, NJ: Erlbaum.

Bleiberg, E. (1984). Narcissistic disorders in children. *Bulletin of the Menninger Clinic, 48,* 501–517.

Blos, P., Jr. (1985). Intergenerational separation-individuation: Treating the mother-infant pair. *Psychoanalytic Study of the Child, 40,* 41–56.

Blum, H. P. (1988). Shared fantasy and reciprocal identification and their role in gender disorders. In H. P. Blum, Y. Kramer, A. K. Richards, & A. D. Richards (Eds.), *Fantasy, myth, and reality* (pp. 323–338). Madison, CT: International Universities Press.

Bowlby, J. (1969). *Attachment.* New York: Basic Books.

———. (1973). *Attachment and loss: Vol. 2. Separation.* New York: Basic Books.

———. (1980). *Loss.* New York: Basic Books.

———. (1989). The role of attachment in personality development and psychopathology. In S. L. Greenspan & G. H. Pollack (Eds.), *The course of life: Vol. I. Infancy* (pp. 229–270). Madison, CT: International Universities Press.

Brazelton, T. B., & Craemer, B. G. (1990). *The earliest relationship.* Boston: Addison-Wesley.

Bretherton, I. (1990). Communication patterns, internal working models, and the intergenerational transmission of attachment relationships. *Infant Mental Health Journal, 11,* 237–252.

———. (1992). Social referencing, intentional communication, and the interfacing of minds in infancy. In S. Feenman (Ed.), *Social referencing and the social construction of reality in infancy* (pp. 57–77). New York: Plenum Press.

———, & Bates, E. (1979). The emergence of intentional communication. In I. Uzgiris (Ed.), *New Directions for Child Development, 4,* 81–100.

———, & Beeghly, M. (1982). Talking about internal states. *Developmental Psychology, 18,* 906–921.

———, Biringen, Z., Ridgeway, D., Maslin, C., & Sherman, M. (1989). Attachment: A parental perspective. *Infant Mental Health Journal, 10,* 203–221.

———, McNew, S., & Beeghly-Smith, M. (1981). Early person knowledge as expressed in gestures and verbal communication. In M. E. Lamb & L. R. Sherrod (Eds.), *Infant Social Cognition: Empirical and Theoretical Considerations* (pp. 333–373). Hillsdale, NJ: Erlbaum.

———, & Waters, E. (Eds.). (1985). Growing points in attachment theory and research. *Monographs of the Society for Research in Child Development, 49*(6, Serial No. 209).

Bruner, J. (1986). *Actual minds, possible worlds.* Cambridge: Harvard University Press.

———. (1990). *Acts of meaning.* Cambridge: Harvard University Press.

Bruner, J. S. (1977). Early social interaction and language acquisition. In H. R. Schaffer (Ed.), *Studies in mother-infant interaction* (pp. 271–289). New York: Academic Press.

———. (1983). *Child's talk: Learning to use language.* New York: Norton.

Buirski, P., & Buirski, C. (1980). The split transference in the simultaneous treatment of mother and child. *Bulletin of the Menninger Clinic, 44,* 639–646.

Burlingham, D. (1951). Present trends in handling the mother-child relationship during the therapeutic process. *Psychoanalytic Study of the Child, 6,* 31–37.

———, Goldberger, A., & Lussier, A. (1955). Simultaneous analysis of mother and child. *Psychoanalytic Study of the Child, 10,* 165–186.

Campos, J. J., & Stenberg, C. (1981). Perception, appraisal, and emotion. In M. Lamb & L. Sherrod (Eds.), *Infant social cognition* (pp. 273–314). Hillsdale, NJ: Erlbaum.

Chazan, S. E. (1992). Merging and emerging realities: Simultaneous treatment of parent and child. *American Journal of Psychotherapy, 46,* 281–296.

Chethik, M. (1976). Work with parents: Treatment of the parent-child relationship. *Journal of the American Academy of Child Psychiatry, 15,* 453–463.

Cicchetti, D., & Aber, J. L. (1980). Abused children—abusive parents: An overstated case? *Harvard Educational Review, 50,* 244–255.

———, & Carlson, V. (1989). *Child maltreatment.* New York: Cambridge University Press.

Clark, R. (1985). *The parent-child early relational assessment.* Unpublished manuscript, University of Wisconsin.

Coates, S., & Person, E. S. (1985). Extreme boyhood femininity: Isolated behavior or pervasive disorder? *Journal of the American Academy of Child Psychiatry, 24,* 702–709.

Combrenick-Graham, L. (1989). *Children in family contexts: Perspectives on treatment.* New York: Guilford Press.

―――. (1989). Family models of childhood psychopathology. In L. Combrenick-Graham (Ed.), *Children in family contexts: Perspectives on treatment* (pp. 67–90). New York: Guilford Press.

Conners, C. K. (1985a). Parent Symptom Questionnaire. *Psychopharmacology Bulletin, 21,* 816–822.

―――. (1985b). Teacher Questionnaire. *Psychopharmacology Bulletin, 21,* 823–831.

Crockenberg, S. (1987). Predictors and correlates of anger toward and punitive control of toddlers by adolescent mothers. *Child Development, 58,* 964–975.

Davies, D. (1991). Conjoint intervention with male toddlers who have witnessed parental violence. *Families-in-Society, 72,* 515–524.

Dodge, K. (1990). Developmental psychotherapy in children of depressed mothers. *Developmental Psychology, 26,* 3–6.

Dumas, J. (1984). Interactional correlates of treatment outcome in behavioral parent training. *Journal of Consulting and Clinical Psychology, 52,* 946–954.

Dunn, J. (1988). *The beginnings of social understanding.* Cambridge, MA: Harvard University Press.

―――, & Plomin, R. (1990). *Separate lives.* New York: Basic Books.

Egan, J., & Kernberg, P. (1984). Pathological narcissism in childhood. *Journal of the American Psychoanalytic Association, 32,* 39–62.

Eisenstadt, T., Eyberg, S., McNeil, C. B., Newcomb, K., & Funderburk B. (1993). Parent-child interactive therapy with behavior problem children. *Journal of Clinical Child Psychology, 22,* 42–51.

Emde, R. N. (1980). Toward a psychoanalytic theory of affect: I. The organizational model and its propositions. In S. Greenspan & G. Pollock (Eds.), *The course of life* (Vol. I, pp. 165–193). Madison, CT: International Universities Press.

―――. (1983). The pre-representational self and its affective core. *The Psychoanalytic Study of the Child, 38,* 165–192.

―――. (1988). Development terminable and interminable: Innate and motivational factors from infancy. *International Journal of Psycho-Analysis, 69,* 23–42.

―――. (1989). The infant's relationship experience: Developmental and affective aspects. In A. J. Somercraft & R. N. Emde (Eds.), *Relationship disturbances in early childhood* (pp. 33–51). New York: Basic Books.

―――. (1992). Social referencing research. In S. Feenman (Ed.), *Social referencing and the social construction of reality in infancy* (pp. 79–94). New York: Plenum Press.

―――, Biringen, Z., Clyman, R., & Oppenheim, D. (1991). The moral self of infancy: Affective core and procedural knowledge. *Developmental Review, 11,* 251–270.

―――, & Buchsbaum, H. K. (1980). Toward a psychoanalytic theory of affect: II. Emotional development and signaling in infancy. In S. Greenspan & G. Pollack (Eds.), *The course of life* (Vol. I, pp. 193–229). Madison, CT: International Universities Press.

Erickson, M., Korfmacher, J., & Egeland, B. (1992). Attachments past and present: Implications for therapeutic intervention with mother-infant dyads. *Development and Psychopathology, 4,* 495–507.

Esman, A. H. (1970). Transsexual identification in a three-year-old twin: A brief communication. *Psychosocial Process, 1,* 77–79.

Fast, I. (1985). *Event theory: A Piaget-Freud integration.* Hillsdale, NJ: Erlbaum.

Feinman, S. (1982). Social referencing in infancy. *Merrill-Palmer Quarterly, 28,* 445–470.

———, & Lewis, M. (1983). Social referencing at ten months. *Child Development, 54,* 878–887.

Feldman, L. (1988). Integrating individual and family therapy in the treatment of symptomatic children and adolescents. *American Journal of Psychotherapy, 42,* 272–280.

Feshbach, N. D. (1987). Parental empathy and child adjustment/maladjustment. In N. Eisenberg & J. Strayor (Eds.), *Empathy and its development* (pp. 271–291). New York: Cambridge University Press.

Fischoff, J. (1964). Preoedipal influences in a boy's determination to be "feminine" during the oedipal period. *Journal of the American Academy of Child Psychiatry, 3,* 273–286.

Fonagy, P. (1993). Psychoanalytic and empirical approaches to developmental psychopathology: An object-relations perspective. *Journal of the American Psychoanalytic Association, 41*(Suppl.), 245–260.

———, Steele, M., Moran, G., Steele, H., & Higgitt, A. C. (1991). The capacity for understanding mental states: The reflective self in parent and child and its significance for the security of attachment. *Infant Mental Health Journal, 13,* 200–216.

Fraiberg, S. (1980). *Clinical studies in infant mental health: The first year of life.* New York: Basic Books.

———. (1987). Pathological defenses in infancy. *Psychoanalytic Quarterly, 51,* 612–635.

———, Adelson, E., & Shapiro, V. (1975). Ghosts in the nursery: A psychoanalytic approach to the problems of impaired infant-mother relationships. *Journal of the American Academy of Child Psychiatry, 14,* 387–421.

Fredrich, W., & Wheeler, K. (1982). The abusive parent revisited. *Journal of Nervous and Mental Disease, 170,* 577–587.

Freud, A. (1950). Introduction to simultaneous analysis of a mother and her adolescent daughter by Kata Levy. *Psychoanalytic Study of the Child, 15,* 378–380.

Freud, S. (1909). Analysis of a phobia in a five-year-old boy. *The standard edition of the complete psychological works of Sigmund Freud* (Vol. 10, pp. 3–149). London: Hogarth Press, 1955.

———. (1913). Totem and taboo. *The standard edition of the complete psychological works of Sigmund Freud* (Vol. 13, pp. 1–161). London: Hogarth Press, 1955.

———. (1914). Remembering, repeating, and working through. *The standard edition of the complete psychological works of Sigmund Freud* (Vol. 12). London: Hogarth Press, 1958.

———. (1920). Beyond the pleasure principle. *The standard edition of the com-*

plete psychological works of Sigmund Freud (Vol. 18). London: Hogarth Press, 1955.

———. (1926). Inhibitions, symptom and anxiety. *The standard edition of the complete psychological works of Sigmund Freud* (Vol. 20). London: Hogarth Press, 1959.

Gaensbauer, T. J. (1982). Regulation of emotional expression in infants from two contrasting caretaking environments. *Journal of the American Academy of Child Psychiatry, 21,* 163–171.

Galenson, E. (1986). Some thoughts about infant psychopathology and aggressive development. *International Review of Psychoanalysis, 13,* 349–354.

———. (1991). Treatment of psychological disorders in early childhood: A tripartite therapeutic model. In S. Akhtar & H. Parens (Eds.), *Beyond the symbiotic orbit* (pp. 323–336). Hillsdale, NJ: Analytic Press.

———. (1993). Infant psychiatry with high-income and low-income multirisk families, 1980–1990. In H. Parens & S. Kramer (Eds.), *Prevention in mental health.* Northvale, NJ: Jason Aronson.

———, & Fields, B. (1989). Death of a young child's father: Effects on separation-individuation. In *The psychoanalytic core: Essays in honor of Leo Rangell, M.D.* (pp. 301–312). Madison, CT: International Universities Press.

George, C., & Main, M. (1979). Social interactions of young abused children: Approach, avoidance, and aggression. *Child Development, 50,* 306–318.

Gergen, K. J., & Gergen, M. M. (1983). Narratives of the self. In T. R. Sarben & K. E. Scheibe (Eds.), *Studies in social identity* (pp. 254–273). New York: Praeger.

Gilpin, D. C., Roaza, S., & Gilpin, D. (1979). Transsexual symptoms in a male child treated by a family therapist. *American Journal of Psychotherapy, 33,* 453–463.

Gottsegin, M., & Grasso, M. (1973). Group treatment of the mother-daughter relationship. *International Journal of Group Psychotherapy, 23,* 69–81.

Green, R. G., Newman, L. E., & Stoller, R. J. (1972). Treatment of boyhood "transsexualism." *Archives of General Psychiatry, 26,* 213–217.

———, R. G., & Stoller, R. J. (1971). Two monozygotic twin pairs discordant for gender identity. *Archives of Sexual Behavior, 1,* 237–321.

Greenacre, P. (1959). On focal symbiosis. In L. Jessner & E. Parenstedt (Eds.), *Dynamic psychology in childhood* (pp. 243–256). New York: Grune & Stratton.

———. (1971). Early physical determinants in the development of the sense of identity. In P. Greenacre (Ed.), *Emotional growth* (Vol. 1, pp. 113–127). New York: International Universities Press.

Greenspan, S. L. (1981). *Psychopathology and adaptations in infancy and early childhood.* New York: International Universities Press.

———. (1989). *The development of the ego.* Madison, CT: International Universities Press.

———, & Lieberman, A. (1989). Infants, mothers, and their interaction: A quantitative clinical approach to developmental assessment. In S. Greenspan & G. Pollack (Eds.), *The course of life* (Vol. I, pp. 503–561). Madison, CT: International Universities Press.

Hirshfeld, D. R., Rosenbaum, J. F., Biederman, J., Bolduc, E., Faraone, S., Snidman, N., Reznick, S., & Kagan, J. (1992). Stable behavioral inhibition and its association with anxiety disorder. *Journal of the American Academy of Child and Adolescent Psychiatry, 31,* 103–111.

Hobson, R. P. (1993). The intersubjective domain: Approaches from developmental psychopathology. *Journal of the American Psychoanalytic Association, 41*(Suppl.), 167–192.

Hoffman, M. L. (1978). Empathy: Its development and prosocial implications. In C. B. Keasey (Ed.), *Nebraska symposium on motivation:* Vol. 25 (pp. 169–218). Lincoln: University of Nebraska Press.

———. (1982a). Measurement of empathy. In C. Izard (Ed.), *Measurement of emotions in infants and children* (pp. 279–296). New York: Cambridge University Press.

———. (1982b). Development of prosocial motivation: Empathy and guilt. In N. Eisenberg (Ed.), *Development of prosocial behavior* (pp. 281–313). New York: Academic Press.

Holden, C. (1980). Identical twins reared apart. *Science, 207,* 1323–1328.

Holman, S. (1985). A group program for borderline mothers and their toddlers. *International Journal of Group Psychotherapy, 35,* 79–93.

Hopkins, J. (1992). Infant-parent psychotherapy. *Journal of Child Psychotherapy, 18,* 5–17.

Hurvitz, M. S. (1989). Traumatic moment, basic dangers, and annihilation anxiety. *Psychoanalytic Psychology, 6,* 343–366.

Jacobson, E. (1950). Development of the wish for a child in boys. *Psychoanalytic Study of the Child, 5,* 139–152.

———. (1964). *The self and object world.* New York: International Universities Press.

Kagan, J. (1981). *The second year: The emergence of self-awareness.* Cambridge, MA: Harvard University Press.

———. (1989). *Unstable ideas.* Cambridge, MA: Harvard University Press.

Kalmanson, B., & Pekarsky, J. (1987). Infant-parent psychotherapy with an autistic toddler. *Zero to Three, 7,* 1–6.

Kaufman, J., & Zigler, E. (1987). Do abused children become abusive parents? *American Journal of Orthopsychiatry 57,* 186–192.

Kellman, L. (1960). Simultaneous analysis of mother and child. *Psychoanalytic Study of the Child, 15,* 359–377.

Kernberg, O. F. (1966). Structural derivatives of object relationships. *International Journal of Psycho-Analysis, 47,* 236–253.

———. (1975). *Borderline conditions and pathological narcissism.* New York: Jason Aronson.

———. (1980). *Internal world and external reality.* New York: Jason Aronson.

———. (1984). *Object relations theory and clinical psychoanalysis.* Northvale, NJ: Jason Aronson.

———. (1991). Some comments on early development. In S. Akhtar & H. Parens (Eds.), *Beyond the symbiotic orbit* (pp. 103–120). Hillsdale, NJ: Analytic Press.

Kernberg, P. F. (1989). Narcissistic personality disorders in childhood. *Psychiatric Clinics of North America, 12,* 671–694.

———, Chazan, S. E., Frankel, A., Rosenberg-Hariton, J., Kruger, R. S., Saunders, R., & Scholl, H. (1991). *Children with conduct disorders.* New York: Basic Books.

————, Chazan, S. E., Normandin, L., Blum, E., & Kruger, R. Cornell play therapy scale. Unpublished manuscript, New York Hospital–Cornell Medical Center, Westchester Division.

————, Clarkin, A. J., Greenblatt E., & Cohen, J. The Cornell interview of peers and friends: Development and validation. *Journal of the American Academy of Child and Adolescent Psychiatry, 31*(3), 448–483.

Kleeman, J. A. (1965). A boy discovers his penis. *Psychoanalytic Study of the Child, 20,* 239–266.

Klein, M. (1946). Notes on some schizoid mechanisms. *International Journal of Psycho-Analysis, 27,* 99–110.

Klinnert, M. D., Campos, J. J., Sorce, J. F., Emde, R. N., & Svejda, M. (1983). Emotions as behavior regulators: Social referencing in infancy. In R. Plutchik & H. Kellerman (Eds.), *Emotion: Theory, research and experience: Vol. 2. Emotions in early development* (pp. 57–86). New York: Academic Press.

————, Emde, R. N., Butterfield, P., & Campos, J. J. (1986). Social referencing. *Developmental Psychology, 22,* 427–432.

Kochanska, G. (1991). Patterns of inhibition to the unfamiliar in children of normal and affectively ill mothers. *Child Development, 62,* 250–263.

Kohlberg, L. (1966). A cognitive developmental analysis of children's sex role concepts and attitudes. In E. E. Maccoby (Ed.), *The development of sex differences.* Stanford: Stanford University Press.

Kohn, B. (1976). Simultaneous analysis of child and parent by the same therapist. *Journal of the American Academy of Psychoanalysis, 4,* 481–499.

Kohut, H. (1972). Thoughts on narcissism and narcissistic rage. *Psychoanalytic Study of the Child, 27,* 360–400.

Kolansky, H., & Moore, W. T. (1966). Some comments on the simultaneous analysis of a father and his adolescent son. *Psychoanalytic Study of the Child, 21,* 237–268.

Lane, R. C., & Chazan, S. E. (1989). Symbols of terror: The witch/vampire, the spider, and the shark. *Psychoanalytic Psychology, 6,* 325–342.

————, & Chazan, S. E. (1990). On fixing and being fixed. *Contemporary Psychotherapy, 20*(2), 16–20.

Lazarus, A. (1992). The multimodal approach to the treatment of minor depression. *American Journal of Psychotherapy, 46,* 549–554.

Levy, K. (1960). Simultaneous analysis of a mother and her adolescent daughter: The mother's contributions to the loosening of the infantile objective. *Psychoanalytic Study of the Child, 15,* 378–391.

Lieberman, A. (1992). Infant-parent psychotherapy with toddlers. *Development and Psychopathology, 4,* 559–574.

————, Westin, D., & Paul, J. (1991). Preventive intervention and outcome with anxiously attached dyads. *Child Development, 62,* 199–209.

Loeb, L., & Shane, M. (1982). The resolution of a transsexual wish in a five-year-old boy. *Journal of the American Psychoanalytic Association, 10,* 419–434.

Mack-Brunswick, R. (1940). The preoedipal phase of the libido development. *Psychoanalytic Quarterly, 9,* 293–319.

Maddux, J. E., Eyberg, S. M., & Funderburk, B. (1989). Parent-child interaction therapy. In M. Roberts & C. E. Waller (Eds.), *Casebook of child and pediatric psychology* (pp. 161–175). New York: Guilford Press.

Mahler, M. S. (1949). Sixteenth Congress of the International Psychoanalytic Association, Zurich, Switzerland. Cited by B. Kohn (1976), p. 483.

――――. (1961). On sadness and grief in infancy and childhood. *Psychoanalytic Study of the Child, 16,* 332–351.

――――. (1965). On the significance of the normal separation-individuation phase. In M. Schur (Ed.), *Drives, affects and behavior* (Vol. 2, pp. 161–169). New York: International Universities Press.

――――. (1968). *On human symbiosis and the vicissitudes of individuation.* New York: International Universities Press.

――――, & Furer M. (1960). Observations on research regarding the symbiotic syndrome of infantile psychosis. *Psychoanalysis, 2,* 317–327.

――――, & Gosliner, B. J. (1955). On symbiotic child psychosis: Genetic, dynamic and restitutive aspects. *Psychoanalytic Study of the Child, 10,* 195–212.

――――, Pine, F., & Bergman, A. (1970). The mother's reaction to her toddler's drive for individuation. In E. J. Anthony & T. Benedek (Eds.), *Parenthood* (pp. 257–274). Boston: Little, Brown.

――――, Pine. F., & Bergman, A. (1975). *The psychological birth of the human infant.* New York: Basic Books.

Main, M. (1983). Exploration, play and cognitive functioning related to infant-mother attachment. *Infant Behavior and Development, 6,* 167–174.

――――. (1991). Metacognitive knowledge, metacognitive monitoring, and single (coherent) vs. multiple (incoherent) models of attachment: Findings and directions for future research. In C. M. Parkes, J. Stevenson-Hinde, & P. Marris (Eds.), *Attachment across the life cycle* (pp. 127–159). London: Routledge.

――――. (1993). Discourse, prediction, and recent studies in attachment: Implications for psychoanalysis. *Journal of the American Psychoanalytic Association, 41*(Suppl.), 209–244.

――――, & Goldwyn, R. (1984). Predicting rejection of her infant from mother's representation of her own experience: Implications for the abused-abusing intergenerational cycle. *Child Abuse and Neglect, 8,* 203–217.

――――, & Hesse E. (1990). Parents' unresolved traumatic experiences are related to infant disorganized attachment status: Is frightened and/or frightening parental behavior the linking mechanism? In M. Greenberg, D. Cischette, & M. Cummings (Eds.), *Attachment in preschool years* (pp. 161–182). Chicago: University of Chicago Press.

――――, Kaplan, N., & Cassidy, J. (1985). Security in infancy, childhood and adulthood: A move to the level of representation. In L. Bretherton & E. Waters (Eds.), Growing points of attachment theory and research (pp. 66–104). *Monographs of the Society for Research in Child Development, 50*(1–2, Serial No. 209).

――――, & Westin, D. (1982). Avoidance of the attachment figure in infancy: Descriptions and interpretations. In C. P. Parkes & J. Stevenson-Hinde (Eds.), *The face of attachment in human behavior,* New York: Basic Books.

Meltzer, D., Bremner, J., Hoxter, S., Weddell, D., & Wittenberg, I. (1975). *Explorations in autism.* Perthshire, Scotland: Clunie Press, 1991.

References

Mitchell, S. A. (1991). Contemporary perspectives on the self: Toward an integration. *Psychoanalytic Dialog, 1,* 121–149.

Modell, A. H. (1990). *Other times, other realities.* Cambridge, MA: Harvard University Press.

Nagara, H. (1966). *Early childhood disturbances, the infantile neuroses and the adult disturbances.* New York: International Universities Press.

Neubauer, P. B. (1960). The one-parent child and his oedipal development. *Psychoanalytic Study of the Child, 15,* 286–309.

Newman, L. E., & Stoller, R. J. (1974). The oedipal situation in male transsexualism. *British Journal of Medical Psychology, 44,* 295–303.

Nottelmann, E., Martinez, P., Fox, M., & Belmont, M. (1992). Young children of affectively ill parents. *Journal of the American Academy of Child and Adolescent Psychiatry, 31,* 68–77.

Ogden, T. H. (1979). On projective identification. *International Journal of Psycho-Analysis, 60,* 357–373.

Ornstein, A. (1981). Self pathology in childhood: Developmental and clinical considerations. In K. Robson (Ed.), *The psychiatric clinics of North America: Development and pathology of the self* (Vol. 4, pp. 435–453). Philadelphia: Saunders.

Parens, H., & Kramer, S. (Eds.). (1993). *Prevention in mental health.* Northvale, NJ: Jason Aronson.

Person, E., & Ovesey, L. (1974). The transsexual syndrome in males: I. Primary transsexualism. *American Journal of Psychotherapy, 27,* 4–20.

Piaget, J. (1954). *The construction of reality in the child.* New York: Basic Books.

Radke-Yarrow, M., Cummings, M. E., Kuczynski L., & Chapman, M. (1985). Patterns of attachment in two- and three-year-olds in normal families and families with parental depression. *Child Development, 56,* 884–893.

————, Nottelmann, E., Martinez, P., Fox, M. B., & Belmont, B. (1992). Young children of affectively ill parents. *Journal of the American Academy of Child and Adolescent Psychiatry, 31,* 68–77.

————, Zahn-Waxler, C., & Chapman, M. (1983). Children's prosocial dispositions and behavior. In P. H. Mussen (Ed.), *Handbook of child psychology* (Vol. 4). New York: Wiley.

Rinsley, D. B. (1980). Diagnosis and treatment of borderline and narcissistic children and adolescents. *Bulletin of the Menninger Clinic, 44,* 147–170.

Robinson, E., & Eyberg, S. (1981). The dyadic parent-child interaction coding system: Standardization and validation. *Journal of Causality and Clinical Psychology, 49,* 245–250.

Roiphe, H., & Galenson, E. (1973). The infantile fetish. *Psychoanalytic Study of the Child, 28,* 147–168.

Rothbaum, F., & Schneider-Rosen, K. (1988). *Parental acceptance scoring manual: A system for assessing interactions between parents and their young children.* Unpublished manuscript, Tufts University and Boston College.

Sameroff, A., & Emde, R. (Eds.). (1989). *Relationship disturbances in early childhood.* New York: Basic Books.

Sander, L. W. (1962). Issues in early mother-infant interaction. *Journal of the American Academy of Child and Adolescent Psychiatry, 1,* 141–166.

———. (1964). Adaptive relationships in early mother-child interaction. *Journal of the American Academy of Child Psychiatry, 3,* 164–321.

———. (1975) Infant and caretaking environment: Investigation and conceptualization of adaptive behavior in a system of increasing complexity. In E. J. Anthony (Ed.), *Explorations in child psychiatry* (pp. 129–166). New York: Plenum Press.

———. (1983). Polarity, paradox, and the organizing process in development. In J. D. Call, E. Galenson, & R. L. Tyson (Eds.), *Frontiers of infant psychiatry* (pp. 333–346). New York: Basic Books.

Sandler, A.-M. (1994). *Grand rounds in child psychiatry.* New York Hospital–Cornell Medical Center, Westchester Division, April 13, 1993.

Sandler, J. (1960a). The background of safety. *International Journal of Psycho-Analysis, 41,* 352–356.

———. (1960b) On the concept of the superego. *Psychoanalytic Study of the Child, 15,* 128–162.

———. (1961). Identification in parents, children and doctors. In R. MacKeith & J. Sandler (Eds.), *Psychosomatic aspects of paediatrics.* London: Pergamon Press.

———. (Ed). (1987). *Identification, projection, projective identification.* New York: International Universities Press.

———. (1993). Fantasy, defense and the representational world. *Bulletin of the Anna Freud Centre, 16,* 337–348.

———, & Jaffe, W. G. (1967). The tendency to persistence in psychological function and development with special reference to fixation and regression. *Bulletin of the Menninger Clinic, 31,* 257–271.

———, & Rosenblatt, B. (1962). The concept of the representational world. *Psychoanalytic Study of the Child, 17,* 128–145.

———, & Sandler, A. M. (1978). On the development of object relationships and affects. *International Journal of Psycho-Analysis, 59,* 285–296.

Sarnoff, C. A. (1987). *Psychotherapeutic strategies in the latency years.* Northvale, NJ: Jason Aronson.

Satir, V. (1967). *Conjoint family therapy.* Palo Alto: Science & Behavioral Books.

Schafer, R. (1992). *Retelling a life.* New York: Basic Books.

Segal, H. (1974). *Introduction to the work of Melanie Klein.* New York: Basic Books.

Shapiro, V., Fraiberg, S., & Adelson, E. (1980). Billy: Infant-parent psychotherapy on behalf of a child in a critical nutritional state. In S. Fraiberg (Ed.), *Clinical studies in infant mental health* (pp. 197–220). New York: Basic Books.

Sholevar, G., Burland, J. A., Frank, J. L., Etezady, M. H., & Goldstein, J. (1989). Psychoanalytic treatment of children and adolescents. *Journal of the American Academy of Child and Adolescent Psychiatry, 28,* 685–690.

———, & Schwoeri, L. (Eds.) (1994). *The transmission of depression in families and children.* Northvale, NJ: Jason Aronson.

Short, A. (1984). Short-term treatment outcome using parents as co-therapists for their own autistic children. *Journal of Child Psychology and Psychiatry, 25,* 443–458.

Sorce, J. F., & Emde, R. N. (1981). Mother's presence is not enough: Effect of emotional availability on infant exploration. *Developmental Psychology, 17*, 737–745.

Sperling, M. (1950). Children's interpretation and reaction to the unconscious of their mother. *International Journal of Psycho-Analysis, 31*, 1–6.

———. (1951). The neurotic child and his mother. *American Journal of Orthopsychiatry, 21*, 351–364.

———. (1954). Reactive schizophrenia in children. *American Journal of Orthopsychiatry, 24*, 506–512.

———. (1959). A study of deviate sexual behavior in children by the method of simultaneous analysis of mother and child. In L. Lessuer & E. Pavenstedt (Eds.), *Dynamic psychopathology in childhood* (pp. 221–242). New York: Grune & Stratton.

———. (1970). The clinical effects of parental neurosis on the child. In E. J. Anthony & T. Benedek (Eds.), *Parenthood* (pp. 539–569). Boston: Little, Brown.

———. (1982). The major neuroses and behavior disorders in childhood. New York: Jason Aronson.

Spitz, R. (1965). *The first year of life.* New York: International Universities Press.

Sroufe, L. A. (1983). Infant-caregiving attachment and patterns of adaptation in preschool: The roots of maladaptation and competence. In M. Perlmutter (Ed.), *Minnesota Symposium on Child Psychology* (Vol. 16, pp. 41–81). Hillsdale, NJ: Erlbaum.

_____ (1988). The role of infant-caregiver attachment in development. In J. Belsky & T. Nezworski (Eds.), *Clinical implications of attachment* (pp. 18–39). Hillsdale, NJ: Erlbaum.

———, & Fleeson, J. (1986). Attachment and the construction of relationships. In W. W. Hartrup & Z. Rubin (Eds.), *The nature and development of relationships.* Hillsdale, NJ: Erlbaum.

———, Jacobvitz, J., Mangelsdorf, S., DeAngelo E., & Ward, M. J. (1985). Generational boundary dissolution between mothers and their preschool children: A relationship systems approach. *Child Development, 56*, 317–325.

———, & Waters, E. (1977). Attachment as organizational construct. *Child Development, 48*, 1184–1199.

Steele, B. F. (1983). Child abuse and neglect. In J. D. Call, E. Galenson, & R. L. Tyson (Eds.), *Frontiers of infant psychiatry.* New York: Basic Books.

Stern, D. N. (1985). *The interpersonal world of the infant.* New York: Basic Books.

———. (1990). *Diary of a baby.* New York: Basic Books.

Stern-Bruschweiler, N., & Stern, D. N. (1989). A model for conceptualizing the role of the other's representational world in various mother-infant therapies. *Infant Mental Health Journal, 10*, 142–156.

Stoller, R. J. (1966). The mother's contributions to infantile transvestic behavior. *International Journal of Psycho-Analysis, 47*, 384–395.

———. (1968). *Sex and gender.* New York: Science House.

Sullivan, H. S. (1953). *The interpersonal theory of psychiatry.* New York: Norton.

Thomas, A., & Chess, S. (1977). *Temperament and development.* New York: Brunner/Mazel.

———, Chess, S., & Birch, H. G. (1968). *Temperament and behavior disorders in children*. New York: New York University Press.

Trad, P. V. (1986). *Infant depression, paradigms and paradoxes*. New York: Springer-Verlag.

———. (1991a). Intervention paradigms for parents: The application of previewing. *American Journal of Psychotherapy, 45*, 243–260.

———. (1991b). Previewing: A preventive strategy that promotes adaptive development. *American Journal of Psychotherapy, 45*, 231–242.

———. (1992). Using parent-infant dyads as models for interpreting the parallel process. *Journal of Contemporary Psychotherapy, 22*, 107–130.

———. (1993a). Previewing. *Journal of Clinical Psychology, 49*, 261–277.

———. (1993b). *Short-term parent-infant psychotherapy*. New York: Basic Books.

Trevarthen, C. (1980). The foundations of intersubjectivity: Development of interpersonal and cooperative understanding in infants. In D. R. Olson (Ed.), *The social foundations of language and thought* (pp. 1–34). New York: Norton.

———, & Hubley, P. (1979). Secondary intersubjectivity: Confidence, confiding, and acts of meaning in the first year. In A. Lacke (Ed.), *Action, gesture and symbol* (pp. 183–229). New York: Academic Press.

Tustin, F. (1990). *The protective shell in children and adults*. London: Karnac.

Urist, J. (1977). The Rorschach test and the assessment of object relations. *Journal of Personality Assessment, 41*, 3–9.

van der Waals, H. G. (1965). Problems of narcissism. *Bulletin of the Menninger Clinic, 29*, 293–311.

Volkan, V. D. (1973). Transitional fantasies in the analysis of a narcissistic personality. *Journal of the American Psychoanalytic Association, 21*, 351–376.

Vygotsky, L. S. (1978). *Mind in society*. Cambridge, MA: Harvard University Press.

Wasserman, G., Gardier, K., Allen, R., & Shilansky, M. (1987). Interactions between abused infants and strangers. *Journal of the American Academy of Child and Adolescent Psychiatry, 26*, 504–509.

Wasserman, S. (1973). The abused parent of the abused child. *Children, 14*, 175–179.

Weil, N., & Boxer, A. (1990). Who mothers young mothers? In *Adolescent psychiatry* (Vol. 17, pp. 451–472). Chicago: University of Chicago Press.

Weiss, E. (1950). *Principles of psychodynamics*. New York: Grune & Stratton.

Weston, J. A. (1993). A legacy of violence in nonorganic failure to thrive. *Child Abuse and Neglect, 17*, 709–714.

Williams, D., Nover, R., Castellan, J., Greenspan, S., & Lieberman A. (1987). A case of double vulnerability for mother and child: Louise and Robbie. In S. I. Greenspan (Ed.), *Infants in multirisk families* (pp. 39–79). Madison, CT: International Universities Press.

Winnicott, D. (1951). Transitional objects and transitional phenomena. In *Through paediatrics to psycho-analysis* (pp. 229–242). New York: Basic Books, 1975.

———. (1958). The capacity to be alone. In *The maturational processes and the facilitating environment* (pp. 29–36). New York: International Universities Press, 1965.

———. (1960a). String: A technique of communication. In *The maturational processes and the facilitating environment* (pp. 153–157). New York: International Universities Press, 1965.

———. (1960b). The theory of the parent-infant relationship. In *The maturational processes and the facilitating environment* (pp. 37–55). New York: International Universities Press, 1965.

———. (1963). The development of the capacity for concern. In *The maturational processes and the facilitating environment* (pp. 73–83). New York: International Universities Press, 1965.

———. (1971). *Playing and reality*. New York: Basic Books.

Zager, B. (1970). The role of familial factors in persistent effeminate behavior in boys. *American Journal of Psychiatry, 126,* 1167–1170.

Zahn-Waxler, C., Cummings, E. M., McKneur, D. H., & Radke-Yarrow, M. (1984). Altruism, aggression, and social interaction in young children with a manic-depressive parent. *Child Development, 55,* 112–122.

———, & Radke-Yarrow, M. (1990). The origins of empathic concern. *Motivation and Emotion, 14,* 107–130.

Zeanah, C. H., & Anders, T. F. (1987). Subjectivity in parent-infant relationships: A discussion of internal working models. *Infant Mental Health Journal, 8,* 237–250.

———, & Barton, M. L. (1989). Introduction: Internal representations and parent-infant relationships. *Infant Mental Health Journal, 10,* 135–141.

———, & Klitzke, M. (1991). Role reversal and the self-effacing solution: Observations from infant-parent psychotherapy. *Psychiatry, 54,* 346–357.

———, & Zeanah, P. D. (1989). Intergenerational transmission of maltreatment: Insights from attachment theory and research. *Psychiatry, 52,* 177–196.

Zilbach, J. (1986). *Young children in family therapy*. New York: Brunner/Mazel.

———. (1989). The family life cycle: A framework for understanding children in family therapy. In L. Combrenick-Graham (Ed.), *Children in family contexts* (pp. 146–166). New York: Guilford Press.

Zucker, K. (1982). Childhood gender disturbance: Diagnostic issues. *Journal of the American Academy of Child Psychiatry, 21,* 274–280.

———, & Green, R. (1992). Psychosexual disorders in children and adolescents. *Journal of Child Psychology and Psychiatry, 33,* 107–151.

Zucker, K. J. (1985). Cross-gender identified children. In B. W. Steiner (Ed.), *Gender dysphoria: Development, research, management* (pp. 73–174). New York: Plenum Press.

Index